CHARISMATIC CHALLENGE

CHARISMATIC CHALLENGE

FOUR KEY QUESTIONS

John Napier

PROVIDENCE HOUSE PUBLISHERS
Franklin, Tennessee

Originally printed in Australia

Copyright 1991 by John Napier

Copyright 1995 by John Napier

Revised edition copyright 2003 by John Napier

Printed in the United States of America

08   07   06   05   04   03   1   2   3   4   5   6

ISBN 1-881576-52-3

Published by
PROVIDENCE HOUSE PUBLISHERS
238 Seaboard Lane • Franklin, Tennessee 37067
800-321-5692

*To Dr. F. Merle May
who for over forty years of ministry
has placed the approval of Christ
before the applause of men.*

Contents

Foreword

Dr. Deane J. Woods
Principal of the Adelaide College of Ministries
Adelaide, Australia

The charismatic issue, with its many and varied ramifications, is one which the church has had to face down through the centuries.

The Apostle Paul was confronted by charismatic phenomena at Corinth. The Montanists of Phrygia, Asia Minor, raised the same issue shortly after the middle of the second century. Continuing outbursts of a charismatic nature were known amongst the Cevenols of Southern France in the late seventeenth century. In the nineteenth century, an outburst of tongue-speaking occurred in England, among Edward Irving's followers. By the beginning of the twentieth century, the charismatic experience of Agnes N. Ozman and others were being reported in Kansas, Missouri, and Texas. By 1906, tongue-speaking was practiced in Los Angeles. Soon, twenty-six contemporary church bodies (with two million plus in membership) traced their origin to Los Angeles. Since then, it has made rapid gains. Today, the charismatic issue has spilled across denominational lines on all continents.

This movement is presently the major talking point of contemporary Christianity. The issue is real. Many well-meaning, well-intentioned Christians are finding themselves challenged by it. Others are being caught up in it. The issue does not lie merely in the theological areas of the controversy alone. It also embraces its practical implications. It is no wonder, then, that legitimate, fundamental questions are being asked by many well-motivated believers.

From such a context, my good friend and colleague, John Napier, draws upon four of the central questions and discusses them in the light of Scripture. He focuses on four crucial areas:

1. *Where does it say in the Bible that tongues, the other sign, and revelatory gifts are not for today?*

9

2. *Why do good, dedicated Christians experience these phenomena if they are not for today?*

3. *Why do these charismatic experiences normally produce a positive effect in one's Christian life, if such is not from God?*

4. *If tongues, other sign and revelatory gifts are not for today, if they are not from God, how does one explain the growth and blessings of God upon the charismatic churches?*

The author takes these questions and deals with them theologically and practically. For him, a basic issue is at stake. In the charismatic climate of today, the bottom-line question is not whether one would like to *believe* in the charismatic phenomena, or whether one has *witnessed* its mind-boggling ramifications, nor even *experienced* its blessings; the primary question in all these matters (as indeed any other) is whether it is *true according to Scripture*. What does the Bible have to say on the matter? The Protestant Reformers were right in their positive assertion: "*Sola Scriptura*" (Scripture alone).

When the Scriptures speak, God speaks. God's Word must ever be regarded as the final court of appeal in all matters of faith and conduct. Any and every challenge, whether theological or practical, must pass the touchstone test of Scripture. What is more, biblical doctrine must ever determine practice. Experience must always be interpreted by Scripture, not vice versa.

In these pages, John Napier faces the charismatic issue fairly and squarely. He tests its claims and challenges according to his understanding of God's revealed Word. Throughout the treatment of the "Four Key Questions," the author addresses a fifth question which he terms "The Silent Question"—that is, what elements of the charismatic movement meet with the God's blessings and stand as a positive challenge to evangelical and conservative believers at large. This book, therefore, contains a message for all believers, whether charismatic or non-charismatic in orientation.

John Napier's motivation is not to surreptitiously fuel the controversy further, but to grapple with both the doctrinal issues and practical questions which many people are asking. This he does, not primarily for those who have had the privilege of formal theological training (though there are plenty of "meaty sections" for such Bible students to consider), but for the ordinary layperson. With this in mind, the reader will find the *Review of Key Concepts* at the end of each chapter to be especially helpful. This is also true of *Appendix A* which deals with additional questions arising from this study.

In this volume, one will find the combination of three elements which characterize John Napier's life and ministry: scriptural scholarship, a heart aflame for Christ, and a passionate concern for the salvation of souls. He is a scholar, lecturer, church-planter, and beloved pastor. But above all, John is a man of God—a designation with which all who know him will readily concur.

In treating the charismatic issue in the way he does, the author thus draws attention to a vital, topical, and contemporary subject. It is my hope that what he writes will be read by many, and that all who read his words will be helped and encouraged as much as I have been in reading the draft copies. It has been a privilege for me to work with John, Senior Lecturer in Bible Exposition at the Adelaide College of Ministries, in preparing a course by the same name as this book's title as a part of the college's curriculum. I commend both the author and his book to all interested in, confronted by, or associated with the charismatic challenge facing the church at this time. It is my prayer that God will use both the author and this publication for His glory and for the salvation and blessing of many souls around the world, but especially across the land of John's birth, the United States, and his adopted homeland, Australia.

Preface

When *Charismatic Challenge: Four Key Questions* was first published in Australia (Lancer Press, 1991), the charismatic movement was experiencing explosive growth. A sampling of data from the *Dictionary of Pentecostal and Charismatic Movements* confirms this point:

United States (Decadal Membership Growth Rates 1974–84): In the United States, the growth rate for independent charismatic churches . . . was an amazing 1,467 percent. This, of course, did not include charismatic growth within the denominational structures.

Australia (Decadal Membership Growth Rates 1976-81): The highest rate of recorded growth among denominational groups was 24 percent. However, Pentecostal churches recorded a growth rate over the same period of 385 percent.

Korea (Decadal Membership Growth Rates 1969-82): While other Protestant groups recorded growth rates as high as 240 percent over the period, the charismatic churches experienced a growth rate of 742 percent.

Singapore (Decadal Membership Growth Rates early 1970s to early 1980s): All major Christian groups experienced growth with Bible Presbyterian showing an increase of 242 percent. Again, the Pentecostal churches far outdistanced these other groups by recording a growth of 635 percent.[i]

Other sources supported this same pattern of growth worldwide—especially so in Brazil, Africa, Latin America, Europe, and former Eastern Bloc countries. Indeed, it was estimated that when all the statistics would become available for the period surveyed, *Pentecostal-Charismatic churches would be found to be the fastest-growing group of churches in at least 80 percent of the nations of the world.*[ii]

While the percentage growth of the charismatic movement decreased markedly in the decade of the nineties, the influence and

13

impact of the movement continues to grow exponentially. As new questions have arisen in regard to the myriad of issues spawned by the movement, the basic *core questions* originally addressed in *Charismatic Challenge: Four Key Questions* still remain. Such continued inquiry and controversy calls for this third printing of the book.

I wish to express appreciation to friends, both charismatic and non-charismatic, who have given encouragement. Critiques have also been welcomed and have further confirmed the Biblical conclusions contained in the work. In a world where "tolerance" seeks to accord legitimacy to *any* idea, philosophy, or religious orientation, the truth-claims of Scripture need to be heard as never before.

The early church highly valued doctrine—yes, and doctrine held *dogmatically*. Our Lord and the early church knew that doctrine *determined* one's destiny (Matt. 7:21–27; John 14:6; Acts 2:21, 36; 4:12); *defined* fellowship (Gal. 1:6–9; 2 John 9; Rom. 16:17; 2 Cor. 6:14–18); *directed* the church (2 Tim. 2:1–2; 4:1–5; Titus 2:10; 3 John 4); and *drove* discipleship (Matt. 28:18–20; John 14:21). Indeed, doctrine coupled with the power of the Holy Spirit served as the dynamic force in the early church. It was equally true that *doctrine partnered with devotion* in the lives of those truly desiring to experience the fullness of the Christian life.

In conclusion, I offer praise to the Lord that Bible colleges, Bible Institutes, and churches in the United States, Australia, and in various parts of the world are using *Charismatic Challenge* as a textbook and resource. May the Lord continue to use this work to edify and strengthen believers and to "rescue" many who embrace certain experiential phenomena that stand in direct contrast to the Word of God. To God be the glory. Amen.

Acknowledgments

Any writer knows the indebtedness one has to a host of people who make the writing and publishing of a book possible. So, I would pause a moment and express deep appreciation to those particularly involved in this project. First, special thanks to my family (Emma, Rebecca, and James) who gave so much encouragement and understood the necessity of addressing the issues at hand. They lived through many of the experiences and stories detailed in this work. Deep appreciation is expressed to Dr. Deane Woods, principal of the Adelaide College of Ministries, whose insights and evaluation of the original manuscript enhanced its preparation. Despite heavy commitments, he was always available to listen and give needed advice. His own contribution in the appendices strengthened the present work. Deep appreciation is also expressed to Nick Hodge of Random Access Pty. Ltd. [Adelaide, Australia] whose expertise in computer software and manuscript presentation was invaluable—Nick often went beyond the "call of duty" in assisting the work; to John Burfield who crystallized the concept of the book into the cover design and was there in the early days of the project to give instruction; and also to Bill Gilliver and Charles Deweese whose editorial comments and advice served to keep me accountable to sound argumentation and a spirit seasoned with Christian love.

Introduction

Throughout the course of church history, mighty winds of controversy have blown across the Christian landscape.[1] Today, another such wind is blowing across professing Christendom. Once again there is major controversy, and a call for clarification and understanding cries out from the hearts of many. Much has been written on the charismatic movement. It has been lauded, explored, analyzed, experienced, criticized, and placed ever before the Christian public. The movement, and all that it embodies, has come to the center stage of Christianity. The issues which are raised by the movement touch all aspects of professing Christendom. Churches which have never before even addressed the issue of *tongues*, *laughing in the Spirit*, the *sign gifts* or *revelatory gifts* (prophecy, words of knowledge, visions, dreams) are having to make a response to this movement.

Sometimes the response is forced by those in various churches inquiring of their leaders about the experience which they or those whom they know have had. If responses are not carefully formed, they often fail to adequately address the issues. A few Scripture passages will not suffice to answer key questions that are being raised. Indeed, many a correct doctrinal answer does not satisfy some of the more practical questions pressing the hearts of sincere saints. On the other hand, some responses often are formed on the basis of experience or relational considerations, rather than on doctrinal truths. Even to those churches which have traditionally rejected the claims of the charismatic movement, key questions are being asked which deserve answers. No longer are people asking easy questions, expecting easy answers.

The situation is complicated by the fact that in recent years well respected Christian writers such as J. I. Packer, D. Martyn Lloyd-Jones, C. Peter Wagner, and John White have given certain aspects of the charismatic movement their qualified or full endorsement.[2] We are urged to "get in step with the Spirit," and to participate in the new "wave" of the Spirit's power. These endorsements are crucial for they are giving a semblance of biblical support for the charismatic movement.

17

Moreover, in 1988, shock waves reverberated through evangelical and fundamental circles when Dallas Theological Seminary lost three of its esteemed faculty members. The reason? They had embraced certain charismatic views which were unacceptable to the seminary.[3] One of the professors, Jack Deere, later became the "in-house" theologian for John Wimber's Vineyard Movement.

Deere would go on to write one of the most powerful defenses of the charismatic movement: *Surprised by the Power of the Spirit* [see Appendix A for a brief response].[4] While John Wimber has privately repudiated some of his former teachings (a point to be discussed later in this book), Jack Deere's earlier involvement in the Vineyard Movement gave its adherents a champion well schooled in biblical exegesis. Thus, credibility for the charismatic movement has gained momentum in many quarters.

Emotional Time Bomb

Maybe the subtitle is a bit dramatic, but when anyone enters into a discussion of the charismatic movement, one is immediately faced with a myriad of emotional considerations. Veteran missionaries, pastors, friends, and relatives are experiencing the various phenomena associated with the charismatic movement. Even people who do not seek the phenomena are being exposed to tongues, laughing in the Spirit, miraculous healings, exorcism of demons, new revelations given through prophecy, visions, and dreams. Yet, many hesitate to scripturally evaluate the current wave of sign and revelatory gifts sweeping across the churches. Why?

First of all, there seems to be an ever growing consensus that such is a genuine movement of the Spirit of God. Secondly, these charismatic phenomena seem to engender an enthusiasm for the things of the Lord. Because no sincere Christian wants to stand against a genuine movement of the Spirit of God or be seen as quenching the zeal of fellow believers, many emotional forces are brought to bear when one begins to discuss these matters. To make a judgment against these present-day experiences is interpreted by many as an attack against the integrity of dear saints and loved ones. This can be a wrenching emotional experience. Thus I realize that any call for a fresh evaluation of the subject will meet some readers who find the conclusions threatening.

From the very beginning of this study, I wish to say that I believe **the Lord is using many in the charismatic movement to reach others for the kingdom**. Yet, this does not mean that one should shy away from examining practices which are unscriptural and dangerous to Christians at large. Deception wears many disguises and may even touch those in key leadership positions. Remember that one of the dynamic leaders of the early church, the apostle Peter, was rebuked publicly by Paul over Peter's refusal to identify with Gentile believers (Gal. 2:11-21). Peter was used mightily of God, but slipped into error in refusing to eat with Gentiles. Paul loved Peter, but Paul could not allow such error to persist without addressing his brother. Not only did Paul call Peter a hypocrite before the church at Antioch, but he called Peter a hypocrite in Scripture as well, and sent this denunciation to the churches of Galatia.

How would you respond if another Christian called you a hypocrite, and then published his statement, and sent it to all the churches in your city? Most of us could not take that kind of public rebuke. However, Peter took the rebuke, later coming to Paul's defense at the Jerusalem Council (Acts 15:7-11) and commending Paul's writings in his own epistles (2 Pet. 3:14-16).

What does the matter of Peter's rebuke have to do with the subject at hand? Simply this: there are many good men and women caught up in a deception that is mushrooming among the churches. What is the source of this deception? Is it human in origin or, possibly, satanic? To scripturally face the issues will require fighting through some real emotional prejudices as well as relationship ties. To rebuke a brother or a movement does not necessarily mean a lack of love or care—Paul's example proved that. Again, to balance the perspective, there are many things in the charismatic movement which are good, and which serve to challenge the Body of Christ for the better. Yet, how is one to discern between the true and the false elements, between the good and evil?

God Still Works Miracles

I can remember attending a conservative evangelical church when I was a young boy. The pastor preached the essentials of the faith. There was warmth and love in the church, and people were coming to a saving knowledge of the Lord Jesus Christ. I distinctly remember one particular Sunday. I was about ten or twelve years old, and I sat in the balcony where most of the kids my age retreated to pass the service. It wasn't that we were anti-Gospel, or anti-church, or anti-preacher; the balcony was just a safe place where we could experience the warmth of the church service, but not be held accountable for paying attention all the time. But this was a Sunday where I could not help but be absorbed in an unfolding drama.

A lady in her thirties or forties was moving through each aisle of the church shaking hands with everyone and saying something to them! For a few moments I was very pleased that I was in the balcony, watching this lady make her personal procession. I was safe from this strange encounter. However, soon after I settled in for the service, that same lady appeared in the balcony! She was shaking everyone's hand and thanking them. Soon she was shaking my hand and saying, "thank you so very much," "thank you so very much." I had never seen this lady before and did not understand why she was shaking everyone's hand. On the way home from church, I asked about the lady and was told that she had just recently been healed of cancer—that the church had been praying for her. I did not even know then the real meaning of prayer or the serious- ness of cancer, but I walked away that Sunday wondering about a great deal of things: the power of prayer; the character of God; the joy in the heart of this lady; how healing takes place; why some are healed and others are not. As days turned into months and years, the significance of that Sunday became shelved among other childhood memories. It was not until I became a Christian that the memories came again—especially as I grappled with the same issues of prayer, the Person and Character of God, the promises of Scripture, and the practical day-to-day living of the Christian life.

Yes, our God is a miracle-working God! "Jesus Christ: the same yesterday, today, and forever" (Heb. 13:8). "I am the Lord, I do not change" (Mal. 3:6). Certainly, the same God who worked mighty mira- cles in the Old Testament record, and who in the Person of the Lord Jesus Christ worked miracles as recorded in the Gospels, still works mightily in the lives of people today. The experience of healing which that lady had was real! Praise the Lord that the God of Scripture does move in power today: transforming lives through the blessed Gospel; moving in response to the prayers of God's people as those prayers touch His will; blessing, strengthening, encouraging, and healing. **The essential question is not "Does the Lord still heal and perform miracles today?"** (For the answer to that is a resounding "YES.") **Rather, the question is, "How is the Lord working today?"** Does the Lord work through individuals who have a certain gift of healing or power to work miracles? Does the

Lord give new revelation through prophecy, tongues, dreams, and visions? These are the essential questions before us.

Experiential Limitations

Allow me to share two other examples. My greatest prayer warrior during the formative years of my Christian life was a dear lady who was a member of a Pentecostal church. She touched many lives through her witness; she purposely never married so she could give her life to prayer, visiting the sick, door-to-door witnessing and evangelism. Of course, we differed over the issue of tongues. One day I asked this dear saint why she endorsed a practice which was so different from the biblical tongues of the first century. Her response went something like this: "I was in a church service and really questioning the practices which were going on in the service. I picked out a man in the choir and asked the Lord, 'If this tongues is of you, have that man come on the last refrain of the hymn, stand in front of me, and speak in tongues.'" According to her testimony, on the last refrain, the man did exactly that! *Thus, this saint of God came to a conclusion on the present-day tongues movement, not by an in-depth study of the Word of God, but rather by one experience vindicating another experience.*

Experience is a dangerous ground upon which to test ultimate truth, because our experiences may vary, and our interpretation of an experience, however genuine, may be wrong. Scripture clearly says to "test the spirits, whether they are of God" (1 John. 4:1). No human can test spiritual realities without the Word of God. That is why the Word is called the Sword of the Spirit (Eph. 6:17).

Finally, some time ago, my family and I had the privilege of hosting in our home one of the great soldiers of the faith. He is known for his defense of the fundamentals of the faith. In conversation, he confided that he had spoken in tongues and has continued to use such as a private prayer language. He spoke of how his entire life changed after the experience: i.e., the holy life became more attainable; the prayer times were more vibrant; the excitement level about the Christian faith attained new heights. In the midst of our exchanging views, he asked one of the most important questions regarding the tongues experience: "HOW COULD SOMETHING WHICH PRODUCED SUCH A DRAMATIC AND POSITIVE EFFECT IN MY LIFE FOR CHRIST COME FROM SATAN?" He went on to tell how he had not sought the gift; it just came. Certainly, as he awaited a response in our lounge room, the emotional element was clearly present.

The response that was shared that evening has been shared in Bible college classrooms, seminars in various church settings, and on tape. What follows in this book is a response to the aforementioned question and several others. I do not offer this as the final word on the subject. Yet, this material does come from one who has wrestled with the issues and who, as both a pastor and college lecturer in biblical studies, sees the effect which the charismatic movement is having upon the lives of believers. A cry emerges from both charismatic and non-charismatic churches for answers to key questions. These questions must have answers that address BOTH biblical and experiential concerns.

The Four Key Questions

As noted above, when one speaks of the sign gifts and revelatory gifts, especially those of tongues, healing, and prophecy, one immediately steps into an emotional plane. Realizing the emotional and scriptural aspects of this subject, I will try to answer four key questions. Some of these questions engender subsidiary questions and thus are presented in Appendix A. Nevertheless, these four basic questions comprise the main chapter divisions of this study:

Question #1 *Where does it say in the Bible that laughing in the Spirit, tongues, and the other sign gifts are not for today? And what about the revelatory gifts of prophecy, knowledge, visions, and dreams? How is one to regard the supernatural acts of God that have been documented on third-world mission fields and in charismatic circles around the world?*

Question #2 *Why do good, dedicated Christians experience these phenomena if they are not for today? Even pastors, veteran missionaries, and Bible teachers who do not seek these experiences have them. Why would God allow His children to experience something which some suggest is from Satan? Furthermore, is it so serious an issue as to merit such concern?*

Question #3 *Why do these charismatic experiences normally produce a* *positive effect in one's Christian life if such is not from God? How does one explain the increased interest in the Bible, the renewed boldness to witness, the increased vitality in the prayer life, and the greater overall joy in living the Christian life? Again, how could something which is not from God produce positive effects in the spiritual lives of Christians?*

Question #4 *If tongues, manifestations of the Spirit, other sign and revelatory gifts are not for today, if they are not from God, how does one explain the growth and blessings of God upon the charismatic churches? They are the fastest growing churches around the world. Surely God would not bless such churches with growth and genuine converts if these churches were spreading a lie?*

The aforementioned questions are being asked by charismatic and non-charismatic alike. They are usually directed at those who reject the claims of the charismatic movement. These are fair questions, often asked by those who are sincerely wrestling with the issues. This book is written with the layperson in mind, and the writer trusts that the material presented will be of help to those grappling with essential questions. Where does one find the answers? The Scriptures contain the answers— for it is there where all experiences find their true meaning and interpretation.

Before moving on in our study, let us pause to ask one final question. Let us term this *The Silent Question,* for it will weave itself in and through our entire discussion. No single chapter will be devoted to answering this question. However, it deserves a place in our study. What is the *silent question?* Simply this: *What elements within the charismatic movement are being blessed of the Lord?*

I have already stated that the Lord is using many in the charismatic movement to reach souls for the kingdom of God. This book, therefore, does not stand as a blanket condemnation of *every* aspect of the movement. Truth demands that believers identify the redeeming elements in the movement as well as the most deceptive and dangerous. One should judge how these redeeming elements stand as a positive challenge to evangelicals and conservative Christians. Any study of the *charismatic challenge* remains incomplete without addressing this last consideration as well. Now, with the road clearly mapped out for our inquiry, let us begin.

Question One

Where does the Bible teach that tongues, the sign gifts, revelatory gifts, and other manifestations of the Spirit are not for today?

Biblical Truth, the Inductive Method, and the "Quick Fix" Generation

We, in the western world, live in the generation of the *quick fix* . While many starving children search days for a morsel of food, we have our instant soups, coffees, potatoes, and our meals on wheels bringing pizza to our doors. Our microwave society lingers only a few minutes for its food. We zoom to work in our fast lanes (most of the time!), and we shop for services where time is the real commodity by which we measure service. We want it *now*! And we are used to getting it *now*!

It is very hard in the midst of the "quick fix" generation to slow down and invest time in diligently studying the Word of God. Many sincere Christians are choosing the "quick fix" in their Bible study; many are bowing before the god of experience, or self-esteem, without carefully checking the labels or the manufacturer who made up the instructions. But we must give Scripture attention. We must labor long and hard. We must treat the Word correctly because we are commanded by the Holy Spirit to do so!

Most Bible students are aware of the truths stated in 2 Timothy 2:15, "Be diligent to present yourself approved to God, a worker who does not need to be ashamed, rightly dividing the word of truth." The Greek word, *orthotomounta,* translated "rightly dividing" literally carries the meaning, "cutting straight," Perhaps Paul, the tentmaker, used this word to graphically portray a craftsman, cutting and trimming his material most carefully so that the pieces would fit together. In like manner, the child of God is charged to be a workman, a laborer, correctly handling the Word of God: searching, comparing, compiling, analyzing, and interpreting the total scriptural evidence on any given subject. In other words, it takes work! It is this process of searching, studying, and "cutting straight" the Word of God that is so lacking in church circles today.

Some of the most important doctrines of the Christian faith have their foundation, not in a single statement of truth, but in a mosaic of various Scriptures which together set forth a single position. For example, the doctrine of the Trinity draws its substance from numerous Scriptures; and it is the total evidence of these separate passages which give a wholeness and clarity to the fact that we worship one God in three Persons. One comes to the doctrine of the Trinity through the process of induction (i.e., logical reasoning that a general truth or law exists because particular cases which parallel or illustrate this truth exist). In other words, by comparing Scripture with Scripture, one comes to a common conclusion that correctly explains all cases.

The same process of induction is used in answering the question: *Where does the Bible say that tongues, manifestations of the Spirit (i.e., spiritual laughter), the sign gifts, and revelatory gifts (i.e., prophecy, words of knowledge, visions, dreams) are not for today?* There is no single statement in Scripture which completely settles this issue. However, when one compares Scriptures which deal with the revelatory and sign gifts, one can see a definite answer to this question. One will have to dig, to labor, to "cut straight," and properly interpret the various passages, and then put them all together to see the unified testimony of Scripture. Do not settle for the "quick fix" on this issue of tongues, the sign gifts, the revelatory gifts, or other manifestations of the Spirit. And as has already been asserted, never discern spiritual truths on the basis of the senses or experience; rather test all experience in the light of Scripture.

ATTENTION DEAR READER: By design, this chapter is a bit "meaty." So let me encourage you to persevere and be like the Bereans. Remember that they were the ones who "received the word with all readiness, and searched the Scriptures daily to find out whether these things were so" (Acts 17:11). Once the foundation has been laid for our present study, then we will deal with the other three questions in a more relaxed style and format.

THE BIBLICAL NATURE OF TONGUES

As tongues appears to be the most apparent and controversial aspect of the charismatic movement, I will focus on this issue. Moreover, many of the same arguments and scriptural passages that relate to tongues also relate to the sign and revelatory gifts, and to other manifestations of the Spirit.

Known Languages to Communicate the Wonders of God to Unbelievers

The type of tongues that is being evidenced in churches today is entirely different from the tongues described in the Bible. Note the comments of J. I. Packer regarding the type of tongues most prevalent today in charismatic circles:

> The gift is regarded as mainly, though not entirely, for private devotional use. Subjectively, it is a matter of letting one's vocal chords run free as one lifts one's heart to God, and as with learning to swim, confidence in entrusting oneself to the medium (the water in the one case, babbling utterance in the other) has much to do with one's measure of success and enjoyment.[5]

This personal tongue is often referred to as ecstatic speech (i.e., spontaneous speech, accompanied by emotion, and without linguistic form). While the phrase "ecstatic speech" may legitimately describe current tongues speaking, the qualification by Packer is instructive:

> Glossolalia is not, as is often thought (and as the NEB mistranslations in 1 Corinthians 14 suggest), an ecstatic thing. "Christian speaking in tongues is done as objectively as any other speaking, while the person is in full possession and control of his wits and volition, and in no strange state of mind whatever" and once the novelty has worn off, "at times the glossolalic feels a singular lack of emotion while speaking in tongues." Usually, though not invariably, glossolalia persists in the experience of those who have once begun it, as a mode of prayer that seems real and right for them, into which they can slip at will; and though they allow it to be a lesser gift, according to Paul's estimate in 1 Corinthians 14:1-19, yet they prize it because of the devotional help it brings them. Whether one's first entry into it was spontaneous and involuntary or by learning a vocal technique for it (both happen) does not affect its devotional value once one can manage it.[6]

In direct contrast, the biblical tongues of the first century were *known languages* which communicated the wonders of God publicly to unbelievers (see Appendix B). They served as an authenticating sign that the gospel message was true. *Their function far transcended a personal and devotional use on the part of the speaker.* In the first recorded instance of tongues, these principles are clearly seen.

> And they were all filled with the Holy Spirit and began to speak with other tongues, as the Spirit gave them utterance. . . . Then they were all amazed and marvelled, saying to one another, "Look, are not all these who speak Galileans? And how is it that we hear, each in our own language in which we were born? . . . We hear them speaking in our own tongues the wonderful works of God" (Acts 2:4, 7, 8, 11).

Once the sign of tongues had accomplished the purpose of gaining a hearing from the Jewish multitude, Peter went on to proclaim the gospel. Thousands responded to the message of the Lord Jesus Christ.

Please note four important considerations regarding biblical tongues:

1. **They were known languages.**
2. **They were a sign to unbelievers—unbelieving Jews in the case of Pentecost.**
3. **The content of the tongues was the "wonderful works of God."**
4. **They occurred in the context of a gospel presentation.**

Again, at Pentecost, Scripture presents tongues as languages which were understood by the crowd: "each one heard them speaking in his own language" (Acts 1:6). They were not unintelligible sounds; they did not go beyond the bounds of human comprehension. People understood what was being said! Moreover, the content of the tongues was *"the wonderful works of God"* (Acts 1:11). We are not told the nature of these "wonderful works," but certainly such must have been in line with the gospel message. Obviously this revelation concerning the wonderful works of God spoke to the hearts of these unbelieving Jews, for about three thousand people came to embrace the message of grace later preached by Peter (cf. Acts 2:41).

As one comes to the second recorded instance of tongues in Acts (i.e., at the conversion of Cornelius in Acts 10), one finds it is equated with that which happened at Pentecost. Scripture strongly suggests these manifestations were exactly the same. The comments of Peter to the brethren in Jerusalem are very instructive: "And as I began to speak, the Holy Spirit fell upon them, *as upon us at the beginning*" (Acts 11:15; italics mine).

Could wording be any plainer? If there had been any difference in the manifestation of tongues at the conversion of Cornelius, Luke would have recorded the difference. Instead, he records the testimony of Peter that the manifestation of the Spirit was the same as occurred in Acts 2. This time, however, the recipients were Gentiles instead of Jews. The implication is clear: the tongues of Cornelius and his company were exactly the same as that experienced by believers in Acts 2.

In Acts 10:46, Luke records that the content of these tongues focused on God: "For they heard them speak with tongues and magnify God." The four key elements which were present at Pentecost were present in this instance: they were known languages; they focused on the Person and Work of God; they occurred in the context of the gospel being presented to unbelievers. These tongues were given as a sign to confirm the gospel message. They were also given as heaven's testimony to the fact that Gentiles were now recipients of grace just as the Jews. Moreover, it was essential that Jews be present even at the conversion of Cornelius to witness the sign.[7] Even though the Jews present were believers (cf. Acts 10:23, 45; 11:12), the event in Cornelius' home would serve as a sign to both unbelieving Jews and Gentiles that God's grace was extending beyond the boundaries of Judaism.[8]

Some maintain that the tongues of the Corinthian experience were different from that which occurred at Pentecost. Yet, there is no change in the word for "tongues" or the context to suggest that the tongues experienced by the Corinthian believers were anything different from that which occurred in Acts.[9]

Public Language—Never a Private Prayer Language

Some well-meaning saints would point to several passages to support a tongues gift which manifests itself in a private prayer language. They maintain that God enables them to pray in an unknown language and that this experience heightens their fellowship with God and invigorates their Christian walk. Some of the passages upon which they draw support are the following:

> Likewise the Spirit also helps in our weaknesses. For we do not know what we should pray for as we ought, but the Spirit Himself makes intercession for us with groanings which cannot be uttered (Rom. 8:26).

Though I speak with the tongues of men and of angels, but have not love, I have become as sounding brass or a clanging cymbal (1 Cor. 13:1).

Pursue love, and desire spiritual gifts, but especially that you may prophesy. For he who speaks in a tongue does not speak to men but to God, for no one understands him; however, in the spirit he speaks mysteries. But he who prophesies speaks edification and exhortation and comfort to men. He who speaks in a tongue edifies himself, but he who prophesies edifies the church. I wish you all spoke with tongues, but even more that you prophesied . . . (1 Cor. 14:1-5a).

The wording of the Romans passage prevents any application to the tongues issue or that of a private prayer language. One will note that it is the Holy Spirit who prays with groans which cannot be expressed in words. There is no room in the passage for applying this to human experience. Granted, a form of the word *groans* occurs in Romans 8:22 and 23; yet, in these instances Paul speaks of the "whole creation" groaning or believers groaning "*within ourselves*, eagerly waiting for the adoption, the redemption of our body" (italics mine). No outward verbalization is implied in either sense.

Regarding the "tongues of angels" reference in 1 Corinthians 13, there are two major considerations. There is no biblical evidence of a special language for angels. Every place in Scripture where angels are recorded as speaking, they speak in intelligible languages understood by humans. The burden of proof rests upon those who would state that there is a special angelic language. The second consideration has to do with the structure and purpose of the passage. MacArthur's comments are instructive on this point:

What was Paul saying here? He was not necessarily stating factual reality. He was using hyperbole—exaggeration—to make a point. In Greek, verses 2 and 3 of 1 Corinthians 13 use subjunctive verbs. Normally, when the subjunctive is used in the Greek, it indicates an improbable, a hypothetical hyperbolic situation. In order to make his point about the necessity for love, Paul was trying to stretch his comments about speech to the outer limits. He was saying, "No matter how fine or wonderful or miraculous your speech might be—even if you talk angel talk—if you don't have love, you are nothing but noise."[10]

Thus, Paul was merely using heightened comparison to give preeminence to love, an important theme throughout his writings.

Paul used the same heightened comparison involving revelatioi from men and angels in Galatians 1:8, "But though we, or an angel from heaven, preach any other gospel unto you than that which we have preached unto you, let him be accursed." In the Galatians passage, Paul is not talking about two different *forms* of communication. He is, however, talking about different *levels* of communication. Obviously the preaching by men or angels in this verse would be in languages intelligible to mankind. There is no mysterious tongue implied. The purpose of the passage is to give heightened emphasis to sources of a false gospel—it could come through men or through angelic beings. And as angels are said to be on a higher creative plane than mankind (cf. Ps. 8:5), the comparison underscores the varied avenues through which revelation can come. Again, that is all Paul is doing in 1 Corinthians 13 when he speaks of tongues of men and of angels. The writer of the Book of Hebrews also draws similar comparisons (Heb. 2:1-4). He compares and distinguishes revelation spoken by angels, the Lord, and men. Again the emphasis stresses *levels* of communication, *not differences in kind.*

Many charismatic teachers make reference to 1 Corinthians 14:1-5 to support a private prayer language. They note that Paul clearly states that those who speak in tongues speak to God and not to men, that the content of the tongues are "mysteries" and not able to be understood by men, and that the person exercising the gift is edified. On the surface this appears to be the case. Yet, one must remember the entire tone of 1 Corinthians, plus the fact that one must filter this passage through that context.

What was the tone of 1 Corinthians? It was a letter of rebuke; of strong rebuke. Paul firmly asserted that the church in Corinth was "carnal" (1 Cor. 3:1). The church was beset by divisions, sexual perversion, enmity to the point of brother taking brother to secular law courts, idolatry, marital conflict, drunkenness, desecration of the Lord's Table, and doctrinal questions regarding the resurrection. Amidst this entire carnal picture, there was the abuse, misuse, and misunderstanding surrounding spiritual gifts—especially tongues.

Carnal believers can employ spiritual gifts—this is obvious from the Corinthian account. However, the carnal exercise of spiritual gifts does not produce spiritual blessings. Paul's rebuke of the Corinthian church focused upon the false equation that gifts equal spirituality. When 1 Corinthians 14 is seen in this light, as well as a rebuke regarding excesses in public worship, there is no room for a private prayer language in 1 Corinthians 14: 1-5. What then is the Lord saying through these Scriptures?

clear that the praying in tongues of verses 1-5 is
given in a public worship service—albeit in a house-
...t. This is not talking about a private prayer language.
...e force of verses 14-16 (italics mine):

> For if I pray in a tongue, my spirit prays, but my understanding is unfruitful.
> What is the result then? I will pray with the spirit, and I will also pray with the
> understanding. I will sing with the spirit, and I will also sing with the under-
> standing. Otherwise, if you bless with the spirit, *how will he who occupies the
> place of the uninformed say "Amen" at your giving of thanks*, since he does not
> understand what you say.

Do not miss the thrust of this passage. Paul stresses that when one prays
in a tongue or sings, he should do so in such a manner that the *entire
congregation* can say, "Amen." Obviously then, Paul is not addressing the
issue of a private prayer language.

Some may raise the point that Scripture says the person is edified in
the speaking of tongues to God (1 Cor. 14:4). Therefore, they maintain,
it must be an acceptable practice. However, the entire context is rebuke,
not commendation. Every time a believer exercises his or her spiritual
gift, that person will be edified. That is a by-product of employing a spiritual gift. Yet, the primary purpose of spiritual gifts is that of edifying the
Body of Christ, the Church (1 Cor. 12:7; 14:4). When the former element (edifying self) takes preeminence over ministering to the Body of
Christ, one is misusing what has been given by God for the benefit of all.
That is what was happening in the Corinthian church. Some would be
praying or speaking in tongues and the only one in the assembly who
could understand would be that particular unbeliever for whom the
tongue was meant. To other unbelievers or believers in the assembly, the
one using the tongue would only be speaking to God. They could not
understand the tongue, and since an unbeliever could not speak or
address the church assembly, the tongues speaking was not benefiting
the church. That is why later in the passage, Paul would regulate the
speaking and praying in tongues and insist that someone with the gift of
interpretation be present. In that manner the entire assembly could be
edified, believer and unbeliever alike.

J. I. Packer admits that the tongues of today do not fit the biblical
pattern. Nevertheless, he goes for the middle ground in asserting that
since the practice is personally edifying, it is harmless. For Packer, it

doesn't matter whether tongues fits the biblical model as long as it makes one "feel" closer to God. He likens it to singing in the shower or bath after a rough day at the office in that it gives one a psychological release and is good for the soul.

> . . . It does not seem inconceivable that the Spirit might prompt this relaxation of rational control at surface level in order to strengthen control at a deeper level. Wordless singing, loud perhaps, as we lie in the bath can help restore a sense of rational well-being to the frantic, and *glossolalia might be the spiritual equivalent of that; it would be a Godsend if it were.* Also, if its effect really is to intensify and sustain moods of praise and prayer that otherwise one could not sustain because of wandering thoughts, it could be a positive character builder and lead into what exponents of mystical prayer term *contemplation.* This might be specially beneficial to folk who, as victims of the bustle, superficiality, and unauthentic brittleness of modern living, are not in touch with themselves at a deep level and whose Christianity is in consequence more formal, notional, conventional, stereotyped, imitative and secondhand than it should be. (The charismatic movement is, after all, a mainly urban phenomenon, and it is in towns that these pressures operate most directly.)

> In this way glossolalia could be a good gift of God for some people at least, on the basis that *anything that helps you to concentrate on God, practice his presence, and open yourself to his influence is a good gift* (italics mine).[11]

J. I. Packer has been used of the Lord in many previous writings to strengthen believers in their commitment to the Lord and His Word. For this he is to be commended. Yet, on the present subject, he has allowed emotive issues and his personal evaluations to replace sound biblical exposition. Such a "neutral" position on tongues is not only untenable, and against Scripture, but opens one to a dangerous position.

When the "laughing revival" came to Toronto in January of 1994, few could have foreseen the worldwide effects of this phenomena. As word of the "Toronto Blessing" spread, so did its influence. Even *Newsweek* covered the growing movement:

> On a RECENT WEEKNIGHT IN TORONTO, 1,500 worshippers gathered in the Vineyard Christian Church and had a good laugh. It began when a dozen pilgrims from Oregon got up to introduce themselves and then began to fall to the floor, laughing uncontrollably. An hour later, the huge new church looked

like a field hospital. Dozens of men and women of all ages were lying on the floor: some were jerking spasmodically; others closed their eyes in silent ecstasy. . . . These communal laugh-ins have been going on six nights a week, every week, for over a year at the charismatic congregation near Toronto's Pearson International Airport. In all, more than 100,000 people have experienced "the Toronto Blessing," which believers interpret as *an experience of the Holy Spirit much like the "speaking in tongues"* mentioned in the New Testament. Hundreds of visiting pastors have taken the Blessing home to roughly 7,000 congregations in Hong Kong, Norway, South Africa, and Australia, plus scores of churches in the United States (italics mine).[12]

DO NOT MISS THE PARALLEL made between tongues and this so-called "laughter in the Spirit." Those seeking to defend the phenomena could say, like Packer, that the experience helped them to *focus upon God, practice His presence, and open up to His influence.* Yet, such becomes a tragic commentary when no appeal is made to Scripture to evaluate the nature of this "happening."

In the same *Newsweek* article, the author reported that some of those touched by the Toronto Blessing were heard making ANIMAL SOUNDS:

Recently the laughter has taken a beastly turn. Now some people who get the Toronto Blessing are beginning to roar like animals as well. To Hank Hanegraaff, who hosts a California radio show as "The Bible Answer Man," such fearsome noise suggests possession by the Devil—and the need for exorcism. But pastor Arnott can point to plenty of holy shaking and quaking at revival meetings in the 18th century. Indeed, some proponents of the Blessing believe that roaring may be a prophetic sign. After all, in the Bible God is called the Lion of Judah.[13]

Incredible! Such superficial appeals to past revivals and Scripture will not do. Neither history nor Scripture vindicates the Toronto Blessing. To the contrary, the manifestation of animal sounds amidst laughter DOES suggest demonic influence.

Believers are commanded to "test the spirits, whether they are of God . . ." (1 John 4:1). This "testing" is not accomplished through intuition, feeling, human consensus, or reason; rather such can only be done through Scripture. While the Holy Spirit does indeed manifest Himself in many special ways today, questionable practices must be judged in light of the Word of God, the ultimate written authority.

THE SIGN AND REVELATORY GIFTS
Given to confirm the SPOKEN WORD and part of a passing cluster

In any discussion of tongues, it is important to note that they were not just spiritual gifts. They also were designated as a "sign gift" and part of a cluster of gifts named by Jesus in Mark 16. These sign gifts were given to *individuals* to authenticate the message of the gospel. The early Christians had no New Testament in the early years following the ascension of Christ. As the gospel went to Jew and Gentile alike, it needed the witness of the signs to undergird its authority, until the written Scriptures established that authority base. Let us look closer at these principles.

The Testimony of Jesus

When one traces through the narrative portions of Scripture describing the advance of the gospel and the growth of the early church, one immediately sees a pattern developing regarding the sign gifts. What are the sign gifts? They are first mentioned in Mark 16:15-20 (boldface mine):[14]

> And He said to them, "Go into all the world and preach the gospel to every creature. He who believes and is baptized will be saved; but he who does not believe will be condemned. And these **signs** will follow those who believe: In My name they will cast out demons; they will speak with new tongues; they will take up serpents; and if they drink anything deadly, it will by no means hurt them; they will lay hands on the sick, and they will recover." So then, after the Lord had spoken to them, He was received up into heaven, and sat down at the right hand of God. And they went out and preached everywhere, the Lord working with them and **confirming the word through the accompanying signs. Amen!**

Note the clearly stated purpose of the sign gifts. *They confirmed the Word of God. More specifically, they confirmed the SPOKEN WORD*, for Scripture states that the signs accompanied the preaching. All gave witness that the Lord (The Incarnate Word) was still ministering on the earth through His disciples in whom He had invested much responsibility.

As this is the first mention of the sign gifts, including tongues, one would do well to make some observations.

1. **They were gifts given to individuals.**
2. **Tongues was part of a cluster of sign gifts.**
3. **The sign gifts would be given to those who "believe."**
4. **The sign gifts confirm the spoken Word.**

Note: For those who insist that tongues is a valid sign today, let them also venture into the rest of the sign gifts which make up this cluster. For instance, regarding the picking up of snakes, the voice of the Greek verb is active which means a conscious act on the part of a believer to pick up a poisonous snake as a sign. This is not talking about accidental snakebite as some claim. Charismatics often accuse non-charismatics of picking and choosing what gifts apply today, what Scriptures apply today. For the sake of integrity, if one claims tongues are for today, then one should make the same claim for the other sign gifts in the cluster—including snake handling! The "**CLUSTER CONNECTION**" stands as a vital consideration.

The Continuing Testimony of Scripture

This emphasis on confirming the spoken word of God continues throughout the early witness of the church. Note the following passages where there is a definite link between the signs and the spoken Word of God.

Acts 2:1-11 There are several important facts in this passage. Not only is this the first recorded account of tongues, but such occurs in the context of preaching the gospel. Pentecost was in full accord with the stipulations of Mark 16:20. Tongues was given as a sign gift to confirm the spoken Word. As the Apostles spoke of the "wonderful works of God" (2:11), the people heeded the message. Some mocked, but 3000 came to a saving knowledge of the Lord Jesus Christ. The sign had accomplished its purpose. It set the stage for Peter's sermon, which no doubt was in the **common language** of the people.

Acts 4:29-31 Peter and John have just been released from custody and their appearance before the Sanhedrin. As they are reunited with other believers, they all break forth in prayer to the Lord. Note the role of the sign gifts in this prayer:

> "Now, Lord, look on their threats, and grant to Your servants that with all boldness they may *speak Your word* by stretching out your hand to heal, and that *signs and wonders* may be done through the name of Your holy Servant Jesus." And when they had prayed, the place where they were assembled together was shaken; and they were all filled with the Holy Spirit, and they *spoke the word of God with boldness* (italics mine).

The disciples asked the Lord to assist them in speaking the Word of God with boldness. In their prayer, they asked the Lord to accompany the speaking of the Word with signs. Why? Because the signs would do exactly what had been recorded in the Gospel of Mark—i.e., they would confirm the spoken Word.

Acts 6:1-8 When Stephen and the other men were chosen to assist the Apostles in the church at Jerusalem, Scripture attests that "the word of God spread, and the number of disciples multiplied greatly in Jerusalem, . . . and Stephen, full of faith and power, did great *wonders and signs* among the people" (Acts 6:7-8; italics mine.). Note that the spread of the Word of God is directly tied to the display of the signs and wonders. Again, they continue the pattern of confirming the Word of God.

Acts 8:6 The setting for this verse is Philip preaching in the city of Samaria. In response to the preaching, many believed in the Lord Jesus Christ. Again, note the relationship between the sign gifts and their role of confirming the spoken Word: "And the multitudes with one accord heeded the things *spoken* by Philip, *hearing and seeing the miracles which he did*" (italics mine). Because there were no New Testament Scriptures at this time, it was essential that the Lord confirm the gospel message of grace with signs and wonders. The Jews would challenge the disciples over their "new" message, and they would point to the Old Testament Scriptures and twenty centuries of religious history to vindicate their Judaism. The early church, therefore, needed "credentials" to confirm that their message and ministry were of the Lord. As they had no Scriptures which particularly defended their position, the signs and wonders became the necessary credentials to show the multitudes that their message was from God. The implication is clear: when the New Testament Scriptures would come, there would be no need for the sign gifts. Scripture would stand as a self-validating witness to the truth which it embodies. Again, there would be no need for signs to confirm the Word of God, once it was delivered to the believers in scriptural form.

Acts 9:36-42 The occasion is the raising of Dorcas from the dead by Peter. Following the miraculous restoration of Dorcas to life, news of the event spread throughout Joppa. The result was that many came to believe in the gospel. Again, the miracles confirmed the spoken word. They were not done for the sake of personal benefit alone, but for furthering the gospel witness. Note the Scripture account: "And it became known throughout all Joppa, and many believed on the Lord" (Acts 9:42).

Acts 13:1-12 Paul and Barnabas are on the island of Cyprus. This is the beginning of Paul's first missionary journey. As he shares the gospel with a certain Roman proconsul, Sergius Paulus, a sorcerer by the name of Elymas seeks to turn the proconsul away from the faith (13:8). In response, Paul rebukes Elymas for perverting the "straight ways of the Lord" and strikes the sorcerer blind. Sergius Paulus witnesses the miracle and believes. Yet, note the emphasis that the Scripture places on the entire incident: "Then *the proconsul believed, when he saw what had been done, being astonished at the teaching of the Lord*" (Acts 13:12; italics mine).

If we were describing this event, we would probably have said, "Sergius Paulus believed because he was astonished at the miracle which Paul had done." But again, the miracle pointed to the truth of Paul's message. *The miracle confirmed the spoken Word!* That is why Scripture notes that Sergius Paulus was astonished at the teaching. Surely, he was astonished at the miracle. However, the miracle led him to listen to the message of the Cross, the Resurrection, and redemption through the Lord Jesus Christ. It was that message which astonished Sergius Paulus.

Acts 14:1-3 The setting is the first missionary journey of Paul and Barnabas. The two men are ministering in Iconium which is in Asia Minor. The pattern of sign gifts confirming the spoken Word of God continues to unfold. Note the following verse:

> Therefore they stayed there a long time, *speaking boldly in the Lord, who was bearing witness to the word of His grace, granting signs and wonders to be done by their hands* (Acts 14:3; italics mine).

This is one of the clearest passages in the Bible on the purpose of the sign gifts. The Lord granted signs and wonders to "bear witness to the word of His grace." As these messengers of God's grace preached in the synagogue of Iconium, many Jews and Greeks believed (14:1). Yet, a number of Jews remained in unbelief. They had their two thousand years of special favor from God; they had their God-ordained ceremonies and civil practices; and they had their Scriptures. They must have wondered: "Why would God suddenly do away with the ceremonies and laws of Moses that God Himself instituted some 1500 years ago?" They must have asked Paul and Barnabas the same question that Jesus was asked when He ministered: "By what authority are You doing these things? And who gave You this authority?" (cf. Mt. 21:23). **That is why the signs and wonders were needed—they gave witness that the spoken message did have the authority of heaven behind it. This testimony to the authority of the spoken gospel was essential until such a time as the gospel could become a part of the New Testament Scriptures.**

Heb. 2:1-4 The book of Hebrews sets forth the preeminence of Christ and the New Covenant of grace over the Old Covenant of the Law. Indeed, in Hebrews 8:8-13 the writer clearly ties the advent of the gospel of the Lord Jesus Christ to the prophesied New Covenant of Jeremiah 31:31-34. Scripture goes on to affirm that the Old Covenant was made obsolete by the New, and that the obsolete was ready to vanish away (Heb. 8:13). In other words, *change was the order of the day!* The old was passing away; the new was taking its place. During this *period of transition* between the Old and the New, it was necessary for the New Covenant to have a special witness from the Lord. The Old would not die easily. Thus, the writer urges Christians to hold on to the vital truths of Christ and to ponder the signs which confirmed the gospel message:

> Therefore we must give the more earnest heed to the things we have heard, lest we drift away. For if the word spoken through angels proved steadfast, and every transgression and disobedience received a just reward, how shall we escape, if we neglect so great a salvation, which at the first began to be *spoken* by the Lord, and was *confirmed* to us by those who heard Him, God *also bearing witness both with signs and wonders, with various miracles, and gifts of the Holy Spirit*, according to His own will? (Heb. 2:1-4; italics mine.)

The conclusion from this and the aforementioned passages is obvious.

As believers exercised their sign gifts, they did so not for personal benefit; rather they employed sign gifts as proof that their spoken message had the authority of God behind it. The sign gifts were therefore a witness to unbelievers and served to point them to the blessed message of the gospel.

A passage in the book of James further illustrates that sign gifts were not to be used for the benefit of believers. James does not instruct the church to find someone with the gift of healing if there are any sick among the brethren. He clearly says: "Is anyone among you sick? Let him call for the elders of the church, and let them pray over him, anointing him with oil in the name of the Lord. And the prayer of faith will save the sick and the Lord will raise him up" (James 5:14, 15). Additional scripture passages reveal that several other believers experienced sickness, yet were not healed by those possessing the healing gift. Paul had to leave Trophimus sick at Miletus (2 Tim. 4:20; cf. Epaphroditus, Phil. 2:25-27); and Timothy had to contend with a long standing stomach ailment and frequent bouts with illness (1 Tim. 5:23). All of these saints had contact with the Apostles and would surely have appealed to them for assistance. Even Paul himself had to contend with his thorn in the flesh that would not be removed (2 Cor. 12:7-10). **All of these accounts further stress the fact that the sign gifts, as defined in Mark 16:17, 18, were given to confirm the Gospel to unbelievers. They were never designed to minister to the church body.**[15]

Now that the gospel stands confirmed through Scripture, there is no need for the sign and revelatory gifts. God still heals today; but He does so through the corporate prayers of God's people and in accordance with His will—not through some believer with the gift of healing. The Lord still leads personally in the lives of believers; yet such is done through the Scriptures, through internal leadings and impressions by the Spirit of God, and not through visions, dreams, or prophecies (see Appendix A for discussion of some instances where there may be exceptions to this general principle). The Lord's power to cast out demons is still available today; but again, such is done through the corporate prayers of God's people and through the Name of the Lord Jesus Christ—not by someone who has a special gift or ministry of deliverance. Prayers for healing and deliverance are not the property of a few; rather they belong to the entire Body of Christ. Such is the heritage of the saints throughout the Christian community.

THE "ABRAHAM CONNECTION"
Heaven's Declaration

In view of the biblical evidence, most would agree that the sign gifts were given to confirm the spoken Word of God. However, many would question the conclusion that the sign gifts ceased when the written Word of God was completed. Some would charge that this is only a logical deduction, that there is no scriptural proof to support the link between the written Word and the cessation of sign gifts. This is an appropriate question. While deduction is a valid means of approaching truth, direct Scripture evidence is much more to be desired. So, is there a scriptural bridge that binds this concept together? Yes, and the passage is found in the Gospel of Luke.

In Luke 16:19-31, we find ourselves in one of the most dramatic passages in all the Bible. It is the only time the Lord takes a TV camera into Hell itself. We see the historical account of a rich man's experience in torment. Amidst the cries of agony, the rich man makes an appeal to Abraham whom he sees in paradise. Note the cry for help, but especially the response:

> "Then he said, 'I beg you therefore, father, that you would send him to my father's house, for I have five brothers, that he may testify to them, lest they also come to this place of torment.' Abraham said to him, 'They have Moses and the prophets; let them hear them.' And he said, 'No, father Abraham; but if one goes to them from the dead, they will repent.' But he said to him, '*If they do not hear Moses and the prophets, neither will they be persuaded though one rise from the dead*'" (Luke 16:27-31; italics mine).

What does this passage have to do with the sign gifts? It reveals Heaven's viewpoint regarding the preeminence of Scripture, and **the denial of signs to confirm belief when the written Word of God is available**. This is crucial for us to see. It is not, therefore, mere deduction to say that when the New Testament was completed the sign gifts were no longer necessary. This passage is Heaven's commentary on the issue. Significantly, it is the only passage in the New Testament that clearly reveals Heaven's denial of signs when the written Word is available.

Granted the context is a pre-Cross setting, yet the principle does not change. The rich man in the story had access to the written Word of God. So did his brothers. That was enough to engender faith. They needed no further signs to assist their belief. Yet, some may be wondering: "Did not Jesus and His disciples do miracles to authenticate the spoken gospel message?" "Did not these signs assist in belief unto salvation?" "Why did God deny signs to the rich man's brothers, yet permit signs when Jesus walked the streets of Palestine?" "The written Word of God was available to the people in both instances. How does one explain that in light of the Luke 16 passage?"

The answer is simple. Jesus and the disciples were bringing *new revelation*. This new revelation did need authenticating signs (Mark 16:20). Yet, where revelation was already in place, there needed to be no signs to assist belief. Such was the historical situation facing the rich man and Lazarus.

A number of writers have stressed the fact that in the biblical record, there were primarily three periods in which signs and miracles were the order of the day: the time of Moses and Joshua; the prophetic age highlighted by the ministries of Elijah and Elisha; and the time embraced by the ministry of Jesus and the Apostles. What is the common thread which links these three periods, each lasting about one hundred years? Primarily two elements were present in each period: (1) new revelation was being given in major proportions; and (2) signs and miracles were needed to authenticate this new revelation so that men and nations would receive the message.[16] Yet again, once the new revelation had become part of Scripture itself, available to God's people as well as the unbelieving world, the signs and miracles decreased in preeminence. Their role was finished. It was not that miracles ceased, for God continued to intervene in the affairs of men. However, the role of miracles authenticating the spoken Word was no longer needed when the written Word was in place. That is the essential thrust of the passage in Luke 16. Heaven's reply to the cry of the rich man was essentially: *"the Scripture is there, it is enough; even the resurrection of the dead cannot do more than the written Word of God in bringing men to faith"* (cf. Rom. 10:14-17).

A recent publication entitled, *Signs and Wonders and Evangelicals*, exposes the errors of John Wimber and his Vineyard Movement.[17] The book was written shortly after Wimber held a series of meetings in Sydney, Australia. The writers point out that, for Wimber, the finished work of Christ proclaimed in the gospel message is not sufficient in and of itself to be effective. Signs, wonders, and attendant revelations must accompany proclamation if the gospel is going to have maximum impact.[18] Such an emphasis runs counter to Scripture for the Bible affirms that the gospel DOES have the power, *in and of itself,* to bring forth maximum impact (cf. Rom. 1:16; 1 Cor. 1:18, 22-24; 2:1-5; 15:1-3).

One final comment on this point is in order. Jesus recognized the bent of man for the sensational. He knew that the sign gifts were essential to authenticate the new revelation that He and the disciples were giving. Yet, He also knew that some would seek signs as a requirement for belief, rather than responding to signs out of a humble heart. It was the seeking and demand for signs that brought strong rebuke from Jesus. The Lord declared, *"An evil and adulterous generation seeks after a sign . . ."* (Matt. 12:39).

On a trip to Jerusalem during the earlier part of His ministry, Jesus ministered to many through miracles and signs (cf. John 2:23-25). Even though many believed in His name when they saw the signs that Jesus did, the Scriptures assert the following: "But Jesus did not commit Himself to them, because He knew all men, and had no need that anyone should testify of man, for He knew what was in man" (John 2:24-25). In John 6:26 and 27, Jesus rebuked the crowd for their selfish motives in response to the miraculous feeding of the multitudes. In so doing, He gave preeminence to faith in His claims, devotion to His teachings and the need to "feed" upon His Person. Many of the disciples left Jesus when confronted with these spiritual realities (cf. John 6:66; 20:29). Note the insightful comments of Warren Wiersbe on these passages in John's Gospel:

> While in Jerusalem for the Passover, Jesus performed miracles that are not given in detail in any of the Gospels. It must have been these signs that especially attracted Nicodemus (John 3:2). Because of the miracles, many people professed to believe in Him; but Jesus did not accept their profession. No matter what the people themselves said, or others said about them, He did not accept human testimony. Why? Because, being God, He knew what was in each person's heart and mind.

> The words *believed* in John 2:23 and *commit* in John 2:24 are the same Greek word. These people believed in Jesus, but He did not believe in them! They were "unsaved believers"! It was one thing to respond to a miracle but quite something else to commit oneself to Jesus Christ and continue in His Word (John 8:30-31).

> John was not discrediting the importance of our Lord's signs, because he wrote his book to record these signs and to encourage his readers to trust Jesus Christ and receive eternal life (John 20:30-31). However, throughout the

book, John makes it clear that it takes more than believing in miracles for a person to be saved. Seeing the signs and believing in them would be a great beginning; in fact, even the disciples started that way and had to grow in their faith (compare John 2:11 and v. 22). . . .

It is important to see that Jesus tied His miracles to the truth of His message. He knew that the human heart is attracted to the sensational. The 5,000 that He fed wanted to make Him King—until He preached a sermon on the Bread of Life, and then they left Him in droves! "Grace and truth came by Jesus Christ" (John 1:17). In grace, Jesus fed the hungry; in truth, He taught the Word. The people wanted the physical food but not the spiritual truth, so they abandoned Him.

"He knew what was in man" is a statement that is proved several times in John's Gospel. Jesus knew the character of Simon (John 1:42). He knew what Nathanael was like (John 1:46ff.), and He told the Samaritan woman "all things" that she had ever done (John 4:29). He knew that the Jewish leaders did not have God's love in their hearts (John 5:42), and that one of His disciples was not truly a believer (John 6:64). He saw the repentance in the heart of the adulteress (John 8:10-11) and the murder in the hearts of His enemies (John 8:40ff.). Several times in the Upper Room message, Jesus revealed to His disciples their own inner feelings and questions.

As you follow our Lord's ministry in John's Gospel, you see Him moving gradually out of the bright light of popularity and into the dark shadows of rejection. At the beginning, it was easy for people to follow the crowd and watch His miracles. But then, His words began to penetrate hearts, with conviction following; and conviction either leads to conversion or opposition. It is impossible to be neutral. People had to decide, and most of them decided against Him.

Yes, Jesus knows the human heart. "Except ye see signs and wonders, ye will not believe" (John 4:48). People who want His works but not His Word can never share His life. "Seeing is believing" is not the Christian approach (John 11:40; 20:29). First we believe; then we see. Miracles can only lead us to the Word (John 5:36-38), and the Word generates saving faith (Rom. 10:17).[19]

Jesus was especially concerned that His own disciples had a proper perspective on the signs and wonders. These signs and wonders were never to occupy a place of preeminence in their own hearts; rather, the disciples were instructed to rejoice primarily in the saving of souls. Note the following exchange between Jesus and the disciples in Luke 10:17-20 (italics mine):

> Then the seventy returned with joy, saying, "Lord, even the demons are subject to us in Your name." And He said to them, "I saw Satan fall like lightning from heaven. Behold, I give you the authority to trample on serpents and scorpions, and over all the power of the enemy, and nothing shall by any means hurt you. Nevertheless, *do not rejoice in this, that the spirits are subject to you, but rather rejoice because your names are written in heaven."*

The disciples were never to lose sight of the marvellous fact that redemption is the miracle above all miracles (cf. Luke 15:10).

The Apostle Paul also underscored the **sufficiency** of the Word, apart from signs, to engender faith: "For Jews request a sign, and Greeks seek after wisdom; but we preach Christ crucified, to the Jews a stumbling block and to the Greeks foolishness, but to those who are called, both Jews and Greeks, Christ the power of God and the wisdom of God" (1 Cor. 2:22-24). So once again, it is more than a logical jump to say when the Written Word is given, the need for signs will cease. It is a biblical principle.[20]

THE SIGN AND REVELATORY GIFTS
Given until the revelation of the Lord Jesus was completed

One of the most important considerations regarding the cessation of the sign and revelatory gifts is that regarding the ministry and revelation of the Lord Jesus Christ. Jesus is the highest revelation of God to mankind (see Appendix C). When one of Jesus' own apostles asked Him to reveal God the Father, Jesus declared: "He who has seen Me has seen the Father . . . " (John 14:9). He went on to say, "The words that I speak to you I do not speak on My own authority; but the Father who dwells in Me does the works" (John 14:10). Other passages clearly affirm the preeminence of Jesus in revealing God to man. Note the emphasis of Hebrews 1:1-4 and 2:1-4:

> God, who at various times and in different ways spoke in time past to the fathers by he prophets, has in these last days spoken to us by His Son, whom

He has appointed heir of all things, through whom also He made the worlds; who being the brightness of His glory and the express image of His person, and upholding all things by the word of His power, when He had by Himself purged our sins, sat down at the right hand of the Majesty on high, having become so much better than the angels, as He has by inheritance obtained a more excellent name than they (Heb. 1:1-4).

Therefore we must give the more earnest heed to the things we have heard, lest we drift away. For if the word spoken through angels proved steadfast, and every transgression and disobedience received a just reward, how shall we escape if we neglect so great a salvation, which at the first began to be spoken by the Lord, and was confirmed to us by those who heard Him, God also bearing witness both with signs and wonders, with various miracles, and gifts of the Holy Spirit, according to His own will? (Heb. 2:1-4.)

Yes, God revealed Himself through prophets and through angels. However, the highest revelation of Himself was through Jesus at His incarnation and through Scripture, the Word of God. Jesus' revelation superseded that of the angels and the prophets. Even though He ascended to the right hand of the Father, He continued to give new revelation to the Church through the Scriptures and through the ministry of the Holy Spirit. Once revelation was completed, the need for confirming signs and wonders ceased.

By divine design, the Scriptures closed with the *Revelation of Jesus Christ*. Because of Jesus' preeminence in the realm of revelation as the Incarnate Word of God (cf. John 1:1-14; Rev. 19:13), the closing of Scripture had to highlight the Lord Jesus. Moreover, the warning at the close of the New Testament must be viewed as extending beyond the parameters of the Book of Revelation:

For I testify to everyone who hears the words of the prophecy of this book: If anyone adds to these things, God will add to him the plagues that are written in this book; and if anyone takes away from the words of the book of this prophecy, God shall take away his part from the Book of Life, from the holy city, and from the things which are written in this book (Rev. 22:18, 19).

Although this warning does serve as a capstone to the Book of Revelation, such also serves as a warning to all who would claim to be the vessel for new revelation. Scripture, and thus revelation itself, closes with the book bearing the name of the Lord Jesus Christ. Jesus spoke His last words to the Church as recorded in The *Revelation of Jesus Christ*. Therefore, those who claim to speak new revelation from God today stand against the preeminence of Christ as the highest revelation of God. The words of Walter Chantry are instructive on this point:

> Failure to see Jesus Christ as the final revelation of truth is a major error that will open the door of the church to a multitude of heresies, taught in the name of truth. Every true movement initiated by the Spirit of God leads men back to the words of Christ which were inscripturated by his own inspiration.

> Some men have ridiculed an appeal to Revelation 22:18, 19 when discussing the close of the canon (the end to divine messages from the Lord). However, in the context of all that the Bible says about Jesus being the final prophet, the climax of revelation, the words are most significant. It is this same Jesus Christ who speaks in the last chapter of the Bible, "If any man shall add unto these things, God shall add unto him the plagues that are written in this book." Our Lord makes this comment in the closing verses of the last confirming witness to his revelation. The Saviour gave his warning through the last living apostle at the conclusion of his ministry.

> Some would prefer to weaken our Lord's warning signal by saying that it only applies to the Book of Revelation. But such strong and unusual language must be more than a prohibition to tamper with that one writing. We must see it as did Matthew Henry. He wrote, "This sanction is like a flaming sword to guard the canon of the Scripture from profane hands."

> Revelation is no usual book. It is a sweeping analysis of history from the first advent of Christ to the second. Jesus had promised that the Spirit would teach his apostles "all things" [John 14:26].The Spirit had come and fulfilled the promise. Apostles had communicated the authoritative word. The task of revelation was finished. The Book of Revelation is the last apostolic word to the church. The Almighty Saviour, seated at God's right hand, opens his sovereign lips personally to declare that nothing is to be added to what has been recorded. Beware of meddling with Christ's revelation![21]

The dynamic connection between the Lord Jesus Christ and the Word of God is clearly established in Scripture (cf. John 1:1-14; Rev. 19:13; John 5:39). In John 5:39, Jesus set forth this relationship when he declared to the Pharisees: "You search the Scriptures, for in them you think you have eternal life; and *these are they which testify of Me*" (italics mine). Not only do the Scriptures testify to the Lord Jesus Christ, but this testimony is said to be the very heart of prophecy.

When the apostle John was receiving the marvellous revelations of Jesus on the Isle of Patmos, the angelic messenger responded in the following manner when John fell at his feet:

> And I fell at his feet to worship him. But he said to me, "See that you do not do that! I am your fellow servant, and of your brethren who have the testimony of Jesus. Worship God! *For the testimony of Jesus is the spirit of prophecy*" (Rev. 19:10; italics mine).

> Now I, John, saw and heard these things. And when I heard and saw, I fell down to worship before the feet of the angel who showed me these things. Then he said to me, "See that you do not do that. For I am you fellow servant, and of your brethren the prophets, and of those who keep the words of this book. Worship God! " (Rev. 22:8, 9.)

In the very midst of revelation, John is reminded that while angels and prophets serve as vessels for revelation, the highest preeminence must be given to God. It is most befitting therefore, that since the Scriptures bear testimony to Jesus (John 5:39) and since the "testimony to Jesus is the spirit of prophecy" (Rev. 19:10), prophecy should close with the last book of Scripture, *The Revelation of Jesus Christ*. One should be very careful, therefore, in claiming to speak further revelation for God. The **Christ Connection** renders any claim of new revelation to be a spurious counterfeit. Moreover, as new revelation has ceased, the need for confirming signs and wonders (cf. Mark 16:20) also has ceased. (For a more in-depth discussion of this point, see Appendix C.)

THE SIGN AND REVELATORY GIFTS
Signifying blessing on believers; judgment on unbelieving Israel

One must remember that in showing the sign gifts and revelatory gifts have ceased, one is dealing with a mosaic of Scripture passages. Another key passage is 1 Corinthians 14:18-22. Paul is dealing with the exercise of tongues in the Corinthian assembly. He had already referred to the

Corinthians as carnal and spiritual babes (3:1); now he points to the path of maturity regarding tongues. His argument is crucial.

> I thank my God I speak with tongues more than you all; yet in the church I would rather speak five words with my understanding, that I may teach others also, than ten thousand words in a tongue. Brethren, do not be children in understanding; however, in malice be babes, but in understanding be mature. In the law it is written: "With men of other tongues and other lips I will speak to this people; And yet, for all that, they will not hear Me," says the Lord. Therefore tongues are for a sign, not to those who believe but to unbelievers; but prophesying is not for unbelievers but for those who believe (1 Cor. 14:18-22).

In pointing the Corinthians to maturity, Paul quotes from Isaiah 28:11, 12. Why? What is he saying and why does he go all the way to the Old Testament to make a point when tongues are strictly a New Testament phenomenon?

The Parallel Between Tongues and the Parables of Jesus

We have already seen that tongues was a special evangelistic gift given to the early church to break through language barriers and share the wonderful works of God. Thus, tongues had a very beautiful element. Yet, there was the other side of tongues as well. An analogy can be made with the parables of Jesus. The parables had a twofold purpose. For those with open hearts, the parables gave instruction on the deeper truths of the kingdom of God and the Person of Christ. However, the parables also had a judgmental factor—this upon unbelieving Israel. Jesus taught in parables to purposely hide the truths of the kingdom from those who refused to open their hearts to His teachings. Note the words of the Lord Jesus on this matter in Matthew 13:10-15:

> And the disciples came and said to Him, "Why do You speak to them in parables?" He answered and said to them, "Because it has been given to you to know the mysteries of the kingdom of heaven, but to them it has not been given. For whoever has, to him more will be given, and he will have abundance; but whoever does not have, even what he has will be taken away from him. Therefore I speak to them in parables, because seeing they do not see,

and hearing they do not hear, nor do they understand. And in them the prophecy of Isaiah is fulfilled, which says: 'Hearing you will hear and shall not understand, and seeing you will see and not perceive; for the heart of this people has grown dull. Their ears are hard of hearing, and their eyes they have closed, lest they should see with their eyes and hear with their ears, lest they should understand with their heart and turn, so that I should heal them.'"

In like manner, tongues also had a twofold purpose. The *Isaiah Connection* which Paul placed before the Corinthians reveals a purpose of tongues which is often overlooked. And this purpose relates to the overall argument as to why biblical tongues have ceased.

THE "ISAIAH CONNECTION"
Tongues as a sign of judgment on unbelieving Israel

Paul quoted from Isaiah to drive home the point to the Corinthians that tongues was also a sign of judgment upon unbelieving Israel. Just as Isaiah had come with a message from God and was rejected by Israel, so Jesus had come to the nation and was also rejected. Because Israel of old had rejected the message and ministry of Isaiah, the Lord gave a prophecy to Israel that He would get their attention through the tongues of foreigners. In other words, because of Israel's unbelief, foreign powers would come and conquer Israel. Foreign languages (i.e., tongues) would be heard in the villages, towns, and cities of Israel. Thus, because Israel refused to hear the voice of God through His prophets, God would speak to them in judgment through foreign conquerors. History confirms that Isaiah was talking about the coming Assyrians. So what was Paul's intent in presenting the *Isaiah Connection?*

Because Israel had refused the Messiah, and continued to spurn the witness of the apostles, the Lord had now turned to the peoples of the world. He would use them as vessels and stewards of His truth. Israel would no longer be in a special place of favor (cf. Rom. 3:1, 2). Instead, Jews of the dispersion and the Gentiles would hear the gospel in their own languages. Tongues therefore would serve to authenticate the universal aspect of the gospel message and the messenger as well. This was a sign that the Lord was no longer dealing exclusively with Israel. The fact that God was speaking through other languages continued to confirm this reality to all persons willing to listen.

While tongues communicated God's wonderful works to various language groups, Israel stood condemned because of her rejection of the gospel. Such was the judgmental aspect which Paul wanted the Corinthians to see. He wanted to reaffirm that tongues was a sign gift to testify to unbelievers, not a gift to be exercised within the church for the sole benefit of believers. Paul emphasizes this truth another time in 1 Corinthians 14:22-24:

> Therefore tongues are for a sign, not to those who believe but to unbelievers; but prophesying is not for unbelievers but for those who believe. Therefore if the whole church comes together in one place, and all speak with tongues, and there come in those who are uninformed or unbelievers, will they not say that you are out of your mind? But if all prophesy, and an unbeliever or an uninformed person comes in, he is convinced by all, he is judged by all.

When the armies of Titus destroyed Jerusalem and the Temple in A.D. 70, the judgmental aspect of tongues was no longer needed. Neither the Jew nor the Gentile world needed any further sign or confirmation that Israel stood under the judgment of God. This was evident to all. The destruction of Jerusalem and the dispersion of the Jewish population sealed the temporary aspect of tongues as a judgmental sign.[22]

Even though Israel is back in their land today, they still have no temple and no sacrifices. The judgment continues, and during this church age God is dealing mainly with the Gentiles.[23] So in view of Paul's call to maturity on the issue of tongues, his argument is relevant for today. He stresses the judgmental aspect of tongues to confirm that tongues are for a sign to unbelievers. Sadly, most tongues speaking today takes place in the midst of a church assembly, and is directed to believers, or in a private devotional context. These two aspects alone should raise questions regarding the validity of the tongues experience.

THE SIGN AND REVELATORY GIFTS
Given until the "Perfect" is come

Any discussion of tongues or the sign gifts must address 1 Corinthians 13:8-13. A proper understanding of this passage is crucial to the overall question regarding the cessation of sign gifts. In this chapter, Paul has just given instruction on the preeminence of love among the body of believers and how the principle of love must govern the exercise of spiritual gifts (vv. 1-7). Now in the following verses, Paul asserts that there will come a time when tongues will cease and the gifts of prophecy and knowledge will pass away.

> Love never fails. But whether there are prophecies, they will fail; whether there are tongues, they will cease; whether there is knowledge, it will vanish away. For we know in part and we prophesy in part. But when that which is perfect has come, then that which is in part will be done away. When I was a child, I spoke as a child, I understood as a child, I thought as a child; but when I became a man, I put away childish things. For now we see in a mirror dimly, but then face to face. Now I know in part, but then I shall know just as I am known (1 Cor. 13:8-12).

Crucial Questions Regarding 1 Corinthians 13

A number of questions arise regarding this passage: (1) When will the gifts of tongues, prophecy, and knowledge cease? (2) Who or what is the "perfect" and what is the relationship between the coming of the "perfect" and the cessation of gifts? (3) Are tongues, prophecy, and the gift of knowledge treated as a group in this passage, or is there some differentiation in treatment? Let's take these questions in the order in which they are stated.

When Paul wrote 1 Corinthians, only about five books of the New Testament had been written: James, Matthew, Galatians, 1 and 2 Thessalonians.[24] Indeed, there was still more prophecy to come; there was still the need for the gift of knowledge. One can easily understand therefore why Paul declares, "we know in part and we prophesy in part." Clearly from the passage, the gifts of prophecy and knowledge were to continue until the "perfect has come." When the "perfect" comes, that which was in part (i.e., prophecy and the gift of knowledge) would be abolished. Why? An obvious conclusion follows: the coming of the "perfect" would coincide with the completion of prophecy and the gift of knowledge.

There is an interesting grammatical consideration, however, regarding the issue of tongues. The gifts of prophecy and knowledge are associated with the same verb (*katargeo*) and each is in the passive voice. The force of this verbal construction is "to be abolished" or "to be rendered inoperative." On the other hand, the gift of tongues is linked to a different verb (*pauo*) and this is in the middle voice in the Greek. The construction in this instance means "to cease, in and of itself." While prophecy and knowledge would be removed or abolished at the coming of the "perfect," tongues would cease independently of these two other revelatory gifts. Since verse 9 omits any reference to tongues, it would appear that tongues would cease before the removal of prophecy and knowledge.

What about the identification and time frame regarding the coming of the "perfect"? A number of suggestions have been advanced regarding the identity of the "perfect"—or the "complete." The primary options are the following:

1. **The Person of Jesus Christ at His Second Coming**
2. **The perfected state of the believer in the Resurrection**
3. **The new heaven and new earth**
4. **The mature state of the early church**
5. **The completed Scriptures**

As one considers this list of options, two groupings become apparent. The first three are associated with the Second Coming of Christ, and the last two focus on the completed Scriptures. Our discussion will follow these basic groupings.

The "Perfect": The Person of Jesus Christ at His Second Coming (or the Glorified State of the Believer)

This view has a number of things to commend it. First there is the link between gifts of revelation (i.e., prophecy and knowledge) and Jesus Himself. Indeed, Jesus is the Word made flesh (John 1:14). Jesus' Second Coming is a revelation of Himself (Rev. 1:1) and is the fulfillment of all prophecy. Scripture states that "the testimony of Jesus is the spirit of prophecy" (Rev. 19:10). At His coming all prophecy will find its ultimate fulfillment and completion. One is reminded of the book of Revelation which closes with a capstone on all further prophecy (Rev. 22:18, 19). Then, too, with the coming of Christ for the church (1 Thess. 4:13-18), the gifts of prophecy and knowledge would no longer be needed. Why? The church is no longer present upon the earth.

Although prophecy will continue to be exercised during the Tribulation (Joel 2:28-32; Rev. 11), such a ministry will proceed on a different basis than that during the church age.

The very imagery of the passage seems to support the "perfect" as being Christ. The wording of verse 12 seems to argue that when the "Perfect" (i.e., Christ) comes we will see Him "face to face," and then we will "know even as we are known." Some emphasize that the expansion of believers' knowledge (i.e., to know as we are known) can only happen in the glorified state.

Then, too, Paul would identify the "perfect" or "completed state" in other passages with the believer's standing in Christ. It was a future hope for the Apostle Paul and linked to the Person and Second Coming of Christ (Col. 1:28; Phil. 3:12-14, 20, 21). Thus, the gifts of prophecy and knowledge would continue until the coming of Christ. However, one must remember that the gift of prophecy had two components: fore-telling future events and thus giving new revelation; and "forth-telling," with power and boldness, truths that had already been given in previous revelation. The prophetic gift included both of these activities. So if one takes the "perfect" of 1 Corinthians 13 as a reference to the coming of Christ, one must understand these distinctions within prophecy. Given the restriction in Revelation 22:18, 19 on further revelation, only the forth-telling aspect of prophecy can be operative till the coming of Christ.

Will prophecy be practiced after the rapture of the church? As noted above, Joel 2:28-32 and Revelation 11 reveal that prophecy, dreams, and visions will be the order of the day during the tribulation period. MacArthur cites these passages and others that indicate a continuation of prophecy well into the millennium.[25] That is the reason MacArthur feels the "perfect" of 1 Corinthians 13 is the eternal state—only then will the exercise of prophecy be abolished.

There is a problem, however, with equating the "perfect" with the eternal state. The subject under consideration in 1 Corinthians 13 is that of spiritual gifts to the church. The coming of the "perfect" must thus be related in some way to the church age. To extend the parameters of 1 Corinthians 13 past the church age (or the coming of Christ at the Rapture) is to lose sight of the focus of the passage. Again, the passage is dealing with the spiritual gifts of prophecy and knowledge which have been given to the church. While prophecy was operative before the church age, and certainly will be exercised during the Tribulation and Millennium, Paul's focus is not concerned with these general ministries. He is focusing on spiritual gifts as they relate to the Body of Christ.

While there is scriptural evidence for equating the "Perfect" of
1 Corinthians 13:10-12 with the Lord Jesus Christ and His coming,
there is a better scriptural alternative.[26] When faced with several legitimate options, it is always best to let Scripture interpret Scripture. And
there is a passage in the Book of James that sheds light on the "perfect"
of 1 Corinthians 13.

THE "JAMES CONNECTION"
The "Perfect" as the Completed Scriptures

We have seen the *Abraham Connection* and the *Isaiah Connection*; now it
is essential for the reader to consider the **James Connection**. This is one
of the most overlooked considerations when dealing with the identification of the "perfect" in 1 Corinthians 13.

Earlier I made reference to the fact that the Book of James had
already been written prior to the time when Paul wrote 1 Corinthians.[27]
Most significantly, many expositors regard James as the first book written
in the New Testament. We know from other passages that Paul would
have had access to the Book of James (cf. Acts 9:26-31; Gal. 1:11-24).
Even if Paul did not have access to James' epistle, the same Holy Spirit
that bore James along in his writing also inspired Paul. In chapter one,
James stresses the need for believers to heed the Scriptures and go
beyond merely hearing them:

> But be doers of the word, and not hearers only, deceiving yourselves. For if
> anyone is a hearer of the word and not a doer, he is like a man observing his
> natural *face* in a *mirror*; for he observes himself, goes away, and immediately
> forgets what kind of man he was. But he who looks into the *perfect law of lib-*
> *erty* and continues in it, and is not a forgetful hearer but a doer of the work,
> this one will be blessed in what he does (James 1:23-25; italics mine).

Do not miss the imagery that the Holy Spirit had James employ. The
written Word of God, the Scriptures, are compared to a "mirror" wherein
one may behold his "face." Moreover, the Scriptures are referred to as the
"perfect law of liberty." The word "mirror" (or its equivalent) only occurs
three times in the entire New Testament: here, 1 Corinthians 13:12, and
2 Corinthians 3:18. Again, in this first reference to "mirror," it is clearly
equated with the Scriptures which enable a man to behold his own

"face" (i.e., to see himself as God sees him, as he really is). Now the *James Connection* is precisely this: the same imagery that the Holy Spirit inspired in James appears in 1 Corinthians 13:10-12. In the Corinthians passage, when the "perfect" comes believers would be able to see clearly, face to face. Why did Paul declare that at that time they could only see through the mirror "dimly?" We know from the Book of James that the "mirror" is the Scriptures. At the time of Paul's writing, only five books of the New Testament had been written. There were twenty-two books yet to be given by the Holy Spirit. That is why believers could only see "dimly" into the "mirror," the Scriptures. We also know from the Book of James that the Scriptures are called the "perfect law of liberty." The word "perfect" in James is an adjectival form of the same word found in 1 Corinthians 13. The "perfect" of 1 Corinthians, therefore, has to be Scripture. The same imagery that the Holy Spirit used in James (i.e., that of a mirror, seeing one's face, and the "perfect") appears here in this passage in Corinthians. Note the following comparison:

James 1:23-25	1 Corinthians 13:10-12
Mirror = Scriptures	Mirror = Scriptures (and because only five books of the New Testament were then written, believers could only see dimly at that time)
Face = A believer seeing himself in the Scriptures as he really is, as only God sees him.	Face to face = A believer, seeing his reflection in the mirror clearly when the "perfect" comes.
Perfect = Perfect law of liberty ("perfect" appears in an adjectival sense).	"Perfect" = The completed Scriptures that will enable man to see himself clearly.

The *James Connection* sheds valuable light on how one is to understand the "perfect" of 1 Corinthians 13. In essence, Paul was sharing with the Corinthians that while the gift of tongues would cease in and of itself, the gifts of prophecy and knowledge would continue until the completion of the Scriptures. When the Scriptures would be complete, man would no longer see dimly, but rather see himself in the full light of God's revelation. That is why tongues were no longer needed either. A completed Scripture is a completed revelation of God.

Some have suggested that 1 Corinthians 13:12 points to the time when we will see the Lord "face to face." However, this rendering of the passage forces a meaning on the phrase "face to face" that is disassociated from the context of looking into a mirror.[28] What does one see when one looks into a mirror? One's own reflection or the reflection of another! Thus, the meaning of this verse exactly parallels that in the James 1:22-25 passage: when one looks into the mirror (i.e., the Word of God), one will see himself as he truly is. Remember, at the writing of 1 Corinthians, only four to five books of the New Testament had been written. One could only see "dimly" as more revelation was yet to come. However, with the completed Scriptures, one would see clearly and would possess full knowledge of that which pertains to life and godliness (cf. 2 Pet. 1:3).

The above interpretation is also consistent with 2 Corinthians 3:18. In this passage, the phrase *"beholding as in a mirror"* also relates to the Word of God—the context from verses 7-17. What do we see in the mirror? We see the "glory of the Lord. " Yet, His image becomes our image as we are changed into His likeness by the Spirit of God. So, even though we behold the glory of the Lord in Scripture (the mirror), we behold the image into which we are being transformed.

When one compares this passage with 1 Corinthians 13:12, one sees the parallel application. With only a few books of the New Testament completed, the glory of the Lord revealed in the Word was not yet complete. We could neither see Him, nor ourselves, in the full light of God's revelation. Believers could see only "dimly." However, with the completion of Scripture, not only would the glory of Christ be revealed in greater fullness, but so would the believer's own reflection. Why? Because the believer is to take on the image of Christ.

One must also remember that Paul viewed his own writings as Scripture (1 Cor. 2:13-15; 1 Thess. 2:13). He knew that new revelation was being given, and that one day this process would cease. In the same way that God had completed the Old Testament, God would complete this new revelation. Paul well understood this. The very fact that Paul used the phrases, *"we know in part and we prophesy in part"* (1 Cor. 13:9), indicates he is dealing with quantitative concerns. That is why the word "perfect" is better equated with the completed Scriptures than with Christ. The very word "perfect" (*telion*) most often embodies the idea of "wholeness" or "maturity" or "that which is complete." And in the structure of this passage, the "perfect" has to be the opposite of that which is "in part." Paul understood this principle well.

BUT WHAT ABOUT THE CORINTHIANS? *What would have been their understanding of Paul's statements regarding the "perfect"?* Indeed, any member of the Corinthian church who heard that passage read in the assembly would never has said to himself, "That refers to the completion of the Scriptures or canon!" What did they know about a "canon" or completed Scriptures! Given their mindset, the Corinthians would most likely have understood the "perfect" to have been a reference to the Lord Jesus or the "perfected state" in the kingdom. The question thus arises: *Should not the first-century audience and their perception of Paul's statements weigh heavily on a proper interpretation of the "perfect"?*

Sound biblical interpretation (*hermeneutics*) always demands that one take into consideration the cultural, linguistic, and historical context in which words are spoken. This certainly embraces audience perception and their understanding of terms and phrases. HOWEVER, AUDIENCE PERCEPTION IS A POOR STANDARD FOR CORRECT BIBLICAL INTERPRETATION WHEN ONE IS CONFRONTED WITH NEW REVELATION OF EPOCHAL PROPORTIONS.

A few examples will help to illustrate the weakness of audience perception as a tool for measuring correct biblical interpretation of a pronouncement. Again, this is especially true when the pronouncement or passage addresses new revelation:

1. *Prophetic statements regarding a suffering Messiah* (Ps. 22:1-21; Isa. 52:13-53:12; cf. Isa. 45:18-25 with Phil. 2:5-11): Even the most orthodox Jewish believer would never have equated these passages with Messiah who would come to suffer. Because of their monotheism and their mindset, they were incapable of a proper understanding of these passages (i.e., that God Himself would become an offering for sin). The same may be said for audience perceptions regarding Isaiah 7:14. Would Jewish audiences have understood the significance of the Virgin Birth? Would their monotheism have allowed them to see a plurality in the Godhead—Jesus coming to earth to be born of a virgin? The answer is obvious.

2. *Jesus' pronouncement concerning the "one flock"* (John 10:16): Neither the Pharisees nor Jesus' own disciples would have grasped the significance of this statement, "And other sheep I have which are not of this fold; them also I must bring, and they will hear My voice; and there will be one flock and one

shepherd." Jesus' immediate audience would never have really understood the coming together of Jews and Gentiles into one body. Only through further revelation do we know that Jesus was talking about the Church (the Body of Christ) where Jew and Gentile would become one. Paul would later write Ephesians 2 and 3 and declare that the full revelation of Jew and Gentile being equal heirs in the one body of Christ was a mystery entrusted to him (cf. Eph. 3:1-6). Even the Apostle Peter needed a special vision from God in Acts 10 to open his eyes to the elementary truths of Gentile acceptance. Again, immediate audience perception is a poor standard for discerning correct exegetical interpretation when one is confronted with new revelation of epochal proportions.

3. *The early church's understanding of and commitment to the Great Commission* (Matt. 28:19-20): Jesus' commission to the apostles and the church was clear: take the gospel to every nation, to Jew and Gentile alike (cf. Mark 16:15; Luke 24:47). Nevertheless, the direct intervention of God into Peter's life through a vision (Acts 10), the conscious delay in believers taking the gospel to the Gentiles (Acts 11:19), and the Jerusalem Council (Acts 15), all testified to the fact that time and further revelation were needed to correct perceptions bound by culture and tradition.

4. *The Thessalonian response to new revelation regarding the Rapture* (1 Thess. 4:13-18): In 2 Thessalonians, Paul had to correct audience perceptions regarding his earlier teaching on the Rapture of the Church (cf. 2 Thess. 1:10-12; 2:1-12). Granted, the situation was complicated by false teaching which greatly disturbed the Thessalonian believers. Nevertheless, such underscores again that audience understanding of a particular pronouncement is not always a reliable standard for correct interpretation. Even when Jesus spoke to the apostles of His return in John 14:1-3, they did not relate this to the Rapture of the Church. They did not possess the scriptural framework to accurately interpret what Jesus meant by the pronouncement. Only the total revelation of a completed canon could give insight into the correct understanding of Jesus' words.

Many other examples could be given. However, even a cursory survey of audience response to pronouncements involving the suffering Messiah, the "one fold" (i.e., the Body of Christ), the Great Commission, and the Rapture, all illustrate that further revelation and instruction were needed to ascertain the correct interpretation of the original pronouncement. In each of these cases, where new revelation of epochal proportions was unfolding, audience perception proved less than satisfactory as a reliable standard for interpretation.

THE SAME MAY ALSO BE SAID FOR THE "PERFECT" OF 1 CORINTHIANS 13. WHY? BECAUSE THE CORINTHIANS HAD NO CONCEPT OF A NEW TESTAMENT CANON UNFOLDING BEFORE THEIR VERY EYES. Only the total testimony of Scripture could afford them with the perspective needed to make a correct interpretation of the "perfect." Again, *new revelation of epochal proportions was unfolding in the Scriptures themselves!*

Certainly, the responsible student of Scripture must address cultural, linguistic, and historical factors when seeking a proper interpretation of a passage. So, what about the Corinthian perception of the "perfect"? Should not their perceptions weigh heavily on interpretive options? *Not really.* Neither they nor other first-century believers had the SCRIPTURAL PERSPECTIVE to correct their initial perceptions regarding the "perfect" of 1 Corinthians 13. They would not have been thinking in terms of a coming "canon." This, in itself, was new revelation of epochal proportions—God was giving a new body of Scripture on par with the Old Testament. While the Thessalonian believers received Paul's words as the Word of God (1 Thess. 2:13), the Corinthians even questioned Paul's apostleship. Thus, when it comes to a choice between audience perception and scriptural continuity in exegesis, one must go with scriptural continuity.

Joseph Dillow, in his excellent work, *Speaking in Tongues: Seven Crucial Questions*, indirectly supports the above conclusion—yet, with an interesting twist. He puts forth the thesis that the "perfect" in 1 Corinthians 13 refers to the mature state of the church.[29] In other words, when the church age reaches maturity, there will no longer be needed those spiritual gifts that were necessary to "nurse" the church through its infancy. Dillow presents a strong argument based upon Paul's contrast between infancy and maturity: "For we know in part and we prophesy in part. But when that which is perfect has come, then that which is in part will be done away. When I was a child, I spoke as a child, I understood as a child, I thought as a child; but when I became a man, I put away childish things" (1 Cor. 13:9-11). Of course, the essential question for Dillow relates to the time when the church reached or will reach maturity.

Dillow would argue that even the verses in 1 Corinthians 13:9-11 seem to equate the coming of the "perfect" with the coming of "maturity." He further supports his thesis by appealing to other passages where Paul contrasts childhood with maturity, e.g., 1 Corinthians 2:6 with 3:1; Ephesians 4:13, 14. What are the characteristics of infancy or childhood? The infant or child lacks knowledge and is dependent (1 Cor. 3:1-3); whereas, maturity is characterized by knowledge, understanding, wisdom (1 Cor. 2:7, 12), and a measure of independence. Dillow puts forth the question: *When did the church move from infancy to maturity?* He then proceeds to underscore three key considerations: (1) when the church moved out from under the umbrella of Judaism—this with the destruction of Jerusalem (A.D. 70); (2) when the Scriptures were completed and the apostolic office ceased toward the close of the first century; and (3) ultimately at the coming of the Lord Jesus Christ.[30] Drawing from Ephesians 2:19-21, Dillow aptly demonstrates that the church *functionally* grew to maturity with the completion of Scripture. Why? Because Ephesians 2:20 links the apostolic office and prophecy with the foundational period of the church:

> Now, therefore, you are no longer strangers and foreigners, but fellow citizens with the saints and members of the household of God, having been built on the foundation of the apostles and prophets, Jesus Christ Himself being the chief cornerstone, in whom the whole building, being joined together, grows into a holy temple in the Lord . . . (Eph. 2:19-20).

It is no coincidence that the apostolic office ceased with the completion of Scripture. Such signified that the foundation of the church was complete. In essence, the church had progressed beyond the point of infancy. And as prophecy was also part of the foundational elements (Eph. 2:20), when the apostolic office was abolished, so too was prophecy. The Scriptures, which contain "all things that pertain to life and godliness" (2 Pet. 1:3), assured the church that it now had the necessary understanding and knowledge to live in maturity. Tongues, the gift of prophecy, and the gift of knowledge were no longer needed. Such is the argument of Dillow.[31]

Dillow's correlation between the maturity of the church and the completion of the Scriptures is correct. However, the scriptural evidence suggests an even more direct correlation between the "perfect" and the written Word of God (cf. James 1:23-25 with 1 Cor. 13:8-12). Nevertheless, both positions hold that the early church passed from infancy into maturity with the completion of Scripture and with the passing of the apostolic office. Thus the gifts of prophecy, knowledge, and tongues which were so needed during the early days of the church passed away by the end of the first century.

The testimony of 2 Timothy 3:16, 17 further underscores the above thesis. Note the force of these verses: "All Scripture is given by inspiration of God, and is profitable for doctrine, for reproof, for correction, for instruction in righteousness, that the man of God may *be complete, thoroughly equipped* for every good work" (italics mine). This passage refutes all who would suggest that believers need new revelation, beyond Scripture, in order to fulfill their calling or ministry.

Many saints in the charismatic movement would give their lives defending the inerrancy of Scripture. And that is commendable. However, what they fail to see is that by opening themselves up to further revelation through tongues, prophecy, or word of knowledge, **they are undermining the authority and sufficiency of Scripture**. Who would not want to be among the privileged to receive some special revelation directly from heaven? Would not that do a great more for one's spirituality than laboring to rightly divide the Word of Truth? The testimonies of many who have come out of the charismatic movement stand as a cry to believers to feed upon the written Word, rather than the short-lived "high" that comes through experiential flirting with the unknown. Scripture must be the authority in all matters pertaining to life (cf. 2 Peter 1:1-5; 2 Tim. 3:16, 17).

THE SIGN AND REVELATORY GIFTS
Passing away with the apostolic office

Charismatic teachers continually criticize non-charismatics over the issue of selectivity. Many charismatics boast in the following fashion: "We take Scripture just as it is. We don't chop it up and say this passage is not for today and this passage is; we just believe the entire Word of God applies to today!" While such statements may be appealing to some, they do not truthfully represent charismatic practice. This writer has already alluded to the fact that few charismatics practice the handling of poisonous snakes or drink poison as a sign to unbelievers. Are not they being selective with which sign gifts they wish to display?

Often when talking with those who are open to the sign gifts, I mention *charismatic selectivity*, that very few practice all of the sign gifts recorded in Mark 16:17-20. The responses which I have received have been amazing: complete silence; attempts to shift the conversation to another subject; denial that such selectivity is a serious blow to the movement. Yet, integrity within the charismatic camp demands that **all** the sign gifts be practiced if adherents are going to maintain all gifts are for today. Scripture, of course, teaches the principle of selectivity. The very advance of biblical revelation testifies to the fact that some former scriptural practices no longer apply to believers, e.g., the Jewish ceremonial law, Sabbath observance, the offering of blood sacrifices.

Moreover, Scripture as well as history attest to the passing of the apostolic office. Granted the word "apostle" applies to others such as Barnabas in Acts 14:14. Nevertheless, he did not occupy the *apostolic office*. A parallel may be made with the word "deacon." The same basic word translated "deacons" (*diakonous*) in 1 Timothy 3:8-11 is used of Jesus (*diakonon*) in Romans 15:8 where our Lord is called a "servant to the circumcision for the truth of God." The word "deacon" carries the idea of a servant or minister. While the word applies to Jesus, Scripture in no way suggests that Jesus held the office of deacon. The same may be said for Barnabas. Though he bears the title "apostle," he never held the *office* of apostle. Indeed, the very foundations of the New Jerusalem limit the number occupying the apostolic office to twelve (Rev. 21:14).

While some charismatics insist that the apostolic office continues even today, there is no biblical foundation for such a position. The very fact that the apostolic office passed off the scene indicates that some things which were common to Christianity as recorded in the Book of Acts ceased. When did the apostolic office cease? Right after the Apostle John penned the last words of Scripture. Shortly after Scripture was completed, the last living apostle died.

The apostles and prophets formed the foundational period of the church age (Eph. 2:20-22; 4:8-16; 1 Cor. 12:28). Once the foundation was in place, those elements so necessary in the infant stage of the church were no longer needed. Thus, with the passing of the apostolic office also went prophecy, tongues, the gift of knowledge, and the other sign gifts. For further study on the significance of the closing of the apostolic office, I refer you to Peter Masters' book, *The Healing Epidemic*.[32] Masters, as well as other writers, gives convincing biblical evidence that the sign gifts, while bestowed upon many believers, were primarily associated with the apostolic office. Thus, the *Apostolic Connection* serves as further evidence that the sign and revelatory gifts are no longer valid for today.

THE SIGN AND REVELATORY GIFTS
Always for the benefit of others

The Pattern in the New Testament Era

The mosaic of Scriptures relating to the cessation of sign gifts is almost complete. The *Christ Connection* underscored the preeminence of the Lord Jesus as THE revelation of God (Heb. 1:1-4; 2:1-4). Jesus' preeminence in revelation is seen in His incarnation (John 1:1-14), in His title "the Word of God" (Rev. 19:13), and in the identification of the testimony of Jesus with the "spirit of prophecy" (Rev. 19:10). Thus, it is befitting that Scripture and thus revelation should close with a book entitled *The Revelation of Jesus Christ*. This "REVELATION" serves as the capstone on all prophecy. Anyone who claims to add new revelation to Scripture counters the preeminence of the Lord Jesus Christ as the One who reveals God to mankind. The *Abraham Connection* (Luke 16:19-31) revealed that where Scripture is available, the Lord will deny sign gifts to bring about or assist belief; the *Cluster Connection* reminds all that tongues occurs in a grouping of sign gifts (Mark 16:17-20). Thus if tongues are for today, so must all of the rest of the grouping be present and practiced with equal emphasis. The *Isaiah Connection* (1 Cor. 14:20-22) stressed the fact that tongues were given as a sign of judgment on unbelieving Israel, and with the destruction of Jerusalem in A.D. 70, the judgmental aspect of tongues was no longer needed. The *James Connection* (James 1:22-25) shed light on the "perfect" in 1 Corinthians 13:8-12, and gave additional proof that when Scripture was completed the need for additional revelation (i.e., gifts of tongues, prophesy, knowledge) ceased. The *Apostolic Connection* drew upon Ephesians 2:20 and showed that the apostolic office and prophecy were part of the foundational period of the church age (cf. Rev. 21:14). The passing of the apostolic office was tied to the completion of Scripture. Moreover, as one passed away (i.e., the apostolic office), so must the other (i.e., prophecy).

There is another consideration: what may be termed the *LOVE CONNECTION*. While this latter consideration does not address the cessation of the sign gifts directly, it does show that the current emphasis on seeking to speak in tongues for self-edification is unscriptural.

As we return to 1 Corinthians 13, we see again that Paul is trying to overcome the Corinthian misuse of gifts by underscoring the preeminence that love is to have in the Body of Christ. Note the following:

> Though I speak with the tongues of men and of angels, but have not love, I have become as sounding brass or a clanging cymbal. And though I have the gift of prophecy, and understand all mysteries and all knowledge, and though I have all faith, so that I could remove mountains, but have not love, I am nothing. And though I bestow all my goods to feed the poor, and though I give my body to be burned, but have not love, it profits me nothing. Love suffers long and is kind; love does not envy; love does not parade itself, is not puffed up; does not behave rudely, *does not seek its own,* is not provoked, thinks no evil; does not rejoice in iniquity, but rejoices in the truth; bears all things, hopes all things, endures all things. Love never fails (1 Cor. 13:1-8a; italics mine).

The principle that deserves special attention is captured by the phrase, "love does not seek its own." In other words, right in the middle of Paul's discussion of spiritual gifts, he reminds his readers that spiritual gifts are for OTHERS. The moment one seeks to use spiritual gifts for personal benefit, that constitutes a misuse of the gift. If someone has the gift of teaching, it is for others; if someone has the gift of exhortation, or giving, or helps, or ministry, or leadership, or evangelism, they all are for the benefit of others. Yet, some would try and convince well meaning saints to seek some private gift of tongues for self-edification. The motive of self-edification alone should point to the false nature of this so-called spiritual gift of tongues. The same would be true for those seeking the gift of healing.

There obviously was a legitimate gift of tongues in the New Testament era. It was an evangelistic gift to communicate the wonders of God to unbelievers. What is being called the gift of tongues among charismatic circles today does not fit the biblical pattern. And when something does not fit the biblical pattern, it should be shunned instead of being embraced. The same principle applies where one claims the gift of healing or the gift of prophecy. It does not matter how positive an experience may seem to be, or how close to God it makes one feel. The essential measurement is always the biblical instruction.

The Pattern for Today and in Third World
Mission Situations

Any discussion of tongues or the sign and revelatory gifts usually leads to the subject of reports from third world mission fields. Even a cursory survey of reports in mission journals, literature, or the testimonies of returning missionaries tells of miraculous phenomena which seem to parallel the *biblical* pattern—tongues (communication of the gospel in other languages to unbelievers), healings, miracles, visions, dreams, and prophecy. Reports from China, Japan, and Eastern Europe also testify to similar miraculous interventions by God. The sources in many cases are credible. *How is one to explain these miraculous events in view of the position that tongues and the sign gifts are no longer for today?* Are they deceptions? Yet, how can they be false when these same phenomena open the door of salvation for a people group or individuals. Moreover, if these miraculous phenomena are from God, then does not that lend question to the entire previous discussion?

Peter Wagner in his book, *On the Crest of the Wave*, documents a number of cases where miracles have occurred in third world settings that opened the door of salvation for many. He takes the reader from China to India and Cambodia, from Central America to Ethiopia and South Africa. The reports cover a wide range of phenomena: (1) a lady crushed in an accident miraculously recovers; (2) the son of an official in the Nishi tribe of India is raised from the dead; (3) a strange man arrayed in light leads a young girl, Kham Put, and others safely past communist border guards in Cambodia to refugee camps in Thailand— there Kham Put sees a picture of Jesus on the wall and realizes the "man" who led them through the jungle was Jesus; (4) through a specific prophecy, a church in Guatemala receives divine guidance on where to dig for a well during a severe drought—the well is dug in the pastor's backyard and an entire village comes to the pastor's home for both physical water and the "Water of Life"; (5) in Ethiopia a believer is being persecuted by communist officials and is told to grasp a high tension wire—the Christian does so while exclaiming "Praise the Lord" and the entire town experiences a blackout while the Christian lives; (6) and in South Africa a man prays for the broken leg of a horse—the horse recovers and many flock to evangelistic meetings which later spawn a number of new churches.[33] How is one to evaluate these events in light of our previous discussion? While some accounts no doubt reflect questionable perceptions, evaluations, reporting, or satanic deception, some carry the imprints of our God working mightily in the affairs of mankind.

The *Worldwide Evangelization Crusade* (WEC) mission agency recently published a booklet entitled *God Still Steps In*. In the booklet, a number of WEC personnel, some of whom I know personally, testify to miraculous interventions of God in their lives and in their work. The twenty-one entries present the Lord moving in a myriad of ways: a missionary is saved from harm as the motorbike on which she is riding is miraculously moved to the side to save her from an oncoming vehicle; the corporate prayers of Christians are victorious in delivering fellow believers from illness and demonic oppression; a foundation for a building is poured through miraculous timing and provision of supplies from God—all in answer to prayer. And the reports go on.[34]

The questions and concerns do not involve the miraculous. Again, our God is a miracle-working God. He steps into our lives at various times in marvellous ways. The crucial question is whether He is working in the same way now as He did through the ministry of Jesus and the Apostles. *Moreover, if the apparent signs and wonders and revelatory phenomena are occurring on mission fields, then why should not believers expect the same movement of God amidst affluent western suburbs?*

The Lausanne Committee for World Evangelization sponsored a meeting in Willowbank, Somerset Bridge, Bermuda in 1978 to discuss the topic, "*Gospel and Culture.*" The conference produced a well known missions document entitled *The Willowbank Report*. Note the comments of the report regarding the need for God to demonstrate His power in Third World settings.

"Jesus is Lord" means more than that he is Lord of the individual convert's world-view, standards and relationships, and more even than that he is Lord of culture. It means that he is Lord of the powers, having been exalted by the Father to universal sovereignty, principalities and powers having been made subject to him (1 Pet. 3:22). A number of us, especially those from Asia, Africa, and Latin America, have spoken both of the reality of evil powers and of the necessity to demonstrate the supremacy of Jesus over them. For conversion involves a power encounter. People give their allegiance to Christ when they see that his power is superior to magic and voodoo, the curses and blessings of witch doctors, and the malevolence of evil spirits, and that his salvation is a real liberation from the power of evil and death.[35]

I can remember sharing in a recent Bible conference. Representatives were present from well established mission boards. At one breakfast meeting, a missionary told about the miraculous recovery of a man in a tribal setting through prayer. The stakes were high. According to the missionary, if God did not intervene miraculously in this situation, the very testimony and success of the gospel witness to these people was in jeopardy. To accounts such as this, one could add other reports of those who have found themselves speaking in a language or dialect which they did not know and communicating the gospel to others—some of whom came to Christ through this experience. Again, how is one to evaluate these reports? How can one maintain that tongues and the sign gifts are no longer valid for today in the face of such overwhelming testimony?

First, one cannot address the myriad of reports that come in from various fields. Remember, however, the continuing testimony of this study: **our God IS a miracle-working God! He still steps in to heal, to answer prayer, to perform His purposes. No doubt many of the reports are true. However, the miraculous reports coming from mission fields do not attest to the fact that biblical tongues and sign gifts still apply to today. Why?**

God is sovereign. He can do anything He wants to do. He can step into time and history in miraculous ways; He can order and change international events, natural laws, and personal lives. He has done so throughout human history and He will continue to do so.

Displays of His miraculous power in third world settings are indeed linked to the fact that in many contexts *there are no Scriptures*. Even if the Scriptures are available, literacy prevents the access of many to them. Thus in a people group bound by demonic forces which operate in the realm of visions, dreams, fetishes, supernatural displays, our Sovereign God can step in in power.

The same may be said for reports of visions, angelic visitations, and dreams in Eastern Europe, Russia, China, and Japan. Even amidst industrial based nations such as Russia and those in Eastern Europe where access to the Scriptures is limited, God may use supernatural means to break through the darkness. This is not to say that the gospel lacks the power for conversion; but this is to acknowledge that such a context puts on into an *Acts situation*—first-century Christianity—where the substance of Romans 15:17-21 is being lived out.

Those missionaries who have experienced parallels to biblical tongues or the sign gifts have had the privilege of experiencing a sovereign act of God. But these are *not* the gift of tongues or sign gifts. Again, why? Because when the missionary leaves the mission context and moves into societies that have a long-standing testimony and access to the Word of God, the "power" to speak in tongues *paralleling the biblical pattern* no longer manifests itself. The individual no longer has the "power to heal." Remember that God still heals through the corporate prayers of God's people. However, the sign gifts and tongues of the New Testament era were the possession of *individuals* used to confirm the spoken word of God.

Moreover, if one hears of visions, dreams, or angelic visitations in third world settings or in countries where the people do not have access to Scriptures, one should not assume this phenomena to be the norm for the Body of Christ worldwide. Why? Because one is faced basically with an *Acts context*. One should not assume that the Lord will impart new revelation through these means, but rather guidance and direction to the source for further instruction (cf. the angel to Cornelius in Acts 10).

So in summary, how should one respond to these instances of miraculous interventions of God in third world settings or in countries where access to Scripture is limited? You praise the Lord for His power and His grace! And how does one explain miraculous interventions of God within one's own society, whether third world or western high-tech cultures? *You accept them, you praise the Lord for His power and His grace, and yet, you also test to see if all spiritual manifestations conform to the biblical pattern. You also remember that the greatest miracle of all is that which occurs when a person accepts the Lord Jesus Christ as personal Savior!* (Luke 10:20.)

What if one finds himself communicating the gospel in a language that was previously unknown? What if one finds that through prayer, one is healed? You test such by the biblical pattern. If such does not contravene the biblical pattern, you accept this as a sovereign act of God *paralleling* New Testament phenomena. **However, such is not the gift of tongues or the sign gifts, for if they were, the recipient could duplicate the same in other contexts.** *Remember that the biblical gift of tongues and sign gifts were given to individuals to confirm the spoken Word of God. There is no scriptural evidence that such was limited by geographical considerations. In those settings which parallel an Acts context, our sovereign God can and will step in through manifestations of His power. Yet, what is necessary in one context is not necessary in another; neither should believers demand such.* **And that is the error of the signs and wonders movement.**

One further caution is in order regarding those who claim to have spoken in tongues after the biblical model—i.e., communicating the wonders of God in another language to an individual or people group. Why would God grant such a miracle in some contexts without the attendant ability to interpret the tongue? Such does not fit the biblical pattern in its entirety, and therefore is suspect. Moreover, one must be sure that the immediate context involves the communication of the gospel? If not, and if such cannot be confirmed, the experience must be questioned further.

Those in charismatic circles and those who embrace John Wimber's *Vineyard Movement*, for example, would argue that the same miracles and gifts which characterized the ministries of Jesus and the apostles in the first century are available to Christians today. A recent healing seminar was titled, *"Learning to Minister Like Jesus."* They would further assert that the signs, wonders, and revelatory gifts are not restricted to third world settings, but are ministered in the Spirit's power today in western societies. Such is needed to break down the rationalistic and humanistic perceptions of reality. Like those writing in *The Willowbank Report*, Wimber, Deere, and others in the Vineyard Movement claim that the gospel needs the accompanying signs if such is going to impact indifferent and contemporary pagan societies. For them, the proclamation of the gospel does not have, in and of itself, sufficient power to transform lives. Signs and wonders are needed to undergird its proclamation for maximum impact. [Note: Even though Deere has distanced himself from his earlier involvement with John Wimber, he still holds to his initial claims and teachings.]

Regarding Wimber and Deere's position, three fallacies immediately present themselves. First of all, the gospel and the Word of God *do* intrinsically possess the power to transform lives regardless of the setting (cf. Rom. 1:16; Luke 16:30, 31; 1 Pet. 1:23; James 1:18). To suggest otherwise stands as an affront to Scripture and to the Lord. Secondly, if signs and wonders are still needed to authenticate the gospel message, then such a position requires that "power evangelism" record a one hundred percent healing rate. Remember the presuppositions of Wimber, Deere, Wagner, and others: the Spirit is granting the signs, wonders, and healings so that pagans will see the power of God and respond to the message. The failure to heal some conditions, especially in animalistic or tribal cultures, would raise questions about the gospel and the character of the "Christian" God. Moreover, the "success rate" and the nature of healings addressed within the Vineyard Movement hardly approach scriptural dimensions. Something is wrong in the very camp of those who teach others to minister "just like Jesus." Thirdly, the claims that Christians should seek the gifts of tongues, healing, prophecy, and other phenomena for personal edification go against the Apostle Paul's teaching in 1 Corinthians 13:5. Many advocates of the signs and wonders movement insist that miraculous and revelatory phenomena occurring on mission fields should be the everyday experience of the Christian who has access to the Word of God . Such a position fails to see the uniqueness of the apostolic era and the power of the Scriptures to bring forth life. (Note: For further response to the *Vineyard Movement*, please see Appendix A, Question 14).

Because God chooses to step into human experience in miraculous ways in one context does not mean He must do the same in other contexts. In areas of the world where people groups do not have the Word of God or access to the Word in their language, the Lord may choose to step in through the very agencies that bind the people. For instance, in animalistic or tribal settings where visions, dreams, and encounters with demonic manifestations stand as the order of the day, the Lord may choose to speak through some of these avenues (dreams, visions, special leadings). He may choose to overcome darkness on its own territory by intervening and giving guidance. *In so doing, the Lord is not establishing a common pattern to be followed in all cultures for all times.*

Saul's encounter with the medium of Endor is instructive (1 Sam. 28:3-25). Saul was facing the forces of the Philistines. However, because of his own refusal to heed the Word of the Lord, the Lord had refused to answer Saul in his hour of need (v. 6). Saul then sought out a medium in order to contact Samuel. He hoped that Samuel would be able to give him advice as to what to do in that situation (vv. 11-15). Even though Saul knew that contact with mediums was forbidden by Scripture (cf. Exod. 22:18; Lev. 19:26, 31; 20:6; 20:27; Deut. 18:10, 11), he still pursued that avenue. To the horror of the medium and to the anguish of Saul, Samuel actually appeared in that context and delivered a prophecy regarding Saul's approaching death and the defeat of Israel (vv. 16-19). The rest of Scripture bears out the fulfillment of that prophecy.

In view of our present discussion, what does this account have to do with miraculous interventions of God—either through miracles or revelatory phenomena—on third world mission fields or in countries where people have little or no access to Scripture? Simply this: in the case of Samuel's prophecy to Saul, God chose to step into history right in the context of a practice which He forbade. Scripture clearly condemns seeking mediums for advice. However, even though Samuel truly appeared in an occultic setting, does this intervention of God put a stamp of approval on consulting mediums? The obvious answer is "NO!" Such merely demonstrates that God can intervene in special ways in any context. Yet, His direct intervention does not put a stamp of approval *on the context itself*. One must consult Scripture for a proper view of the context. In the same manner, if God chooses to intervene in special ways (visions, dreams, special leadings) amidst those people groups which do not have access to the Scriptures, then such directive revelation can be viewed as paralleling an *Acts situation*. However, this does not mean that such an intervention by God is normative for all situations and cultures, nor does it establish the dreams, visions, and leadings as the procedure to permanently adopt in dealing with revelation from God. Such is merely the attendant work of God in bringing forth an infant church—again, much like Acts. As the infant church is introduced to Scripture and the gospel, the need for other avenues of revelation cease.

This does not contravene the closing of revelation with Scripture, for such special revelations may serve to guide one to those who can share the gospel—much like the situation of Cornelius in Acts 10. In Acts 10, the angel could come all the way from the throne of God to give guidance to Cornelius, but the angel could not impart revelation concerning the substance of the gospel. That special revelation had to be given through the agency of man and through the proclamation of the Word of God.

One final comment is in order. What is the reaction of the typical Christian parent living in western high-tech cultures when their young ones become sick or are injured? If we are honest with ourselves, most of us offer a brief prayer *on the way to see our local physician or emergency services at our hospitals*. This is not wrong in itself, because medical advances and availability are as much products of God's grace and sovereign program as His direct intervention to heal. But let us move to a different setting. Suppose you are a Christian parent in a third world village, far away from any medical treatment for your family. Your child becomes critically ill. What is your avenue of assistance? *God and only God! Prayer and only prayer!* Thus, because conscious dependency is greater upon the Lord, and because His avenues of responding to the prayers of His children in this situation may require direct intervention, there is more room for Him to work in miraculous ways.

The challenge and message to us who live amidst material prosperity is simply this: Do not let the blessings of culture rob you of a deeper dependency upon the Lord. Yes, use the facilities and the avenues which are available for health care and for the communication of the gospel.

However, do not allow readily available avenues to dull your dependency on the miracle working power of God. Again, our God IS a miracle-working God. We must always view the Lord as the "first initiative" in our lives, in every situation, rather than being the last resort.

REVIEW OF KEY CONCEPTS

1. The sign gifts, including tongues, were given to CONFIRM the SPOKEN WORD (Mark 16:20; Acts 2:11; 4:29-31; 6:7, 8; 8:6; 9:42; 13:6-12; 14:1-3; Heb. 2:1-4). The implication from these passages is that when the New Testament was completed, the sign gifts would no longer be needed to authenticate the Word of God. The Scriptures would need no other confirming signs. The *Abraham Connection* in Luke 16:29-31 demonstrates that where Scripture is available, the Lord will withhold signs to assist or bring about belief. Only when new revelation is being given will signs and wonders be the order of the day.

2. Tongues occurs in the midst of a cluster of sign gifts in Mark 16:17-20. If the gift of tongues is still operative today, then so should the taking up of snakes and the drinking of poison be practiced as sign gifts as well. The phrase in Mark 16:18, "they will TAKE UP serpents," denotes a conscious, deliberative act on the part of the believer. This is not talking about accidental snakebite—the Greek verb *airo* is active voice, thus indicating deliberate action. Thus, the *Cluster Connection* is an important consideration when dealing with the tongues issue and other sign gifts in the present context.

3. The biblical tongues were known languages that communicated the wonders of God to unbelievers. It was an evangelistic gift, and was never meant to be employed either as a private prayer language, or in an assembly that was exclusively composed of Christians (cf. Acts 2:11; 1 Cor. 14:1-5, 14-16). The tongues which are being pushed in charismatic circles today do not fit the biblical pattern. The ecstatic speech resembles similar phenomena found in pagan religions down through the ages. In fact, the type of tongues being practiced in charismatic circles resembles the same phenomenon occurring in several cults such as the Mormons, The Way International, and smaller groups such as the Adelaide Revival Centre. In addition, the

content of present-day tongues often focuses on mundane matters or minor exhortations, rather than revealing the wonders of God to unbelievers.

4. The *Isaiah Connection* (1 Cor. 14:20-22 with Isa. 28:11,12) and the *James Connection* (1 Cor. 13:10-12 with James 1:23-25) give biblical evidence that tongues have ceased. The *Isaiah Connection* shows that tongues was a sign of judgment on unbelieving Israel. Since Israel had refused the voice of God through the Lord Jesus and the apostles, just as they had refused to hear Isaiah, God would now speak His revelation to Gentiles through their own languages. When Jerusalem was destroyed in A.D. 70 by the armies of Rome, the judgmental aspect of tongues was no longer needed. The *James Connection* sheds light on the identification of the "perfect" in 1 Corinthians 13. The same imagery of "mirror," "face," and "perfect" occurs in James as in 1 Corinthians 13. In James, the "mirror" and the "perfect" are clear references to the Scriptures. Consistency in interpretation demands that the same interpretation be given to the "perfect" in 1 Corinthians 13. Thus, Paul was teaching the Corinthians that because only a part of the New Testament had been given, they saw "dimly." However, when the "perfect" (i.e., Scripture) comes, they would see their reflection clearly, "face to face." At such a time there would be no need for further revelation that comes through tongues, prophecy, or the gift of knowledge. Moreover, the verb "cease" which is associated with tongues in the Corinthian passage is in the middle voice, and is best translated, *"will cease in and of itself."* However, the verb associated with the gifts of knowledge and prophecy is passive in form—meaning the subjects are acted upon by an outside force. Thus, when the "perfect" comes, prophecy and knowledge will be *"abolished,"* or *"rendered inoperative."* Because one is dealing with quantitative concerns, this too points to the "perfect" as being the completed Scriptures.

5. The apostles exercised a spiritual stewardship over the early churches until such time as Scripture was completed. Once the revelation of Scripture was complete, the apostolic stewardship was no longer needed. The cessation of the apostolic office at the close of Scripture strongly argues for the cessation of the sign and revelatory gifts as well. This is especially so in light of Ephesians 2:20 which places both the apostolic office and prophecy in the foundational period of

the church age. As one ceases, so must the other. The ***Apostolic Connection*** is thus another biblical consideration which casts doubt about the authenticity of present claims that the sign and revelatory gifts are for today.

6. The ***Love Connection*** (1 Cor. 13:5) stresses that spiritual gifts are given to a person for the benefit of the Body of Christ. Love "does not seek its own." Any motive to seek a spiritual gift for self-edification is a wrong motive. Yet, in charismatic circles today, that is the primary motive stressed in acquiring the gift of tongues.[36]

7. When one adds up the total testimony of Scripture—the Abraham Connection, the Cluster Connection, the Isaiah Connection, the James Connection, the Love Connection, the Apostolic Connection—there is ample biblical evidence to show that biblical tongues, sign gifts, and revelatory gifts have ceased. One of the most powerful arguments in this whole issue is that of the ***Christ Connection***. Jesus is the highest revelation of God to mankind (Heb. 1:1-4; John 14:9-11; Revelation). His revelation superseded that of angels or the prophets. Even though He ascended to the right hand of the Father, He continued to give new revelation to the Church through the Scriptures. By divine design, the Scriptures closed with the book, *The Revelation of Jesus Christ*. The warning at the close of the New Testament (Rev. 22:18,19) must thus be viewed in this context. Although such serves as the capstone of the Book of Revelation itself, such also serves as a warning to all those who would claim to the be the vehicle for new revelation. Scripture (i.e., revelation) closed with the book bearing the name of the Lord Jesus Christ. Jesus, as the incarnate Word and the highest revelation of God, spoke His last words to the Church as recorded in the Book of Revelation. Any who claim to speak new revelation today stand against the preeminence of Christ as the Revelation of God.

8. Though the Lord in His sovereignty intervenes in third world mission contexts, often with miracles and wonders which parallel the sign and revelatory gifts, such is due to the infancy of a new church and the absence of Scripture in the native language. Such is not the norm where Scripture is in place and readily available. Why? Because in the Scriptures the believer has everything that pertains to life and godliness (2 Pet. 1:3). The entire New Testament verifies that.

Question Two

*Why would God allow dedicated Christians to
experience the sign and revelatory gifts if they are not from Him?*

Even when confronted with the biblical evidence that the sign gifts have
ceased, many refuse to embrace this truth because of practical questions
which remain unanswered. The heading of this chapter captures one of
the more frequently asked questions when one takes the position that
the sign gifts are not for today. It is true that even pastors, missionaries,
Bible teachers, and other dedicated Christian workers who have served
the Lord for years, *and who have not sought the sign gifts,* often experience
tongues or some other aspects of the charismatic movement. Again the
question comes: Why would God allow His children to experience
something which is not from Himself—but rather, as some suggest, from
Satan? Others will say, "Why all the fuss? The issues are not that crucial;
the differences are not that serious."

IDENTIFYING THE TRUE CULPRIT

I have already stated in the opening sections of this book that the charismatic movement has a number of positive elements. While believers
should reject and denounce the apostate and liberal churches which
come under the charismatic banner, they should also realize that the old-
line Pentecostal and Assembly of God churches do seek to honor the
Lord, the gospel, and Scripture. Many of these churches are noted for
their high regard for the Word of God, their commitment to prayer, their
evangelistic fervor, their concern for souls, their willingness to step out
in faith and trust the Lord, and their refusal to let human pride, tradition, or societal expectations inhibit their worship. For these and other
reasons, they are making an impact for the kingdom of Christ.

Charismatic churches are filling a void. Many conservative and evangelical churches which once reverberated with the fires of revival have

77

settled into cold, lifeless formalism. The believer assumes the posture of a spectator, rather than a zealous participant in offering genuine worship to Almighty God. They may be doctrinally right, but the fervent love and practical heart for God is missing. Many of the conservative or evangelical pastors and churches know it, but are too proud to admit their need.

One is reminded of John Warwick Montgomery's rather controversial but true book, *Damned through the Church*.[37] In that book he states that while churches should be a place of accelerated salvation, in many instances they have become a place of accelerated damnation. People sit in the pews, lulled into spiritual death by the sound of soft organ music, assuming they are on their way to heaven simply because they sing the refrain, "Amazing Grace, how sweet the sound. . . ." While some churches drown in their presumption, the charismatic churches are reminding Christians that it is biblical for a congregation to respond with "Amen!" when hearts have been blessed through proclamation of the Word of God or the singing of inspirational hymns;[38] it is biblical and permissible for people to weep for joy, or weep under the burden of sin in a worship service—after all, the Lord never intended His church to be a museum where people go to be seen, but rather a spiritual hospital where the Word of God, the Holy Spirit, and the Body of Christ minister to those in need. It is biblical for people to openly respond to an invitation, to come forward in tears or in meditative silence to reach out for Christ or spiritual assistance.[39] It is biblical to share what the Lord is doing through personal testimonies. It is biblical to allow the Holy Spirit time to do His work in hearts, rather than allowing carnal evaluations of priorities to insist a service close "on time." And the list goes on.

Some people assume that heaven is going to be a quiet place, with soothing harp and organ music, and the saints tip-toeing around. Nothing is further from the truth! There will be shouting in heaven, glorious praise and worship! Uplifted hands will not even be an issue on the other side, because the saints will be so consumed with love for Jesus, not one will try to stop a biblically based form of praise with a phrase, "We just don't do that around here."

I realize that displays of emotion and zeal do not necessarily mean true worship is taking place. Such displays often disrupt and run counter to the reverential call from the Lord: "Be still and know that I am God" (Ps. 46:10). However, churches are different, just like people. Indeed, the Lord can be glorified in a service characterized by meditative silence, conventional hymn singing, and formality just as much as He can be glorified in a more relaxed style of worship. We must respect this fact.

Forms and methods of worship are secondary. While they must be biblical and direct our praise, they should never dominate, intimidate, or diminish the praise arising from a surrendered heart. Genuine worship is always a matter of the heart and it can flourish amidst any setting (cf. John 4:23, 24).

I can remember a dear friend from my seminary days. He had a masters degree in psychology, had been a school teacher, but had surrendered his life to full-time service in the pastorate. He was a reserved and very controlled individual. Yet, at times during those first years of Bible training, when the preaching of the Word of God would touch his soul, you would hear him exclaim, "shake that bush again, preacher!" It was not a show, it was not put on; rather, it was a genuine response of his soul affirming a blessing in the Lord and also affirming his prayer for more fruit to fall from the Word of God upon an expectant heart. And do you know what? His response also prompted a blessing and expectancy among the people seated near him. The speaker was exhorted and encouraged, and the others nearby shared the joy that another brother or sister in the Lord was being blessed. This was in a fundamental Baptist church in the early seventies. That is just the way services were among fundamental Baptist churches in those days. I wonder what response my friend would get today in similar circles. Maybe we have become so "dignified" that many cannot discern whether we are backslidden or spiritually dead.

I am not recommending that every believer should display this kind of expression of praise. Nor am I suggesting that such dynamics should be part of every church service. For the sake of balance, allow me to share another brief account. Years ago our family was befriended by some dear Pentecostal families. Soon we received an invitation to come to their services. We were babes in Christ then, still finding our spiritual legs. I well remember one of the services. One of the men, when obviously blessed by the preaching, would turn around from his seat in front of me, grab my knee, and exclaim, "Glory, that's go-o-o-o-d preachin!" After this scenario had repeated itself at least three times, I began to dodge this fella's hand by moving my knee to the side when I saw him coming! After a while I was more concerned with what this brother was going to do than what was being said. Instead of a blessing, this brother had become a distraction from worship and an annoyance. You better believe if I had gone back to that church again, I would certainly have checked out who was sitting in front of me!

Nevertheless, let us return to the question at hand, and to serious concerns that are being raised by those in the charismatic movement. Amidst the many positive elements of the charismatic churches, there lurks a deceptive cancer that is already undermining the good that is being done. **That cancer is the issue of additional revelation**— whether in the form of tongues, prophecy, word of knowledge, visions, and dreams. Note the testimony of Neil Babcox, a former pastor of a charismatic church, who grappled with the seriousness of claiming to speak new revelation from God:

In my case, there were four simple words that played a decisive role in changing my heart: thus saith the Lord. To me, these were most unsettling words. And the more I comprehended their meaning, the more I understood what the prophets meant when they spoke them and what the Holy Spirit meant when He inspired them, the more unsettling they became.

Thus saith the Lord. It is a rich, a pregnant phrase. When a prophet said "thus saith the Lord," he meant that the very word of God was being proclaimed, and that as such it was invested with divine authority. These words also convey the ideas of infallibility and purity—for could God's word be anything less? And as this phrase became ever brighter and more powerful to me, the prophecies that I had spoken and heard others speak paled and diminished to the point of nothingness. I could not help but think that if the prophecies spoken in our church were actually related to the prophecies recorded in Scripture, then they were distant relatives indeed.

Thus saith the Lord. At first I thought that I could disassociate them from my prophecies altogether. Yes, I would continue to prophesy, but I would not let those dread words pass through my lips again. There would be no "thus saith the Lord" from this prophet. I could no longer make any such claim. I believed that my prophecies were blessed by the Holy Spirit, but they were not inspired. And so I tried to salve my conscience by assuming that contemporary prophecies were characterized by a sort of mid-range inspiration: higher than a good sermon but lower than the Scriptures.

My problem, however, could hardly be solved by simply refraining from speaking the phrase "thus saith the Lord" when I prophesied, or by positing a kind of mid-range inspiration for which I could find no support in the Scriptures. For the very phrase and the meaning it conveys are woven into the whole concept of prophecy. You can't disassociate "thus saith the Lord" from prophecy. Whether or not one speaks the actual phrase when one prophesies is not the point. The truth is that the very act of prophesying speaks a loud and clear "thus saith the Lord" whether the actual words are uttered or not.

Thus saith the Lord. When the prophets in the Bible spoke those words, they were based upon definite revelations that were granted to them by God. In Old Testament times prophets were called seers because of the visions they beheld. But what evidence was there that any of our prophecies had their origin in a revelation given by God's Spirit? Ezekiel protested, "This is what the Sovereign LORD says: Woe to the foolish prophets who follow their own spirit and have seen nothing!" (Ezekiel 13:3). In the final analysis, isn't that what we were—prophets who had seen nothing? What evidence was there that we were not just following our own spirits instead of the Spirit of God? I could find no evidence in the Bible that prophecies were communicated by mere intuition or subjective impressions. And, yet, in nearly all cases this is how ours were received. And these impressions and intuitions could not be authenticated in any kind of objective sense.[40]

Babcox goes on to describe that it was this essential question that led him out of the charismatic movement. Indeed, it is a serious matter to claim to speak special revelation from God.

Babcox has revealed one of the more troubling aspects of the current prophecy and revelation craze. The degree of certainty which characterized the genuine prophets of God finds no parallel today. When one reads the biblical accounts such as Ezekiel 2:1-10, 7:1, or Acts 10:19, 20, it becomes apparent that when men were moved by the Spirit of God to speak, they spoke with certainty regarding every word (cf. Prov. 30:5, 6).

So when I saw it, I fell on my face, and I heard a voice of One speaking. And He said to me, "Son of man, stand on your feet, and I will speak to you." Then the Spirit entered me when He spoke to me, and set me on my feet; and I heard Him who spoke to me. And He said to me: "Son of man, I am sending you to the children of Israel. . . . You shall speak My words to them, whether they hear or whether they refuse, for they are rebellious. But you, son of man, hear what I say to you. Do not be rebellious like that rebellious house; open your mouth and eat what I give you" (Ezek. 1:28b -2:3, 7, 8).

Moreover the word of the Lord came to me, saying, "And you, son of man, thus says the Lord God to the land of Israel. . . " (Ezek. 7:1, 2).

While Peter thought about the vision, the Spirit said to him, "Behold, three men are seeking you. Arise therefore, go down and go with them, doubting nothing: for I have sent them" (Acts 10:19, 20).

Prophets of old did not speak merely at the prompting of their own intuition or some general impression. They knew with **one hundred percent certainty** that they were speaking the very words of God. Many who prophesy and claim to speak revelation from God today know in their own hearts that they do not possess the certainty or preciseness of the biblical prophets. Yet, they continue to speak new revelation. The warnings of Ezekiel 13:1-3, Jeremiah 14:14, and Jeremiah 23:25-40 need to be posted before those who carelessly and freely claim to speak new revelation on behalf of God:

> And the word of the LORD came to me saying, "Son of man, prophesy against the prophets of Israel who prophesy, and say to those who prophesy out of their own heart, 'Hear the word of the LORD!'" Thus says the Lord God: "Woe to the foolish prophets who follow their own spirit and have seen nothing" (Ezek. 13:1-3).

> And the LORD said to me, "The prophets prophesy lies in My name. I have not sent them, commanded them, nor spoken to them; they prophesy to you a false vision, divination, a worthless thing, and the deceit of their heart" (Jer. 14:14).

> "I have heard what the prophets have said who prophesy lies in My name, saying, 'I have dreamed, I have dreamed!' How long will this be in the heart of the prophets who prophesy lies? Indeed, they are prophets of the deceit of their own heart. . . . Therefore behold, I am against the prophets," says the LORD, "who steal My words every one from his neighbor. Behold, I am against the prophets," says the LORD, "who use their tongues and say, 'He says.' Behold, I am against those who prophesy false dreams," says the LORD, "and tell them, and cause My people to err by their lies and by their reckless-ness. Yet I did not send them or command them; therefore they shall not profit this people at all," says the LORD. "And as for the prophet and the priest and the people who say, 'The oracle of the LORD!' I will even punish that man and his house. Thus every one of you shall say to his brother, 'What has the LORD answered?' and, 'What has the LORD spoken?' And the oracle of the LORD you shall mention no more. For every man's word will be his oracle, for you have perverted the words of the living God, the LORD of hosts, our God" (Jer. 23:25, 26, 30-36).

Given the deception that Satan has perpetuated through revelation and prophecies in recent times—Mormonism, The Way International, Children of God, The New Age Movement, and a vast array of heretical groups within professing Christianity—the true believer should be on guard against any new source of revelation.

So often I hear dear brethren say something like this: "If the Lord is using the charismatic movement to reap souls into the kingdom of heaven, should we raise so much fuss over minor areas such as tongues, prophecy, visions, healings, and similar phenomena? Can't we just put aside these minor differences and praise the Lord together?" Again, I affirm that it is no small thing to claim to speak new revelation from God. Given the context of the age in which we live, and the direction that history is taking, such error becomes an even greater evil.

THE "AGE OF REVELATION"

There it was! I couldn't believe it! One of Australia's leading newspapers included a full-page advertisement for the New Age Movement. The caption read, "The 'New Age'—Is It Serious?" This was not an article written by some sensationalist. A host of New Age groups, including the Liberal Catholic Church of St. Francis of Assisi, sponsored the article. Note some of the statements selected from the article:

What is the "New Age?"
Popularly presented as people interested in the psychic realms, from tarot reading to crystal healing, from alternative medicine to prosperity consciousness, one wonders whether this is the totality of the New Age. Or is it possible that there is more to it than this?

Philosophers in the field, Cayce, Jung, Gurdjieff, Brunton, Blavatsky, and Bailey, among others, think so. They highlight the fact that the *New Age is a way of thinking, a philosophy of life with a wholistic approach, from our own inner natures and its unfoldment to matters pertaining to the cosmos.* . . .

The Cosmos within
This greater depth, the Cosmos within, is alluded to by many writers and involves, it would seem, the study of a vast range of subjects. Some such topics deal with human and solar evolution, the cultivation of meditation,

invocation and avocation, the refinement of our inner bodies, the science of telepathy and the laws of manifestation.

Blavatsky, in *The Secret Doctrine* and *Isis Unveiled*, presents before the public mind the synthesis of wisdom down through the ages which is the hallmark of the New Age. Her fusion of the Hermetic, Kabbalah, Egyptian, Rosicrucian, Hindu and Chinese traditions (yet without robbing them of their individuality) adds to our understanding and leaves us in no doubt as to the scope, color and depth of this knowledge.

Can the New Age offer us anything substantial?

Krishnamurti, well known author in this field for many years, says of truth that it is *That Pathless Land.*

He suggests that formulations of truth only serve to blind and distort that which they seek to expose. In this sense he highlights with sages and philosophers down through the ages the view, central to the New Age, that there is still a treasure house of knowledge of which philosophy and symbology are but reflections.

Direct access to this knowledge can only come through meditation, living a spiritual life and the subsequent attunement to the intuition.

It is this to which Krishnamurti refers when he speaks of direct knowledge. And it is this which is the highlight and reward of the seeker of Truth and for which the New Age points the way.

Perhaps one of the characteristics of the New Age is an increasing general interest in the art of meditation.

Discovering the self within.

Meditation, we are taught, is a noble tool for receiving direct knowledge. It unfolds the hidden self. Through raising our consciousness to higher levels we are able, eventually, to penetrate the Transpersonal Self. This opens up a whole inner cosmos (italics mine).[41]

"The New Age Movement: 'Is It Serious?'" the article asks. You better believe that it is serious. Do not miss the italicized portions. The writers declare that Truth is a "Pathless Land"; that formulations of truth only "blind and distort"; and that direct access to Truth can only come through meditation. Do you realize that the entire Bible is propositional truth ("formulations of truth"). The proponents of the New Age Movement would insist that "direct knowledge" received through meditation or intuition is much more to be valued than formulations of truth. *How much more exciting to be zapped in the inner self, than to struggle with truth on a written page!* That is the propaganda line. The sad thing is that an entire generation of Christians is being wooed into giving similar forms of experiential revelation a hearing equal to Scripture.

Before you write me off as being too sensational in warning of a tie between the "new revelations" invading the church and dangers in the religious agenda of the New Age Movement, please consider the rest of the article:

Is there a spiritual church of which the major world religions are aspects?

The New Age, whilst holding no dogma, generally adopts this view. Through its study of comparative religion and anthropology it suggests that all world religions, in their pure form, serve as fundamental tools for following the spiritual life.

It suggests that there is a universal message to be found running through all the religions, namely that:

- of the existence of God; without and within the manifested universe,
- of humanity's relationship to God; that we are all children of the one Father,
- of the concept of immortality, arising from our divinity. *That revelation, in some form or other, has been with us through the ages,*
- of the fact that we, through our common heritage, share a brotherhood with one another and
- of there being a path to God whereby love, meditation and service to others holds the key.

Blavatsky says of religions, that they are outer aspects of an inner spiritual kingdom; that they are living reflections of evolutionary presentations of the one all-encompassing Truth.

With the future direction of religion in mind, Dwal Khul even poses the question as to whether, *one day, the new religion may not be a synthesis of faiths "built by emphasizing essential doctrines and the unity and fellowship of the spirit"* (italics mine).[42]

You see, the issue of new revelation is becoming THE essential question of the coming decades. That is why the context of the times demands that any movement which opens itself up to new revelation, even if it arises within the ranks of evangelical or fundamental Christianity, be treated with serious scrutiny.

THE GROWING WARNING FROM CHRISTIAN WRITERS

By this point some readers may be wondering if the question of dedicated Christians experiencing the revelatory aspects of the charismatic movement will be treated. Yes, but it is important to underscore the seriousness of the total issue confronting believers in the Lord. Throughout man's history periods of time have been marked off which have distinctive features or characteristics. Thus, we often speak of history in terms of "ages" such as the Bronze Age, the Age of Reason, the Nuclear Age, and the Computer Age. Now, we stand on the threshold of a "New Age" characterized by revelations to the inner man. This "Age of Revelation" reaches into every facet of life.

In the past few years, well respected writers have issued warnings regarding the growing emphasis in Christian circles on new revelation. Again, while many in the charismatic movement would defend the inerrancy of Scripture, they fail to see that this emphasis on new revelation actually is undermining the authority of Scripture. David Hunt in his book, *The Seduction of Christianity*—and its sequel, *Beyond Seduction*—raised the cry that many Christian churches were unknowingly embracing sorcery and occult practices.[43] He targeted positive and possibility thinking (characteristic of Paul Yonggi Cho and Robert Schuller), the New Age emphasis on the deification of man, visualization techniques, spirit guides, and various forms of pagan mysticism invading the church. Hunt was clear in warning of the "temptation to power" and the attempt of well-meaning Christians to tap into the visions and revelations programming.[44] An excerpt of his warning follows:

There is an even more subtle and dangerous belief. Previously confined to fringe Pentecostal and charismatic groups, the false teaching concerning "revelation knowledge" is beginning to spread rapidly throughout the church. It is understood in two ways: 1) that a proper understanding of Scripture does not come through *interpretation* but through *revelation* (given only to certain leaders), and 2) that these prophets also receive "ongoing prophetic revelation" that supplements the Bible and must be accepted by the church as the key to a "great move of God" that will establish His kingdom upon earth. For example, the brochure advertising a large conference for pastors and church leaders held near Atlanta, Georgia, in October 1986 stated: "What hinders the release of God's Spirit on earth? Reluctance of [church] leadership to embrace revelation knowledge as God continues to speak to his people."[45]

Again, new revelation is seen by many as essential to the Holy Spirit's movement in the churches of today and tomorrow. This is a serious development.

The warnings continue to come in other articles and books such as Tal Brooke's significant work, *When the World Will Be As One*.[46] He carefully documents an ever-growing web of influence which embraces the New Age commitment to the enlightenment of the inner self. This enlightenment comes from new revelations gained through meditation and contact with spirit guides (in reality, demonic forces). In the ARTS AND MEDIA, Shirley MacLaine carries the banner as she proclaims herself to be a "god" who has contact with special spiritual entities; the ACADEMIC COMMUNITY has its own champion in the person of Dr. Elisabeth Kubler-Ross—author of the best selling, *On Death and Dying*. Like MacLaine, Kubler-Ross also claims personal revelations from spirit guides. She also maintains that a former patient, who died, personally appeared in her office and gave her new revelations that came true. Brooke notes that the BUSINESS COMMUNITY is also being touched by the revelation craze. He documents the fact that many Fortune 500 companies in the United States including General Dynamics, IBM, Boeing Aerospace, Lockheed, McDonald's, and Ford are using New Age seminars to introduce management teams to meditation and visualization techniques. Even some American GOVERNMENT AGENCIES such as the Federal Aviation Administration, Justice Department, and NASA, are employing New Age seminars.[47] Brooke quotes Robert Muller, former assistant secretary general to the United Nations and author of the popular New Age book entitled *New Genesis: Shaping a Global Spirituality*:

The next stage will be our entry into a moral global age—the global age of
love—and a global spiritual age—the cosmic age. We are now moving fast
towards the fulfillment of the visions of the great prophets who through
cosmic enlightenment saw the world as one unit, the human race as one
family, sentiment as the cement of that family, and the soul as our link with
the universe, eternity, and God.[48]

The staggering events which continue to unfold in the former Eastern
Bloc countries and those previously part of the USSR give credence to
Muller's "prophecy." Muller is a political figure of world stature calling
for a new spiritual age—the merging of political and religious streams
into a synthesis for world unity.

John Naisbitt, in his new book *Global Paradox*, also points to a
universal code of conduct emerging for the twenty-first century. Naisbitt,
known for his bestseller *Megatrends*, gained notoriety through his accu-
rate forecasting of economic, social, and political trends. In *Global
Paradox*, he astutely argues that the quantum leap now occurring in
communications technology will force a global ethic. Under the banner
of human rights, environmental issues, and hiring codes in businesses,
a shared ethic is emerging. Corporations throughout the world are
already employing Ethics Officers who are telling employees, "Let OUR
conscience be your guide."[49] While Naisbitt writes from a purely secular point of view, his observations serve as a warning to all who would
hold to dogmatic truth in matters of faith, ethics, and religion.

On another front, the introduction of values clarification classes and
revisionist history texts into PUBLIC SCHOOLS in America, Australia,
and Europe stands as startling development. The emerging global ethic
of unity and tolerance—which fosters intolerance toward any dogmatic
religious faith—weaves its way into the hearts and minds of a new generation. Nurtured by this wave of New Age paganism and mysticism,
students come to value the "global consensus" rather than virtues fostered by a Judeo-Christian ethic. Classes even implement meditation
and visualization techniques. Similar techniques are emerging in the
educational systems of other western nations.

WHAT IS THE SIGNIFICANCE OF ALL THIS? If there is such an
onslaught of demonic phenomena across every aspect of society, if the
world is lovingly embracing spirit guides and intuitive knowledge in the
place of propositional truth, would we be so foolish as to think that
those who call themselves Christians would be immune from this? I
agree with David Hunt when he identifies *this search for experiential truth*

as the coming deception. To put it plainly, it has its origin in Hell. Those who truly know the Lord Jesus Christ—and even that is getting harder and harder to discern—are exhorted to heed the warning that God is giving through these writers.

One writer deserving special mention is Dr. Peter Masters, pastor of Spurgeon's former church in London. Masters' book, *The Healing Epidemic,* not only exposes the excesses and occultic patterns in Paul Yonggie Cho's ministry and that of John Wimber's Vineyard Ministries, but also sounds an alarm at the charismatic openness to revelations.

> Charismatics claim that by maintaining rational control over our minds and actions we are opposing and quenching the work of the Holy Spirit. They say that believers must be prepared to surrender rational control in order that they may be open to direct divine activity in both worship and Christian service. John Wimber observes with concern that—"Fear of losing control is threatening to most Western Christians." He insists that we must overcome our fears, because rational control must be forfeited for tongues-speaking to occur; for soaring ecstatic sensations to be felt in worship; for messages from God to be received directly into the mind, and for miraculous events to happen, such as healing.[50]

Masters closes his book with an appeal for Christians to maintain a "sound mind" so that we may be vigilant to cast down "imaginations and every high thing that exalts itself against the knowledge of God, bringing every thought into captivity to the obedience of Christ" (2 Cor. 10:5).

In an earlier conference on *Spiritual Warfare* sponsored by Wimber's Vineyard Ministries, Jack Deere again and again gave preeminence to "new revelations from God." He stated that intimacy with Christ was not gained through conversion or through the pages of Scripture. Rather, an intimate relationship could only be attained by the "hearing of fresh revelations from God."[51] Then he went on to make the rather startling assertion:

> In order to fulfill God's highest purposes for our lives we must be able to hear His voice both in the written word and in the word freshly spoken from heaven. . . . Satan understands the strategic importance of Christians hearing God's voice so he has launched various attacks against us in this area. One of his most successful attacks has been to develop a doctrine that teaches God no longer speaks to us except through the written word. Ultimately, this

doctrine is demonic even [though] Christian theologians have been used to perfect it.[52]

In another discussion, Deere admitted he was not even sure of the basic content of the gospel. For Deere, the proclamation of the gospel must involve the message of justification by faith; but it must also include proclamation of deliverance from demons and disease.

At this same conference, another speaker, Brent Rue, asserted the following: "God wants to woo us from our minds to our spirits . . . watch out for evaluating what is going on with your mind."[53] This advice clearly goes against a number of Scriptures wherein the Holy Spirit instructs believers to monitor and control their thoughts (cf. Isa. 26:3; 2 Cor. 10:5; Phil. 4:8; Rom. 12:1,2; Ps. 19:14). We are to stand against anything which counters the revelation of the Word of God (2 Cor. 10:5), and we are to test the spirits (1 John 4:1-3; Gal. 1:6-9). We must always evaluate what is going on with our minds. Wimber, Deere, Rue, and others are slicing a wide path into evangelical and conservative ranks. They have unwittingly become the storm troopers of a growing deception and New Age thinking within Christian circles.

Serious heresies are invading the church through the charismatic movement and its excesses. Leading charismatic figures are making the same statements as many in the New Age movement. Walter Martin, R. C. Sproul, Michael Horton, Rod Rosenbladt, and others have well documented the blasphemous teachings of Earl Paulk, Charles Capps, Robert Tilton, Kenneth Copeland, and Kenneth E. Hagin. These false teachers were exposed and critiqued in numerous articles in the publication, *The Agony of Deceit*.[54] More recent works such as D. R. McConnell's *A Different Gospel*, Hank Hanegraaff's *Christianity in Crisis*, and John MacArthur's *Charismatic Chaos* further detail the heresies and errors being promoted within charismatic circles.[55]

Amazing parallels exist between the claim that Christians are "little gods" and New Age teachers who claim the same for their adherents. Kenneth Copeland, claiming that Jesus spoke new revelation to him, makes the following assertions: Jesus did not come to earth as God, but only as a man; Jesus never claimed to be God during His earthly ministry; Jesus had to be "born again" in much the same manner as Christians today.[56] These assertions reflect major departures from biblical truth. Again, new revelation under the guise of a "Christian veil" gets the credit for these new teachings—but these new teachings are *not* from God.

One of the clearest parallels that exists between Copeland's brand of charismatic "reality" and that of the New Age deification of man can be seen in the following revelation which Copeland claims to have received directly from Jesus: "Pray to yourself because I'm in yourself and you're in Myself. We are one Spirit, saith the Lord. . . . Many of you are going to have visitations from the Spirit realm. Many of you will have divinely appointed visions and dreams. . . . You're just part of the times. It's time for spiritual activity to increase."[57] Spiritual activity is indeed on the increase. Yet, no scriptural basis exists for Christians to pray to themselves. Nevertheless, many Christians welcome any and all spiritual experience without subjecting such to the scrutiny of the Word of God. This explains the rise of religious hucksters and the increasing satanic deception within Christian circles.

Norman Geisler's book, *Signs and Wonders*, not only deals with the issue of miracles, but also the revelatory gifts of tongues and prophecy. He clearly shows from Scripture that the New Testament prophets were in the same vein as those of the Old Testament. Geisler charges Christians to examine the type of prophecies and revelations coming into the churches today in light of the biblical prophets. When one does this, one will see there is a vast difference between the "thus saith the Lord" of the biblical prophets and the nature of present-day prophecy.[58]

Christians are being confronted with waves of new revelation on every front. When a well respected author such as John White claims that Jesus Christ personally appeared to him on three occasions, but fails to reveal the monumental occasion for such revelation, something is wrong.[59] White proceeds to describe the feelings that accompanied these encounters and makes parallels to the experiences of Daniel, the apostles on the Mount of Transfiguration, and Paul's encounter with the Lord on the Damascus Road. White fails to underscore the fact that each of these biblical encounters was for the purpose of either giving new revelation which would become part of Scripture, unveiling more of Christ, changing the course of Christian missions, or some other major purpose. The Lord did not appear to believers for frivolous reasons. Who did White encounter then, if it was not Jesus Christ? There is only one alternative: a demonic impostor who knew there was one open to such deception.

J. I. Packer stands on dangerous ground too when he asserts that Christians should not be overly concerned about the tongues or prophesying which characterize the charismatic experience.

Or take glossolalia itself. One man voices the ardor of his praise or the agony of his prayer in tongues, another in his native speech; but is the exercise of heart essentially different? Richard Baer affirms a "fundamental functional similarity between speaking in tongues and two other widespread and generally accepted religious practices, namely, Quaker silent worship and the liturgical worship of the Catholic and Episcopal churches," arguing that in all three the analytical reason rests to allow deeper dimensions of the person to be touched by God. Is this idea obviously wrong?

Or take the Spirit-wrought awareness of how the God of the Bible sees us and how his word in Scripture applies to our life situations. If one man objectifies it by calling it prophecy and announcing it in oracle form, while another expresses it as his personal certainty of what god is saying to him and to others, does that argue any essential difference in the inward work of God in the heart of the two cases?[60]

Packer's observations raise a number of disturbing questions. The first is that throughout his book, *Keep in Step with the Spirit*, he puts Roman Catholics and Liberal Protestants in the same bag with evangelicals and fundamentalists. We are all "brothers" experiencing the Christian faith in different ways. This is one of the dangers of the charismatic focus on unity. Doctrinal distinctives go out the window. Has Packer forgotten that missionaries labor even today in predominant Roman Catholic countries trying to rescue people from the paganism and mysticism of Rome? Has he forgotten that those who deny the inerrancy and authority of Scripture, and those who preach a different salvation, come under the anathema of Galatians 1:6-9, 1 John 5:10, and also Romans 16:17? Moreover, for Packer to suggest that no major difference exists between one claiming to prophesy the very words of God and another sharing merely an impression or "leading" from the Lord is simply untrue. There IS a big difference between sharing the Lord's leading in a matter and claiming that you speak the very words of prophecy—"thus saith the Lord." It is no little thing to claim to speak the very words of God (Deut. 18:20-22; Ezek. 13:3-10; Jer. 14:14; Jer. 23:25-36; Job 42:7, 8). And again, it is no little matter to claim to receive direct revelation from God either through tongues, prophecy, visions, or a personal appearance of Christ.

The faculty at Moore College in Sydney have raised a proper alarm regarding the charismatic emphasis on additional revelation. In countering John Wimber's support for visions, "hunches," and impressions, the faculty correctly observes that Wimber undermines the *sufficiency* of Scripture.[61] Indeed, to undermine the Scriptures' *sufficiency* is to undermine its *authority* as well. For those who would seek new revelation through "hunches," intuition, or impressions, they would do well to heed Ezekiel 13:2-7:

> "Son of man, prophesy against the prophets of Israel who prophesy, and and say to those who prophesy out of their heart, 'Hear the Word of the Lord!'" Thus says the Lord God: "Woe to the foolish prophets, who follow their own spirit and have seen nothing! O Israel, your prophets are like foxes in the deserts. You have not gone up into the gaps to build a wall for the house of Israel to stand in battle on the day of the LORD. They have envisioned futility and false divination, saying, 'Thus says the LORD!' But the LORD has not sent them; yet they hope that the word may be confirmed. Have you not seen a futile vision, and have you not spoken false divination? You say, 'The LORD says,' but I have not spoken."

FLASHBACK TO A LOUNGE ROOM VISIT

Let us return to one of the stories previously recounted—the account of the evangelical Bible teacher who confided that he had experienced ecstatic tongues. He did not seek it. It just happened. According to his testimony, the experience made a memorable impact upon his life and walk with the Lord. What I did not mention was that another guest was in that room. He was a friend of this Bible teacher. After the teacher had related his experience of tongues, and after our ensuing discussion, the teacher then turned to his friend and asked him to relate his experience.

I listened intently as he related to me that the Lord Jesus Christ had appeared to him and had spoken to him for four hours. During that time, revelations were received which later proved to be a personal blessing to him. I was asked by both to give my opinion on the matter. Remember, this was in my home. These were not vicious adversaries seated across from me, but dear brothers in Christ who love the Lord and faithfully serve Him. These were mature men in the ministry. Yet, both had received experiences which they had not sought. And now, knowing my general views on such matters, they wanted my specific opinion.

I shared with my brother that I did not doubt the genuineness of his experience. Yet, I went on to explain that his interpretation of the experience was different from mine. The manner in which "Jesus" appeared, the content of the exchanges, the appearance of the so-called Christ, and the time element itself certainly did not conform to the post-resurrection appearances of the Lord Jesus. My conclusion was that the encounter was perpetrated by a demonic impostor. The Scriptures clearly teach that Satan is able to transform himself into a messenger of light (2 Cor. 11:14). Although demons are not omniscient or omnipresent, they well know secrets of men and the universe and can reveal these to those open to such.

It was not an easy exchange of views in the lounge room that evening. Love still prevailed, and we agreed to differ. Yet, I walked away from that night wondering how many other saints were opening themselves up to such phenomena.

If one fails to rebuke temptation or sin when it arises, then one is open to its influence. Moreover, when something confronts a believer that does not coincide with biblical patterns or guidelines, that idea or revelation is to be cast down (2 Cor. 10:4, 5). And this brings us to the major question at hand: WHY WOULD GOD ALLOW HIS CHILDREN, DEDICATED BELIEVERS, TO EXPERIENCE AND GIVE IN TO INFLU-ENCES THAT ARE NOT FROM HIM?

WHY? WHY? WHY?

The answer is very simple. God will allow his children in their walk with Him to be confronted with many influences, even influences which are not from Him. Every moment the Christian must do warfare with the world, the flesh, and the devil. That is just part of the maturing process. Listen to the words of Scripture on this matter: "Blessed is the man who endures temptation; for when he has been proved, he will receive the crown of life which the Lord has promised to those who love Him" (James 1:12).

Even the most dedicated of God's children must contend with pride, anxiety, fear, disobedience, and sin in a number of dressings. Does God allow his children to sin? The answer is obvious. Therefore, there is no inconsistency between the overall character of living the Christian life in battling sin and God allowing His children to embrace experiences that are unbiblical. The Lord allows his children to choose whether to faithfully bring every experience under the control of Scripture or neglect that duty. And whatever does not meet the biblical pattern is an aberrant pattern and does not have its origin in God.

Again, does God allow His children to disobey, to sin, to be insensitive to the voice of the Spirit, to remain carnal instead of Spirit-filled? Yes!

And this can be the experience of a seasoned soldier in the faith just as it can be true of a babe in Christ. The Lord will allow His children to be confronted with temptation and sin in all forms (cf. James 1:12-18). That includes the temptation to move away from Scripture through indulging in false revelations or signs.

We must remember that the Word of God is called the "sword of the Spirit" (Eph. 6:17). It is the Word of God that is able to bring discernment and power: "For the word of God is living and powerful, and sharper than any two-edged sword, piercing even to the division of soul and spirit, and of joints and marrow, and is a discerner of the thoughts and intents of the heart" (Heb. 4:12). Paul exhorted the Thessalonians to "test all things" (1Thess. 5:21). And this warning came right after exhortations concerning quenching the Spirit and prophecy. The Apostle John was also led of the Spirit of God to write: "Beloved, do not believe every spirit, but test the spirits, whether they are of God; because many false prophets have gone out into the world" (1 John 4:1).

Scripture clearly affirms that signs and wonders can have sources other than God (cf. Deut. 13:1-5; Matt. 24:24; 2 Thess. 2:9-10; Rev. 13:13-14). Indeed one can claim to prophesy or do miracles in the name of the Lord, and yet, be a false prophet (cf. Deut. 18:21, 22; Ezek. 13:1-3; Jer. 28). Moreover, in speaking of the close of this age, Jesus warns believers to "take heed that no one deceives you" (Matt. 24:4).

IF THE POSSIBILITY OF DECEPTION AMONG CHRISTIANS WAS NOT REAL, THEN THE AFOREMENTIONED SCRIPTURAL WARNINGS WOULD NEVER HAVE BEEN GIVEN. And how does one "test the spirits." By feelings? By intuition? By popular opinion or human consensus? By the fulfillment of a particular prophecy, revelation, or miracle? No, none of these. One can only test the spirits by the Word of God. That is God's provision for the saint in spiritual discernment and knowledge. When a Christian lays down this Sword of the Spirit, and substitutes feeling or human logic, that saint has opened the way to dangerous deception.

THE DANGEROUS EXCHANGE

Years ago when I was completing my training to be a Flight Instructor, the day came for my final check ride. I will never forget it. I was in my early twenties and had already obtained my commercial flying license. All of the training, all of the practice, all of the theory, and all of the study came down to a two-hour flight check with a veteran instructor. The instructor looked the part—deeply tanned from hours in the cockpit, calm and controlled manner, and sure of his business. To this day I still remember the maneuvers which I was asked to do, still remember the simulated forced landings and that final approach when all was finished. As I sat in his office waiting for my results and his final comments, I hung on every word. His opening statement went something like this:

> John, I want you to remember that there are two things which kill pilots: pre-sumption and presumption. You see the novice pilot gets a few hours under his belt and then thinks he can fly in any weather. So he ventures out when the weather is marginal, thinking he can handle any situation. He flies beyond his expertise. And when suddenly caught by shifting weather patterns, he dies.

> But John, also remember that there is the pilot who has several thousand hours of flying experience. He has flown for years and never had an accident. He knows he should always follow a written check-list in pre-flight prepara-tions for takeoff; and the same goes for landing where possible. It could be an occasion where friends are there, and there is much excitement about the flight. It could be that for some reason, he is in a hurry and just dispenses with the written check-list. He reviews by memory and does it in haste . . . and he dies. Why? Because presumption or pride led him away from depending on the written check-list. John, I want you to always remember that.

And I have down through the years imparted the same instructions to others. There are times also when a pilot must trust his instrument panel, even more than his senses. Any pilot who has done any extended flying will experience vertigo. It happened to me one time when I was checking some charts amidst the clouds. My attention was on the aero-nautical chart, and when I looked up, all I could see was cloud. There was no reference point. My senses told me I was flying straight and level; but my instruments told me I was in a descending turn to the right. Even though my ears could hear the increase in RPM of the engine, my other senses overruled. Again, it was essential that I trust the instrument readings.

There is a spiritual parallel in all this. This writer and others have already demonstrated that false revelation is invading the churches as never before. The tongues and prophecies abounding in evangelical and fundamental churches do not meet the biblical pattern. They are false manifestations and linked to the overall deception that is sweeping planet earth. That is why it is so important to be guided in spiritual matters by the Scriptures—our "instrument panel" or "written check-list."

The sign gifts being offered today in charismatic circles, and the race by many Christians to experience the revelatory gifts, have an appeal to both the new Christian and the mature veteran in the faith. The reasons and motivations may be different, but the end result is the same. If one replaces the voice of Scripture with inner promptings or feelings, one becomes a mark for spiritual disorientation and deception.

The new Christian knows very little of Scripture, but his heart is ablaze with the love of Christ. He wants more knowledge of the Lord. The Bible is a moment-by-moment treasure chest of new discoveries. Everything is new. Because the new Christian's primary reference point is a few Scriptures, experiential concerns predominate. Soon in living the day-to-day struggles of the Christian life, the young convert finds that being saved did not automatically remove the presence of temptation or sin from his life. The experience of Paul in Romans 7:18ff. now becomes the experience of the new Christian. He longs for more contact with God and more power to gain victory in the daily walk. He has not learned the biblical principles of appropriating the Spirit's power. It is at this point that the young Christian is most vulnerable to the wooing of false spirituality. Rather than depending upon the Word of God as the key to life in the Spirit, he begins to seek the shortcut of tongues, visions, dreams, or prophecy that somehow will open the door to the life in the Spirit. He hears talk of a second work of grace, of baptism in the Spirit, of the sanctified life free from sin, of power evangelism, of the gift of healing, of laughing in the Spirit. Unless the new believer stays with Scripture to guide him, he is open to all sorts of deception.

One often hears certain charismatic teachers telling people to just take Scripture at face value. They urge those inquiring of the gifts to not question, just go with the flow of the Spirit. Bible teachers who take opposing views to the charismatic position are often written off with statements like: "Who did Jesus use? . . . the simple to confound the wise! . . . don't let some scholar in Greek or Hebrew steal your blessing from you. Surely God wouldn't design the Scriptures so that only the scholars could tell you what to believe." Believers are then urged to step out in faith on a few verses, take them as they are, and believe. Amazing is the fact that while undermining the role of Bible teachers in the one instance, these charismatic teachers are telling their converts to follow their own line without questioning the interpretation. Just step out in faith on this Scripture or that Scripture.

While it is true that every believer is a priest before God (2 Pet. 2:9); while it is true that every believer can and should search the Scriptures to discover truth with the assistance of the Holy Spirit (1 Cor. 2:9-16); while it is true that all believers should follow the example of the Bereans who, after hearing the Apostle Paul, searched the Scriptures to see if what he said was true (Acts 17:10, 11); *it is also true that the Lord gave teachers to the church as a gift to edify, perfect, and train people for ministry.*

> And He Himself gave some to be apostles, some prophets, some evangelists, and some pastors and teachers, for the equipping of the saints for the work of ministry, for the edifying of the body of Christ, till we all come to the unity of the faith and the knowledge of the Son of God, to a perfect man, to the measure of the stature of the fullness of Christ; that we should no longer be children, tossed to and fro and carried about with every wind of doctrine, by the trickery of men, in the cunning craftiness by which they lie in wait to deceive, but, speaking the truth in love, may grow up in all things into Him who is the head—Christ—from whom the whole body, joined and knit together by what every joint supplies, according to the effective working by which every part does its share, causes growth of the body for the edifying of itself in love (Eph. 4:11-16).

Somewhere in this charismatic call for people to embrace this or that Scripture without checking its relation to other Scriptures, charismatic proponents have forgotten the above instruction by the Holy Spirit. In so doing, they have slain truth in the hearts of new believers and the Holy Spirit is grieved. In slamming Bible teachers who urge careful study of the Word of God, charismatic leaders have by implication sought to negate the legitimate spiritual gift of teaching. The same Holy Spirit Who gives the gifts and fills believers inspired Paul to write: "Be diligent to present yourself approved to God, a worker who does not need to be ashamed, rightly dividing the word of truth" (2 Tim. 2:15).[62]

The new Christian is exhorted to persevere and stay with a sincere study of the Word of God on any life issue. By all means take Scripture literally as it is given. Approach it with the faith of a child, but the reverence and maturity of an adult standing before the holy and Almighty God. But what if both sides of a particular issue seem to offer equally sound scriptural arguments? What then? One thing is for sure, you do not let experiential concerns swing the pendulum. You stay with the study of the Word until the scriptural arguments of one side prevail.

The sign gifts and revelatory gifts can also be a temptation for the mature Christian. Why? The one who has walked faithfully with the Lord for many years also longs for more of God. This is the way it should be. And no doubt, along the way, there will be the desert times. David had his cave (1 Sam. 22:1); Elijah had his juniper tree (1 Kings 19:4, 5); Job, his ash heap (Job 2:8); and Paul, his despairing of life itself (2 Cor. 1:8). In those dry times when the soul knows it is thirsty, when the spiritual knees are weak, even the mature Christian is open to the tantalizing appeal of a spiritual quick fix. Again, it is much easier to just "go with the flow" or give in to forces from without than to return to the road that originally led one to heights of spiritual communion: confession of sin, cleansing, surrender, feeding on the Word, abiding, and taking up the cross daily. All of the aforementioned require struggle and effort and vigilance. The "pressing on" (Phil. 3:10-20) and the "warfare" (2 Cor. 10:4, 5; 2 Tim. 2:2-4) that Paul talked about were to be the moment-by-moment experience of the Christian until one steps on the other side of glory. There never is a time in the Christian experience when one can settle back into an ethereal state that will carry one through a host of tomorrows. The cross is to be taken up *daily* (Luke 9:23). Abiding is a moment-by-moment challenge. Our spiritual warfare requires the monitoring of every thought. Sometimes veteran saints, dedicated soldiers of the Cross, get tired in the battle. It is then, in the dry times, that many will make an exchange between the Word of God and experience. That is a dangerous exchange.

But what about those dedicated saints who experience the charismatic phenomena when they are walking close to the Lord. They seek neither the sign nor revelatory gifts. The phenomena just "happen" in their lives. What then?

THE ONLY ALTERNATIVE

It is a common practice in charismatic circles for those who claim to have the gift of tongues and prophecy to instruct others in how to obtain the gift or use it. Many forget that it is the Holy Spirit who dispenses spiritual gifts as He chooses (1 Cor. 12:11). Many charismatics will testify that they "received" the gift of tongues through brethren laying hands upon them, praying over them, and urging them to pronounce a few syllables over and over again. As the verbalizations come faster and more enthusiastic, one is suddenly hailed by those around as having the gift. As stated earlier, this type of approach to spiritual gifts has no biblical base. Thus, one may come into the false experience through a *learned response*.

There is also another response, a *psychological response*. Here one has been seeking the fullness of God. The person may or may not be part of a charismatic group, but at least is open to the sign gifts or revelatory gifts. One day he awakes from sleep speaking in ecstatic speech; or it may happen in a prayer time; or it may happen in the context of a worship service as one directs praise to the Lord. Regardless of the setting, it just happens. Because of one's prior expectancy and openness to the gift, the experience is received with great joy and release. Subsequent experiences follow, and one learns to employ the "gift" as the need arises.

However, the question deals with those who do not seek the gift. What is the explanation when one does not seek it, does not practice it as a learned response, and it just happens? There is only one alternative. Such must be viewed as *demonic* and must be rebuked. Pagan religions throughout history have their ecstatic forms of speech as common practices. In our own day, cults such as the Mormons and The Way International practice tongues similar to those found in charismatic circles. And, as "revelations to the inward man" are becoming such common practice and the key emphasis of the New Age Movement, one would expect Satan to manifest himself in the church. Again, if the Lord will allow His children to sin, to walk in disobedience, to ignorantly transgress His commandments, then there is no inconsistency in His allowing his children to embrace a practice that is unscriptural. But why would the Lord allow dedicated saints to persist in error, and perpetuate error, year after year without rebuke? And why do many Christians report such positive growth in their lives after such experiences? These questions will be dealt with in the next chapter, but suffice it to say that Satan is continuing his age old attack against the Word of God. If he can't undermine it directly, he will try and supersede its authority and sufficiency with new revelations.

I am concerned at the stance taken by some well respected writers who see no major problem with tongues speaking, *even if it does not coincide with the biblical model*. Packer seems to approve the practice merely on the basis that it has beneficial aspects: "Glossolalia is sought and used as part of a quest for closer communion with God and regularly proves beneficial at the conscious level, bringing relief of tension, a certain inner exhilaration, and a strengthening sense of God's presence and blessing."[63] While he would admit that some manifestations of tongues have a demonic source, he would regard most displays of tongues today as the product of learned activity, psychological response, or as a gift from the Lord. In all of these cases, Packer would approve of the activity—even if it does not measure up to the biblical pattern.

CHARISMATIC FALLOUT

In the early sixties when the threat of nuclear war screamed at us from television, newspapers, public interest groups, and survivalist campaigns, the word "fallout" always caught one's attention. People were concerned not just about the immediate effects of a nuclear explosion, but about the lingering effects of the radioactive fallout that followed. It was the fallout that threatened more lives than the nuclear blast itself. So people built fallout shelters to sustain life amidst a threatening environment.

The charismatic push for the sign gifts and revelatory gifts have an impact that goes far beyond the experience of individuals. Doctrinal distinctives that define true Christianity become blurred amidst the clamor for shared experiences. Many who hold differing views on salvation, the deity of Christ, and the inerrancy of Scripture come together to proclaim "unity" in the Lord. In actuality, the only basis of unity is their common experience.

The major "fallout" that occurs through charismatic influence is the influx and acceptance of heresy and nominal Christians into the fellowship of the faithful. In many instances, heretics, apostates, and true believers can stand together on the same platform, with hands raised in praise to the one true God, glowing in the "unity and Christian brotherhood" of the moment. The pagan and secular world applauds at this display of love and unity; new babes in Christ or the spiritually immature are persuaded that such a stance is pleasing to God. In reality, God is repulsed and grieved.

By way of example, in 1985 in the city of Adelaide (Australia), a leading charismatic figure held joint meetings with Jack Soulsby, a Catholic priest commissioned to do evangelistic campaigns in the Pacific region and Australia. Charismatic renewal came to Adelaide amidst the slogans, *We are one, We are loved.* The series of renewal meetings was called *Challenge '85,* and many churches within both Roman Catholic and Protestant circles endorsed the joint effort. Press releases affirmed that two men from different ends of the Christian spectrum would speak from the same platform. In further pushing the themes of unity and love, the press releases declared:

> The Christian message preached without Christian unity is not credible!
>
> For this reason Challenge '85 is a rally with two functions—a Celebration of Christian unity (imperfect though it may be) and a Proclamation of the Gospel.
>
> We are one family with one Father. We are one kingdom with one King. We are one body with one Head. We are one church with one Spirit. Christian unity is a reality but we need to learn how to live in that unity . . . and learning is by doing. Unless we are prepared to act in the truth of our God-established unity we are not obeying Jesus' command nor the Father's will. Evangelism without unity is worthless and false.
>
> On Pentecost Eve Challenge '85 will celebrate the reality of our unity. We do not all express our faith in the same words nor worship our God in the same way but the reality of our unity overshadows our diversity and needs to be visible to the world. . . . [64]

Two men from different ends of the spectrum of Christianity? Maybe two men from different ends of "perceived Christianity" or "professing Christianity;" but not two men from different ends of the spectrum of biblical Christianity. The "gospel" that a Roman Catholic priest would preach is not the gospel of Scripture. Moreover, the Scriptures pronounce judgment on any who would pervert that gospel (Gal. 1:6-9).

At the time of Challenge '85, I was pastoring a new church in the hills area south of Adelaide. We were visiting door-to-door in the area and met one of the leaders of the Challenge '85 campaign. He was a Roman Catholic who testified glowingly that he was "born again," that he was a group leader for the campaign, and responsible for training counselors who dealt with people coming forward in the services. As we chatted, he admitted that his salvation was through faith in Jesus Christ. Yet, the more we talked, the more evident it became that he still viewed the sacraments as essential to maintaining his security in Christ; that he still held to the traditional Catholic views on Mary, Papal authority, confession, works, and other dogma with an even greater degree of loyalty than ever before. Sadly, he was a deceived man, still under the condemnation of God. What concerned me was that the heads of all the major denominations in Adelaide (Baptist, Assembly of God, Roman Catholic, etc.) not only came out with a joint statement of unity celebrating Challenge '85, but also held a joint march of unity in the city.

So men of different "faiths" joined hands publicly to display unity in Christ. Even though, biblically, some would not even qualify as true Christians, ecclesiastical unity and humanly orchestrated demonstrations of unity became the order of the day.

Five years later, there was another call for Christian unity in Adelaide. The occasion was the United Charismatic Convention—Action 90. This high profile convention included speakers such as Tony Campolo. The priority given to ecumenical unity at the expense of biblical truth was clearly illustrated in the comments of Barry Chant which appeared in the *Advertiser* :

> When you see Catholic, Baptist, Anglican and Uniting Church people standing side by side or linking arms together as they worship the Lord, you know something special is happening. . . . This is the result of the power of the Holy Spirit. Charismatic people believe the Holy Spirit comes to people today with signs such as the gift of tongues, which is mentioned in the Book of Acts. When people are filled with the Holy Spirit, they are also filled with love and joy so they forget their differences and begin to appreciated one another in a new way.[65]

According to Chant, doctrinal differences are to be forgotten when the Holy Spirit brings about this kind of unity? Has he forgotten that Roman Catholic doctrine teaches a different way of salvation than the biblical message? Is that a small doctrinal difference?

The uniting of forces within the Roman Catholic Church, liberal elements in mainline Protestant denominations, and charismatic churches is not new. Catholic influx into the charismatic movement may be traced as far back as Vatican II (1965). Most Protestant denominations have also been represented in the Charismatic Renewal conferences around the world since the sixties.[66] Why the concern? With the passage of time, evangelicals have become more accepting of this type of affiliation. Unity becomes the byword at the expense of biblical truth.

One of the leading charismatic figures in Hong Kong is Jackie Pullinger. For over twenty years she has maintained a ministry to drug addicts. Working in the slums of Kowloon, she has made a difference in this important international city. The government of Hong Kong has officially recognized her humanitarian efforts and has subsidized her work with property grants and facilities. She is well respected by Christians and non-Christians alike. Indeed, she is to be commended for her sacrifice and work among the needy. However, there are several disturbing aspects of her ministry. She maintains that one must speak in tongues to gain power over drug addiction. Although she preaches salvation by grace through the Lord Jesus Christ, she insists that those who come for help will only be delivered if they speak in tongues.[67] Such teaching has no scriptural foundation whatsoever. Pullinger also disregards the clear scriptural instruction of 1 Timothy 2:12-15, for she pastors the church which she founded. Even more disturbing is the fact that she conducts charismatic conferences with Roman Catholic priests.

In a charismatic conference in 1989, Jackie Pullinger joined in ministry with Tom Forrest—Roman Catholic priest who was former chairman of the International Catholic Charismatic Renewal Office (ICCRO) in Rome. The stated purpose of the ICCRO is to serve as a center of unity for worldwide evangelization and the promotion of charismatic renewal. *But what kind of evangelism; what kind of unity; and what kind of renewal? The message of the Roman Catholic Church and the false gospel which it spreads would fall far short of biblical evangelism (cf. Gal. 1:6-9).* Yet, for some reason, this does not bother Jackie Pullinger who claims to represent evangelical Christianity.

The Dominican Republic also has its own representative spreading the news of charismatic healing to the world. Emilien Tardif, a charismatic priest, is making the headlines in western countries through his healing services. He maintains that healing takes place through the mass. He is welcomed in some Protestant charismatic circles as a brother in Christ. This kind of syncretism and experiential fellowship stands under the rebuke of God.

Around the world, the Catholic Charismatic Renewal (CCR), ICCRO, and charismatic advances among Protestant denominations are forging an ever increasing ecumenical structure. Europe has taken the lead. At Strasbourg in May of 1982, an ecumenical conference sponsored by the CCR attracted over twenty thousand people. The planning committee for the conference included leaders from Catholic, Anglican, Lutheran, Reformed, and Evangelical churches.[68] The ICCRO is committed to sponsoring regional and international conferences to promote charismatic renewal and unity. Most Pentecostals and charismatics would be stunned to know of the degree of planning and support which many of their conferences get from the Vatican. Instead of participating in the "free and sovereign movements of the Spirit of God," *many are mere pawns in a global game of emotional experimentation and ecumenical strategies.*

Vance Havner used to say, "Popularity has slain more prophets of God than persecution ever did." Certainly, such is the condition of Christianity today. Whatever is popular, whatever is accepted, whatever brings good feelings, whatever brings unity, all become the accepted norm for the church. *Many forget the great priestly prayer of Jesus recorded in John 17. Before the Lord ever prayed for unity among believers, He prayed that the Father would sanctify (literally, "set apart") believers by His truth, the Word of God (Jn. 17:17-21). Thus, the basis for unity is truth, the Word of God.* Luther said it centuries ago while standing against the threats of the Roman Catholic Church: "unity without truth is treason." And so it is. That is the fallout which is happening today through the charismatic movement. Truth is being set aside in the name of unity; darkness and light are mingling together and embracing; heaven and hell are meeting on common ground. If one listens closely, one will hear that many of those claiming to be sheep no longer bleat, but rather are beginning to howl. Something is wrong.

J. I. Packer correctly discerns that there is a conscious effort in charismatic circles to place emphasis on unity at the expense of doctrine. Some genuinely feel that fellowship on the basis of common experience will eventually bring forth doctrinal synthesis that will honor God. Note the observations of Packer:

"This movement is the most unifying in Christendom today," writes Michael Harper. "Only in this movement are all streams uniting , and all ministries being accepted and practiced." The claim is true. It is a common complaint that ecumenical energy of the conventional sort is waning; but transdenominational charismatic fellowship, with its international leadership and attendant linking organizations, goes from strength to strength.

Ecumenically its technique is distinctive: It seeks first and foremost to realize oneness in Christ experientially, in celebration and ministry, confident that theological convergence will follow. "This open stance," writes Richard Quebedeaux, "whereby the Holy Spirit is seen to lead people to theological truth *following* (rather than prerequisite to) a common experience, is clearly ascendant throughout Neo-Pentecostalism; it is one reason why [in it] evangelicals, liberals, and Roman Catholics have been joined together (spiritually, at least) for the first time." Though in each main-line denomination charismatics are a relatively small minority, the movement's cumulative impact has been considerable and is likely to be greater rather than less as the future unfolds.[69]

In 1993, the Society for Promoting Christian Knowledge (SPCK) published a book entitled *Charismatic Renewal: The Search for a Theology*. The writers approached their subject matter as "friends" of the charismatic renewal movement. Each had experienced charismatic renewal; yet all also acknowledged their search for a proper theology to define their experience. Two of the authors, Tom Smail and Nigel Wright, stated that before they could experience charismatic renewal, they had to place a "moratorium" on theological activity. Note Wright's comments: "part of my own preparation for renewal in the Spirit was to allow myself to be brought to a point where theological activity was for a time put into suspense."[70] Yet now, having emerged *from* their charismatic experiences, these men are in search for a theology.

This hope of a doctrinal synthesis of truth which follows fellowship on the basis of experience is a false hope. Indeed, it stands as a deception of the devil. Such a strategy reverses biblical guidelines for fellowship, and creates an ever growing confusion among believers.[71] The same Holy Spirit who inspired Paul to write Galatians 1:6-10 and Romans 16:17 would not foster a unity based on experiential concerns which would contradict these Scriptures:

> I marvel that you are turning away so soon from Him who called you in the grace of Christ to a different gospel, which is not another; but there are some who trouble you and want to pervert the gospel of Christ. But even if we, or an angel from heaven, preach any other gospel to you than what we have preached to you, let him be accursed. As we have said before, so now I say again, if anyone preaches any other gospel to you than what you have received, let him be accursed. For do I now persuade men, or God? Or do I seek to please men? for if I still pleased men, I would not be a servant of Christ (Gal. 1:6-10).

> Now I urge you, brethren, note those who cause divisions and offenses, *contrary to the doctrine which you learned, and avoid them* (Rom. 16:17, italics mine; cf. Titus 1:12-14; 3:10, 11).

The alluring call for new revelation, power through sign gifts, and unity in worship with nominal Christians is serious business. We are just beginning to feel the harmful effects of this fallout. Instead of a great renewal, Christianity is experiencing a *great reversal*. Granted, many sincere believers, feeling that they are fulfilling Jesus' teaching in John 13:34, 35 and John 17:20, 21, support ecumenical emphases and programs. Sadly, however, they fail to think through the implications of their stance and they fail to see that true unity can only be based on doctrinal truth (John 17:16-19). [Note: *For a more detailed discussion of the ecumenical movement and its dangers, please see Question 5 in Appendix A.*]

So one more time: Is this issue of the sign and revelatory gifts really that significant? Is it that important a doctrinal matter? Should so much controversy be generated among believers regarding differing positions? Most assuredly. Error must be addressed whenever it raises itself. Moreover, when so many believers are being involved in a growing deception, truth demands that brethren speak to brethren on these issues.

We live in a time when globalism and the call for a New World Order are fostering an emerging world ethic. This ethic gathers momentum under the banners of "unity," "tolerance," "love," and the "brotherhood of man." And what stands in the way of this unity and tolerance? Any system of dogmatic truth that would exclude other philosophies and religions. By its very nature, biblical Christianity is based upon dogmatic truth. That is why the charismatic call for unity, at the expense of truth, is so dangerous. If Christians fail to abide in and abide by the Word of God, they open themselves up to the seductive and deceptive spirit of the age.

REVIEW OF KEY CONCEPTS

1. Although many charismatic churches are being used of the Lord to reach people for the kingdom, there is a growing cancer amidst the charismatic movement: new revelation. This emphasis comes through tongues, prophecy, visions, dreams, and words of knowledge. There is also the misunderstanding regarding sign gifts such as healing and the casting out of demons.

2. The emphasis in charismatic circles on new revelation parallels the primary emphasis of the multifaceted New Age Movement. The authority of propositional truth is being replaced by the "new word" from heaven, freshly delivered through modern prophets.

3. In recent years, numerous writers have come to the foreground to
    warn believers of the dangers of dealing in new revelation: David
    Hunt, John MacArthur, Peter Masters, Norman Geisler, Tal Brooke,
    Neil Babcox—to name a few.

4. At the same time, there has been a softening of some such as J. I.
    Packer, D. Martin Lloyd-Jones, and John White. Anecdotal argu-
    ments rather than scriptural proof is given by these to condone and
    even endorse charismatic practices. Even if tongues and prophecy
    do not meet the biblical pattern, if it makes one feel closer to God
    and "practice His presence," then we are told it is fine. Such rea-
    soning is to be rejected. It opens the Christian to spiritual deception.

5. Tongues can be experienced as a result of learned activity, psycho-
    logical response, or demonic influence. Just as God allows His chil-
    dren to sin, to walk in disobedience, to ignorantly transgress His
    commands, so He will allow His children to embrace unbiblical
    practices (cf. James 1:12). That is just part of living the Christian life.
    The only means by which believers can discern truth, test the spirits,
    and evaluate life's experiences is through the Word of God. If a
    believer chooses to bypass the Sword of the Spirit, then he is open
    to deception.

6. The fallout from the charismatic movement is the strengthening of
    the ecumenical movement. While the pagan and secular world
    applauds this show of unity, while liberal churches and apostate
    churches gain new energy and credibility from mutual affiliation
    with evangelicals, doctrinal truth is pushed aside in favor of orches-
    trated "oneness." Light and darkness stand with each other and the
    forces of hell and heaven intermingle—all to the delight of the god
    of this age.

7. Those who say, "let the charismatics alone . . . their views harm no
    one," are wrong. Their error is affecting the lives of many sincere
    believers and is laying the foundation for an ever growing deception.

Question Three

If the sign and revelatory gifts are not for today, and are not from God, why do these experiences produce positive effects in believers' lives?

The Bible Conference was just coming to a close. And the topic for the conference was the Kingdom of God and the Spirit-filled Life. Before me stood a man in his late forties to early fifties. The side of his face bore traces of recent tears. He stretched forth his hand and then began to pour out his heart.

His words went something like this: "For twenty years I have missed so much from the Lord. I come from a charismatic background. For so many years my spiritual life was dependent upon drawing either from some past experience or waiting expectantly for a new work of God. I never experienced the joy of moment-by-moment abiding in the Spirit, drawing upon the Word of God for my spiritual meat. I feel like a babe in Christ. I know so little of Scripture."

I realize that this is not the experience of every charismatic believer. However, many charismatics do admit to similar struggles in their walk with God. Many admit that they are not *one hundred percent sure* that their tongues are from God; many admit they are not completely certain that their prophecies or words of knowledge have the Lord as their source; many admit they are disturbed at charismatic pronouncements that carry the weight of Scripture but not the substance; many admit they are troubled at healings that take place in stages, or relapses that occur among some who claimed healing. Doubts continue to be raised by those who say they are Spirit-filled, yet live inconsistent lives and never see their witness result in others coming to Christ. Should believers persist in holding to practices and doctrines which occasion doubts in their own hearts?

However, others would counter by pointing to the positive effects which the sign and revelatory gifts have upon the lives of believers. How does one explain the increased interest in Bible study, the greater overall joy that is present in living the Christian life, the renewed boldness to witness to others, the new vitality in the prayer life, and the growth in commitment to the Lord? Joseph Dillow mirrors these same concerns.

> Many Christians who struggled for years in futile attempts to experience the abundant life that Jesus offers, mark the day that they spoke in tongues as the beginning of a new and vital experience with God. I know of numerous cases in which lives have been changed, churches revitalized, and even marriages put back together due to personal spiritual revival that was sparked by receiving the "gift of tongues."[72]

Again, if the sign gifts and revelatory gifts are not for today—indeed, are not from God—why do they produce these positive spiritual results in believers' lives?[73]

THE AGE OLD CONFLICT

One need only turn to the Book of Genesis to see the primary forces at work in man's spiritual pilgrimage in this life. In essence, the contest in the Garden of Eden was between the Word of God and Satan's endeavor to influence the choice of man away from submission and obedience to that Word. This is born out by the first recorded words of Satan in the Bible: "Has God indeed said . . . ?" (Gen. 3:1). From his very first contact with humanity, Satan has sought to undermine the Word of God. In seeking to woo man away from dependency and submission to the revealed will of God, Satan has sought to duplicate his own sin in man (i.e., that of declaring independence from God and His Word). He is a deceiver of deceivers. He promises much in order to bind and enslave.

Scripture reveals that Satan has three basic approaches to man: the lust of the eyes, the lust of the flesh, and the pride of life (1 John 2:16). All three avenues were used in the Garden of Eden to entice Eve to sin; and all three avenues were used in the wilderness as Satan failed in his temptation of Christ. Note the following comparison:

	Garden of Eden	*Temptation of Jesus*
Lust of the Flesh	"the woman saw that the tree	"If You are the Son of God,

	was good for food" (Gen. 3:6)	command that these stones become bread" (Matt. 4:3)
Lust of the Eyes	"the woman saw . . . that it was pleasant to the eyes" (Gen. 3:6)	"Again, the devil took Him up on an exceedingly high mountain, and showed Him all the kingdoms of the world and their glory" (Matt. 4:8)
Pride of Life	"The woman saw . . . that it was . . . a tree desirable to make one wise" (Gen. 3:6)	"If You are the Son of God, throw yourself down. For it is written: 'He shall give His angels charge concerning you'" (Matt. 4:6)

One should note that Satan is not averse to using Scripture. He is not afraid of the Word of God as long as it is quoted out of context or employed to entice one into error or into actions which go against the will of God. His primary desire is to foster independence in the heart from the Word of God.

One should also note the *preeminence which Jesus gave to the written Word in Matthew 4*. In His moment of spiritual conflict, our Lord appealed to the highest authority at His disposal: the written Word of God. Again and again, Jesus confronted temptation and deception with the phrase "*It is written*," and then went on to masterfully employ the Scriptures. This phrase "IT IS WRITTEN" resounds through the centuries as God's guide to His saints. That is so crucial to our present study.

Remember the cosmic contest which surrounded Job? The Lord called attention to Job and declared that Job was His servant, "a blameless and upright man, one who fears God and shuns evil" (Job 1:8). Satan basically charged that Job was a "saint for silver," that God was buying his loyalty and worship by bestowing blessings on him. Satan charged that if God removed the blessings, he could get Job to curse God (Job 1:11).

Now the word "curse" which is used in Job chapter 1, verses 5 and 11, and chapter 2, verses 5 and 9, is a very interesting word. In the Hebrew, the word is *barach* which literally means "to bless." Yet, such a translation would be inappropriate in these verses; therefore *barach* is used as a euphemism for the idea of "curse" or "renounce." This is permissible because the word *barach* is used in other verses of the Old Testament to carry the idea of a parting "good-bye" or "farewell" (cf. Gen. 31:55; Josh. 22:6). Thus, Satan was not out to get Job to merely blaspheme or defy God. He was trying to get Job to say "good-bye" to God, to declare independence, to move away from a conscious relationship of dependence and submission. Though Job would later sin in the midst of his trial, though he would charge God with acts of injustice, Job never declared any desire to move away from God. On the contrary, the more his trial intensified, the more he sought the Lord.[74]

So what does all of the above have to do with the present study? This just confirms that from the Garden of Eden, to the experience of Job, to the temptation of the Lord Jesus Christ, to the present day, Satan has tried to move man away from submission to the authority of God and His Word. If he cannot do it through direct enticement or challenge, he will attempt to do it through all manner of subtlety and deception. That is why one must be careful not to embrace new revelations that come through any avenue: impressions, intuition, visions, dreams, tongues, or prophecy. As noted previously, such undermine both the *authority* and *sufficiency* of Scripture.

Every true believer has experienced the leading of the Holy Spirit at times—this through reading the Scriptures or through impressions in the inward man. Yet, "leadings" must not be accorded the status of new revelation. Again, it is a serious matter to claim new revelation has the authority of "thus saith the Lord." Moreover, every "leading" must be checked by Scripture to see if it carries the marks of deception.

THE POWER OF DECEPTION
Two Life Stories

Surely God's saints know when they are being misled or tempted with deception? The answer is that unless one refers to the Word of God, the Sword of the Spirit, even the most gifted and faithful saint of God can be led into deception. Allow me to give two examples: one from Scripture and another from my own dealings with a new believer who was struggling with deception.

The setting for our first story is found in Matthew 16. Jesus has taken the Twelve away to the mountains of Caesarea Philippi for a time of spiritual renewal. They have left the busy streets of Jerusalem and the multitudes on the hillsides of Galilee; they have left the continued confrontation with the Pharisees, the scribes, and rulers of Israel. They rejoice in just being alone with the Master, surrounded by the beauty of nature. It is in this setting that the Apostle Peter would receive his greatest rebuke from Jesus.

You know the story. Jesus turns to his apostles and says, "Who do men say that I, the Son of Man, am?" (v. 13). The apostles relate that some say Jesus is John the Baptist, or Elijah, or Jeremiah, or one of the prophets. Then Jesus inquires, "But who do you say that I am?" (v. 15). Peter is the first to speak up, and he declares, "You are the Christ, the Son of the living God" (v. 16).

Oh, how joyous Peter must have been when Jesus commended him for his answer: *"Blessed are you, Simon Bar-Jonah, for flesh and blood has not revealed this to you, but My Father who is in heaven"* (v. 17). The other disciples joined in the elation as they heard Jesus declare that the keys to the kingdom of heaven (i.e., the gospel) would be given to them. Though they did not fully understand the significance of that pronouncement, they knew it meant special divine favor and blessing. What a wondrous occasion; what wondrous joy and fellowship! However, none in that group was ready for what was about to happen.

Scripture records that for the first time in His earthly ministry, Jesus began to show His disciples that He must go to Jerusalem, suffer many things from the elders and chief priests and scribes, be killed, and be raised again the third day (v. 21). The scene of joy that a few moments before enveloped this gathering now turned to horror.

If you had been one of the disciples, how would you have responded to the news? Remember, this was the first time Jesus clearly revealed His coming sufferings and death to the apostles. Peter, his heart overflowing with love and devotion for the Master, took Jesus aside and began to rebuke Him saying, "Far be it from You Lord; this shall not happen to You!" Peter was merely voicing the emotion that no doubt was filling the hearts of the other apostles. Again, if you had been present at the scene, you would have commended Peter for his noble gesture of devotion and love. None of the other apostles, and certainly not Peter, was aware of another sinister element in this unfolding drama. But JESUS KNEW. He looked past the love; past the sincere display of emotion; and He saw Satan leading Peter away from the revealed will of God. Such was the occasion for the stinging rebuke, *"Get behind Me, Satan! You are an offense to Me, for you are not mindful of the things of God, but the things of men"* (v. 23). Surely, the disciples were stunned! What they viewed as an expression of love on Peter's part had been, in actuality, a deception of

Satan. Yes, even the emotion of love for Christ, when it stood against the revealed will of God, became sin. For Peter to stand between Jesus and the Cross, regardless of the motivation, was terribly wrong. Only Jesus and the Word of God could detect that kind of spiritual deception. Feelings and emotion and logic were no measurements in a situation like that. Spiritual realities can only be discerned through the Word of God.

Let's zoom some twenty centuries into the future. We find ourselves not in the hills of Caesarea Philippi, but in a rustic setting in the woods of Colorado. We are in the home of a new Christian who just a few weeks earlier had responded to the gospel message we shared. However, tension fills the air. A struggle is taking place for the allegiance of this new Christian. In the room is a mutual friend; but this friend is actually a spiritual adversary at this point, for he is a member of the cult group, the Children of God. He has been in the cult for about two years and is seeking to indoctrinate and unsettle this new believer. This is not the place to go into the doctrines taught by the Children of God cult, but suffice it to say they are heretical.[75]

Conversation rapidly becomes debate, with this new Christian family the prize. We had earlier bathed this situation in prayer, for we knew that on this night there would be a confrontation. As I make a scriptural point, this cultist counters with his own. It is like the game, tug of war—except that it is no game. The future of a young believer and a friend who is caught up in deception hang in the balance. As the emotions begin to build, all of a sudden the cultist almost shouts the following: "To prove that what I am saying is from God, John, your mother is healed right now!" (My mother was at that moment in the hospital recovering from shingles.) At this bold declaration, the new believer who is present literally jumps off the sofa and exclaims, "I FEEL THE POWER OF GOD!" I immediately retort that this is not the power of God. I exhort this brother to remain calm and assure him that God does not display miracles to win a scriptural argument. Yes, He did do miracles to authenticate His messengers of old who were vehicles for new revelation; but not for today when Scripture is complete. Let me hasten to add, however, that the atmosphere in that room is electrifying. You can genuinely feel the presence of something or someone. But it isn't God.

As the drama continued to unfold, I phoned my mother who was in the hospital in another city. As we all gathered around the phone, the cultist kept repeating, "She's healed, she's healed;" and the new believer kept whispering, "I feel the power of God." Now my mother was one of those persons who could be suffering terribly, and yet when asked how she was feeling would respond, "Better." When I asked her how she was feeling, she said, "Better." I went on to ask her how she *really* was feeling. She began to cry and admitted she was in great pain. I consoled her, expressed my love, but did not let her know of the occasion for the call. (Note: Even if my mother had been healed, verses would have been shared to show that the need for confirming signs ceased with the completion of the Scriptures.)

Silence filled the lounge room of that rustic home. The young believer sat slowly and quietly back down on the sofa. The cultist was also silent. Our friendship went back to times before his involvement with the Children of God. He had earlier been partially instrumental in awakening within my own heart a new interest in the Bible. This friend, but spiritual adversary, now walked silently out onto the porch. As I put my hand gently on his shoulder, he began to shake. The night was black in these deep Colorado woods. My friend softly muttered that he was seeing things and then he said almost pathetically, "I'm afraid." He walked slowly down the steps to be alone in the forest near the house. It took that crisis point in his own life to get him to question what he earlier had viewed as being from God. It would take over a year for this friend to break ties with the Children of God movement. However, that night was one of several turning points in his retracing the steps that had led him into deception. Today my friend and the new believer are both vibrant Christians for the Lord.

Am I trying to make a parallel between the Children of God cult and the charismatic movement? No way! The former is composed mainly of deluded souls who are lost; the latter has many vibrant and sincere born again Christians. What I am demonstrating is that the new believer, just like Peter, was not aware of the operation of Satan and the forces of evil in his own life. This is not to suggest that everyone should start looking for a demon under every bush. However, again let it be said that when it comes to discerning spiritual realities, there is only one source that is dependable—the Scriptures. Move away from the Scriptures and you are like a ship cast adrift from the moorings, or a rudderless vessel at the mercy of whatever wind is blowing at the moment. Moreover, for one to seek experiences which he or she cannot absolutely verify from Scripture is to invite deception.

In the early days of my Christian faith, I also experienced the allurements of false teachers and deception. At one point I became enamored of the ministry of Herbert W. Armstrong. He taught with such authority; he quoted the Scriptures with such power; his classy literature brimmed with biblical illustrations and verses. Only personal study of the Scriptures led me out of the labyrinth of deception and revealed that Armstrong was a false prophet, although quite persuasive.

We have seen again and again that the Scriptures stand as the believer's defense against deception. Yet, many saints fail to understand the crucial role which the Scriptures play in assisting one to experience the joy and power of the Spirit-filled life. The following discussion is devoted to those who sincerely seek the victorious Christian life. I do not suggest that I have mastered all of these principles. They stand as the goal for which we all press forward to attain—and this for the glory of the Lord.

THE WORD OF GOD, THE POWER OF GOD, AND ABIDING IN CHRIST

Spiritual power is the possession of every child of God. The very fact that the Holy Spirit indwells believers is a testimony to that power. One does not get more or less of the Holy Spirit—He either indwells or He doesn't (Rom. 8:9, 16). Yet, many believers live powerless lives. Why? Is it because some believers have more "power" than others. Does heaven dispense "power" in measure, in quantities to be discovered by the searching saint? The biblical answer is a strong negative. However, as the child of God seeks the Lord in deeper communion, and as cleansing and surrender accompany this desire, the Spirit's power will become more evident in that life.

Recently I read an interesting account about the sudden loss of power to the tram system in a major city. All the trams had come to a halt. It seems some wires were down at a busy intersection and the circuit which funnelled power from the generators down the lines to the cars was thus broken. The generators did not stop; they continued to produce the power, and there was still sufficient power to run the trams, but the power was not getting through. There was a break in the circuit. So these majestic people-movers stood still. You can almost see the cars all over the city coming to a gliding, gradual halt, as inertia carried them on a little ways after the power was cut.

In much the same way, believers and local churches can glide slowly on, doing their ministry activities without the power of the Holy Spirit. Just as the tram works on the *contact principle,* so must the believer. As long as the tram "abides" in the power source, it moves. If contact is broken, it comes to a halt. Many Christians, charismatics and non-charismatics alike, feel the Christian life works on the *storage battery principle*. What is that? Well, some think if they have their devotional time in the early morning that that will be enough to spiritually carry them through the day. They can draw from that time throughout the day, much like a car would draw from a battery throughout a day's normal operation.

A quiet time or devotional time is essential. It helps us to begin the day with our hearts and minds abiding in Christ. However, much more is needed if one is to successfully negotiate the circumstances, events, people, and temptations that confront the Christian in an average day. Many charismatics feel they must have a vision, a dream, a word of knowledge, a prayer in tongues, a prophecy, or a healing to confirm their Spirit-filled walk with Christ. Rather than a moment-by-moment drawing from the Lord, an expectation develops of having to draw from one experience enough to carry them through to another. The Lord never intended His children to employ such dynamics to assist in living a fulfilled Christian life. *Jesus insisted upon the contact principle.* In the same way that the tram must constantly keep in contact with the power lines, so the believer must constantly be in contact with Christ. Jesus used the term *abide* to illustrate this principle and underscored the Scriptures as an essential element in the abiding process:

> If you *abide in My word*, you are My disciples indeed. And you shall know the truth, and the truth shall make you free (John 8:31, 32; italics mine).

> Abide in Me, and I in you. As the branch cannot bear fruit of itself, unless it abides in the vine, neither can you, unless you abide in Me. I am the vine, you are the branches. He who abides in Me, and I in him, bears much fruit; for without Me you can do nothing. . . . If you abide in Me, and *My words abide in you*, you will ask what you desire, and it shall be done for you (John 15:4, 5, 7; italics mine).

Note how the Apostle John, writing under the inspiration of the Holy Spirit, also stresses this concept of abiding and its tie to the Scriptures:

> Now he who keeps His *commandments abides in Him*, and He in him. And by this we know that He abides in us, by the Spirit whom He has given us (1 John 3:24; italics mine).

People often speak of abiding in Christ, but when asked to

practically explain how this is done, many Christians are at a loss of words. What is involved in abiding in Christ? How is one sure from moment to moment whether he or she is abiding in the Lord? Allow me to become a bit more personal. "Are you abiding in Christ right this moment? Are you sure? How do you know?" Pressing the issues a bit further: "Are you filled with the Spirit of God right now? Are you sure? How do you know?" The Lord would not instruct believers to "abide" or to be "filled" and then fail to give them some measurement by which to know of their spiritual standing at any given moment.

The power of the Holy Spirit, the Word of God, and abiding in Christ are all intertwined. Did you note the preeminence which Jesus gave to the Word of God when He was talking about abiding? You cannot be a disciple of Christ unless you abide in His Word; you cannot abide in Christ unless His words abide in you; and a guide to abiding is your relationship to the commands of Scripture at any given point. If there is any disobedience in the life, you are not abiding in Christ. You may be saved and on your way to heaven, but contact is broken. *The Word of God is the measure and the dynamic of our abiding—and thus the Spirit-filled life. Satan knows that, and he will do everything he can to break the believer's dependency on the Word of God.*

THE MIND OF CHRIST: THE BELIEVER'S POSSESSION

One of the most beautiful passages in Scripture is found in 1 Corinthians 2:16, "'For who has known the mind of the Lord that he may instruct Him?' But we have the mind of Christ." What a marvellous truth! We have the very mind of Christ! But how? And what conditions if any must be met in order for the mind of Christ to be operative in our lives?

First of all we have the mind of Christ through the inward operation of the Holy Spirit (cf. 2 Cor. 3:18; Col. 1:27; Rom. 8:5-11; Gal. 2:20). Secondly, we have the mind of Christ through the Word of God—Jesus is the Word Incarnate and the Word of God is one of His titles (cf. Jn. 1:1-3, 14; Rev. 19:13). Paul pled with the Philippian brethren to be in harmony with the mind of Christ and then proceeded to reveal that mind through Scripture (Phil. 2:5-11).

It is essential for the Christian to understand that with the heart one trusts in Christ unto salvation; with the will one obeys the Lord; and with the mind one abides in Christ.[76] Obviously, the heart and will and mind are not compartmentalized solely into these separate functions. They all three work together in the life of the believer and often intertwine or overlap in their exercise. However, Scripture does attribute a primary function to each. Moreover, our will to obey our Lord is only as strong as our abiding; and our dependence upon the written Word of God is essential in living the Spirit-filled life. Scripture teaches these principles in many passages, but the following will suffice:

Heart - Trust

. . . If you confess with your mouth the Lord Jesus and believe in your heart that God has raised Him from the dead, you will be saved. For with the heart one believes to righteousness, and with the mouth confession is made to salvation (Rom. 10:9, 10).

Will - Obey

. . . For it is God who works in you both to will and to do for His good pleasure (Phil. 2:13; cf. Rom. 6:10-14; Heb. 13:20-21).

Mind - Abide

And do not be conformed to this world, but be transformed by the renewing of your mind, that you may prove what is that good and acceptable and perfect will of God (Rom. 12:2).

For the weapons of our warfare are not carnal but mighty in God for pulling down strongholds, casting down arguments and every high thing that exalts itself against the knowledge of God, bringing *every thought into captivity to the obedience of Christ* . . . (2 Cor. 10:4, 5; italics mine).

Finally, brethren, whatever things are true, whatever things are noble, whatever things are just, whatever things are pure, whatever things are lovely, whatever things are of good report, if there is any virtue and if there is anything praiseworthy—meditate on these things (Phil. 4:8).

When Scripture speaks of the "heart," the idea is the totality of the person—intellect, will, affections, and loyalties. The list is endless. The "will" refers to the determinative aspect of people to move beyond the intellect and the affections into the realm of action and commitment. While references to the "mind" in Scripture often embrace broader concerns than mere cognitive functions, it is the thought processes in view in the aforementioned Scriptures. Indeed, as a man "thinks in his heart, so is he" (Prov. 23:7). Thus, the Lord urges time and time again that believers meditate upon the Word of God; that believers "renew their minds"; that believers bring every thought into captivity, conforming them to the knowledge of God. The link between *abiding with the mind* and Scripture is well attested in the Old Testament as well:

> This Book of the Law shall not depart from your mouth, but you shall meditate in it day and night, that you may observe to do according to all that is written in it. For then you will make your way prosperous, and then you will have good success (Josh. 1:8).

> . . . His delight is in the Law of the LORD, and in His law he meditates day and night. He shall be like a tree planted by the rivers of water, that brings forth its fruit in its season, whose leaf also shall not wither; and whatever he does shall prosper (Ps. 1;2, 3).

> Oh, how I love Your law! It is my meditation all the day (Ps. 119:97).

In view of all the previous Scriptures, one sees that this "abiding" is no simple attainment. Christ placed equal emphasis on a believer's abiding in Him and the Scriptures abiding in the believer (Jn. 15:7). The Psalmist spoke of meditating on the Word of God "day and night." And one of the greatest challenges is given to believers when the Word of God instructs us to bring "every thought" into conformity with the revealed will of God. Yes, *every thought*! Moreover, the context of that exhortation was one dealing with spiritual warfare.

To bring *every thought* into captivity to Christ is a lifelong goal that awaits all Christians every day of their earthly existence—indeed, every moment. And the Word of God is the key to that process. Why? Because it is the Word of God that is a discerner of the thoughts (Heb. 4:12). Remember: "The word of God is living and powerful, and sharper than any two-edged sword, piercing even to the division of soul and spirit, and of joints and marrow; and is a discerner of the thoughts and intents of the heart" (Heb. 4:12). The only way any believer can be sure that his or her contact with Christ is unbroken is to be continually subjecting one's entire life to Scripture. That is the measure of one's abiding. Such requires a conscious vigilance over even the expression of love to the Lord—as Peter's case proves. All of this makes the Spirit-filled life (or the life abiding in Christ) a highly disciplined life, reached only through struggle with the forces of hell itself. This requires spiritual focus.

Some would suggest that the "abiding" and the "Spirit-filled life" are attained by merely "going with the flow" or "letting go and letting God have His way." According to some, the Spirit moves upon you; you experience a life-changing endument of power, and the Christian life becomes a spiritual haven with one high after the other. If some charismatics were writing their version of *Pilgrim's Progress*, Pilgrim's pathway to blessing would have been shortened dramatically. There would be no struggling with the Slough of Despond, By-path Meadow, Doubting Castle, or Vanity Fair; no caution to be exercised with Lady Feigning or Mr. Worldly Wiseman. The only thing Pilgrim would really need in order to make it safely to the Celestial City would be a few quick lessons in "fourth dimensional thinking," "ministries of deliverance," or "power prayer."

Scripture, however, upholds Bunyan's great classic. Words like "warfare," "pressing on," "fight," "endure," "yield not," "work out," and "run the race" are used in regard to Christian progress in this life (cf. Phil. 2:12, 13; Rom. 6:1-14; 2 Tim. 2:3-7). We are exhorted to take up the cross *daily* (Luke 9:23). And throughout the Christian walk, the Sword of the Spirit is needed in order to bring every thought into captivity and to the obedience of Christ. Remember, once again, it was Jesus who said if you were going to abide in Him, His words would have to abide in you. Are you prepared for that kind of commitment to spiritual growth, for that kind of struggle?

The problem is that many Christians never use the Sword of the Spirit in actual spiritual combat. May I ask you another question: When was the last time you can remember quoting Scripture to overcome temptation, to cast down thoughts which stood against the revealed will of God? If you cannot recall having used the Scripture in such fashion of late, then there are only three possible conclusions: (1) you haven't been tempted—which is highly unlikely if you are a Christian; or (2) you are not sensitive to temptation and lack spiritual discernment; or (3) you have failed to follow the example of Christ in Matthew 4 when He was confronted with temptation. What did He do? He quoted Scripture. He quoted it immediately upon recognition of temptation; and He quoted an appropriate Scripture to meet the specific temptation. Indeed, one can measure his or her spiritual maturity by how often the Scriptures are employed to combat spiritual temptation in the personal life.

Many Christians will spend hours in Christian book stores looking for a book that will unlock the secret to victorious Christian living. Believers are hungry today to experience the power of God in their lives. If they cannot find the answer in a book, they will seek it in an experience. All the while, the truths are there in the Bible. It is sad, but true, that the majority of Christians leave the Sword of the Spirit sheathed. It is never used in spiritual conflict; rather, it is only used to answer this or that question, or remains only as a source of comfort and inspiration.

The Bible does not say, "Your Word have I read in my devotional times that I might not sin against You;" it does not say, "Your Word have I carried to church or to the Bible college classroom that I might not sin against You." No, the Scriptures declare: "Your Word have I hid in my heart that I might not sin against You" (Ps. 119:11). When the believer seeks to so internalize the Scriptures that emotions, desires, thoughts, priorities, and motives all come under its scrutiny, then that believer has become spiritually sensitive to maintaining unbroken communion with the Lord. Anything which tries to exalt itself against the revealed will of God will be discerned and cast down. Then and only then does the power of the Spirit become the pattern of an individual's life; then and only then does the mind of Christ become a reality in daily experience.

I do not wish to give the impression that I think I have "arrived." Nor do I wish to give the impression that using the Sword of the Spirit, the Word of God, is the only means to spiritual victory. I am stressing that such is one aspect of a multifaceted approach to victorious Christian living. Often it is the neglected aspect. Certainly prayer, songs of praise, meditation and reflection, and the nurturing of the love of the Lord in our hearts all serve to strengthen us in our heavenly pilgrimage.

For the Christian, the road to perfection extends to the other side of glory. The race will only be finished when we stand in the presence of Jesus (Heb. 12:1, 2). Paul well knew this truth and exhorted believers to press on until the day when the course was completed (Phil. 3:10-21). While none of us has arrived, while none of can say we have mastered all that needs to be done in the Christian life, we can draw from some powerful scriptural principles to help us on our way.

FROM "SPRING CLEANING" TO ABIDING

How is one Spirit-filled in the first place? The Holy Spirit will never fill an unclean vessel. Therefore the believer must welcome the light of the Spirit into the dark recesses of the heart. Only God can know the true condition of our hearts. Our estimation of sin is so superficial. The parallel may be made with what some call "spring cleaning."

For spring cleaning to take place, one must recognize the need; then, one must commit a certain amount of time to do a thorough job of getting the house in order. One has to be prepared to open all the closets, all the drawers, and investigate neglected areas. There will be a few surprises along the way as one discovers forgotten items; choices will have to be made on what to keep and what to throw out; and finally, after the cleaning is complete, a continued vigilance must be maintained, lest the clutter gathers again and one has to go through the entire process. A similar process is involved in one being filled with the Spirit. Scripture commands believers to be filled with the Spirit (Eph. 5:18). That should serve as motivation enough for believers to have a consuming desire for this reality in their lives. Confession of sin, a willingness to yield to the things of God, and a willingness to cast out the things that offend all must precede one's appeal to the Lord for filling.

Once a believer makes a conscious commitment to seek the Lord's filling, he opens himself up to the Spirit's convicting power. As sin is revealed, one confesses this to the Lord and on the promise of 1 John 1:5-9 stands clean before God. One is then able to claim the Spirit's filling on the basis of Galatians 3:3-5, Ephesians 5:18, and 1 John 5:14, 15. One is filled in the same manner as one is saved: recognition of sin and one's spiritual need; confession and repentance; appeal to the grace, the power, and promises of God; and then by faith in the Lord and His Word resting in Christ. Since we are commanded to be filled with the Spirit (Eph. 5:18), we know that we are praying in accordance with God's will when we claim the Spirit's filling (1 John 5:14, 15).

Yes, but didn't the apostles have to be filled again after Pentecost (cf. Acts 2 with 4:29-31)? Certainly. And this brings one to THE great challenge in the Christian life. You see the goal of the Christian life is not to gain the Spirit-filled experience; rather, THE GOAL IS TO REMAIN SPIRIT-FILLED. That should be the normal Christian life. That is why abiding is so crucial. The believer is to move from "spring cleaning" and the Spirit-filled life to a firm commitment to maintain such. We have seen that the Scriptures play a major role in this abiding process. As one lives out an ordinary day, meditating upon the Word and the Lord, seeking to bring every thought into captivity to Christ, filtering every experience through the Word, the Spirit has free reign in the heart and communion with the Lord is vibrant. There will be struggles to maintain this unbroken communion; but, when there are failures, communion can be restored through confession and appropriation of the promises of God.

My wife, Emma, is such a joy and blessing in my life. Throughout twenty-four years of marriage she has been a continual source of support, encouragement, and inspiration. Excuse me for getting a bit sappy, but I want to illustrate some of the above points. There are times when I am away on speaking engagements. On such occasions, I will always find a note from Emma tucked away somewhere. It may be in my Bible; sometimes it is placed in a suitcase—she packs it so I will be sure to find it. Even though Emma is not present with me on these occasions, when I open the note and read the words, there is communion. I know those words are an extension of her being. My intellect, my emotion, and my will all come into play as I read expressions of love. My own love is freshly activated, and even though she is not physically present, we are each abiding with the other. I realize this happens even without the notes—just through reflection or praying for one another. However, the words scribbled on a note act as a catalyst to strengthen communion.

In much the same way, our Lord has left us with His love letter—the Scriptures. In 2 Peter 1:2-4, the Scriptures testify that through the knowledge of Christ we have "all things that pertain to life and godliness." As we internalize the Word of God and as we meditate on it throughout the day and night, our abiding is confirmed and our life enriched.

It is through the Word of God that we are born again (John 6:63; Phil. 2:16); it is through the Word of God that we are made clean (Ps. 119:9; Eph. 5:25-27); it is through the Word of God that we discern thoughts and test spiritual realities (2 Tim. 3:16; James 1:22-25; Eph. 6:17; 1 John 4:1); and it is through the Word of God that we maintain our abiding in Christ and the Spirit-filled life (John 8:31-32; John 15:5-7). Any influence which tries to supplant dependency upon the Word of God is to be rejected; any influence which undermines, dilutes, or contradicts biblical revelation is to be cast down.

THE SCRIPTURES: OUR
SPIRITUAL THERMOMETER

When one speaks of the Spirit-filled life or abiding in Christ, one usually thinks of the fruit of the Spirit. The fruit of the Spirit is the evidence of a consecrated walk and one's communion with the Lord. Moreover, Scripture clearly sets forth what constitutes the fruit of the Spirit:

> But the fruit of the Spirit is love, joy, peace, longsuffering, kindness, goodness,
> faithfulness, gentleness, self-control. Against such there is no law. And those
> who are Christ's have crucified the flesh with its passions and desires. If we
> live in the Spirit, let us also walk in the Spirit (Gal. 5:22-25).

Many believers fail to see in these verses a very practical tool which will assist them in living the Christian life. This description of the fruit of the Spirit is not recorded to satisfy our curiosity; but rather, it is recorded as a guide to our living in the Spirit.

In the early days of my Christian life, when I read Galatians 5:22, I would often think: "What a beautiful verse. Those are the traits that I would so desire to be present in my life. Let's see . . . most of the fruit is present in my life. Well, I guess if seven out of nine manifestations are present, I'm doing pretty well." Then one day it dawned upon my heart, that if ALL aspects of the fruit of the Spirit were not operative in my life at any given moment, I WAS NOT SPIRIT-FILLED! Who was I kidding! It is not a question of majority vote. Again, either all nine aspects of the fruit of the Spirit are operative or I'm not Spirit-filled.

When believers come to view Galatians 5:22 as a very practical checklist to the Spirit-filled life, great strides are taken in the abiding process. If during the course of a day I find that I lack peace, or gentleness; if at some point I am unkind or impatient; then that is a signal to my heart that I am not filled. I do not have the "mind of Christ" as a reality in my life at that moment; for if I did, I would respond to every situation and every person in a Christ-like manner. At the very moment when I recognize my deficiency, I need to confess my sin (i.e., of not being filled, since such is a command of God). Then claiming the promises outlined in the preceding paragraphs, I am to reestablish full contact and communion with the Lord. Who gets the credit for all this? The Lord! He is the One who gives the desire, the measure, and the power for abiding (cf. Phil. 2:12, 13; Heb. 13:20, 21).

More than a little discussion has been devoted to demonstrating the dynamic power of the Scriptures in living the Christian life. Remember that Satan has countered the Word of God from the Garden of Eden. He knows the power of the Word of God. He knows that Scripture is essential for salvation, sanctification, security, and spiritual discernment. He knows Scripture is the Sword of Spirit when used by soldiers of the faith. Yet, he does not hesitate to quote Scripture to entice one into temptation—as evidenced in the temptation of Jesus; he does not hesitate to pervert or confuse the meaning of Scripture—as evidenced in the proliferation of false cults and heresies within Christendom. He uses human emotion to counter the revealed will of God—as evidenced in Peter's blunder in misusing the emotion of love to keep Jesus from the Cross. You had better believe that Satan will do anything to woo a believer away from allegiance and submission to the Word of God. And that brings us to the essential question which forms the heading of this chapter.

THE TREACHEROUS TRADE-OFF

Testimony after testimony can be documented of believers whose personal lives have been "enriched" by the charismatic experience. Many assert that through the tongues experience, spontaneous prophecy, laughing in the Spirit, visions, words of knowledge, ministries of deliverance (i.e., casting out demons), and other sign gifts, their lives have grown closer to God. A resurgence of interest in the Bible takes place; prayer becomes an invigorating experience; and a new-found boldness accompanies one's witness for Christ. To return to the main question: How could such positive spiritual effects flow from phenomena that is not God-given? Surely the positive results of these experiences point to a divine Source! Or do they?

Satan is not afraid of prayer, Bible study, or bold witness. That statement may shock some, but it is true. The "god of this age," the "prince of the power of the air," smiles every time people kneel and offer prayers that are contrary to the Word of God. While you read these words, pagan prayers are being lifted to this false god all over this planet. Even in worship services in Christian churches, liturgical prayers that reach no higher than the ceiling are pleasing to the god of this age. And what of Bible study? Satan loves Bible study. The numerous cults from Mormons, to Jehovah's Witnesses, to Christadelphians, to the Children of God, to the Way International all study the Bible diligently. And as far as witnessing goes, these aforementioned cults are among the most bold in their proclamation. Even in Adelaide, the heretical Adelaide Revival Centre is a perfect example of misplaced zeal. This group teaches that water baptism and speaking in tongues are essential to salvation. Although trapped in a false gospel, they give themselves heartily to prayer, Bible study, and witness. Satan does not fear such a group—many of whom are sincere, wonderful people. *The only time Satan is fearful of prayer and Bible study and bold witness is when such is done in accordance with the will of God—in spirit and in truth.*

The Gospels record many confrontations between Jesus and the religious rulers of Israel. These rulers had access to the Scriptures; they prayed; they witnessed; they claimed to represent the one true God. Yet, all of these activities were condemned by Christ:

Their Prayers

And when you pray, you shall not be like the hypocrites. For they love to pray standing in the synagogues and on the corners of the streets, that they may be seen by men. Assuredly, I say to you, they have their reward. . . . But when you pray, do not use vain repetitions as the heathen do. For they think that they will be heard for their many words (Matt 6:5, 7).

Their Bible Study

You search the Scriptures, for in them you think you have eternal life; and these are they which testify of Me (John 5:39; cf. Matt. 22:23-33).

Their Witness

Woe to you, scribes and Pharisees, hypocrites! For you travel land and sea to win one proselyte, and when he is won, you make him twice as much a son of hell as yourselves (Matt. 23:15).

Again, Satan is not afraid of prayer, Bible study, or bold witness when they foster error and advance his own kingdom. Peter also warned of those who twist the Scriptures to fit their own prejudices and passions:

Therefore, beloved, looking forward to these things, be diligent to be found by Him in peace, without spot and blameless; and account that the long-suffering of our Lord is salvation—as also our beloved brother Paul, according to the wisdom given to him, has written to you, as also in all his epistles, speaking in them of these things, in which are some things hard to understand, which *those who are untaught and unstable twist to their own destruction, as they do also the rest of the Scriptures* (2 Pet. 3:14-16; italics mine).

Now when it comes to prayer, Bible study, and witness that reflect the will of God, these spiritual exercises do shake the foundations of hell. Moreover, Scripture indicates that these exercises take place in the context of spiritual warfare and conflict. Indeed, Satan has always opposed the true exercise of these spiritual privileges.

We have already noted that from the beginning of man's history on this planet, Satan has fought against the Word of God (Gen. 3:1). The very fact that the Word of God is called the Sword of the Spirit (Eph. 6:17) indicates there is spiritual conflict that surrounds its use and interpretation—Matthew 4 confirms this also. In the area of prayer, Daniel 10 is most instructive.

Daniel had been praying to the Lord over the future of Israel. From the moment he began to pray, his words were received in heaven. However, an angel sent from God was held up for three weeks in delivering the answered prayer to Daniel. What interfered with the angel's divine mission? Demonic forces! Read the scriptural account:

> And he said to me, "O Daniel, man greatly beloved, understand the words that I speak to you, and stand upright, for I have now been sent to you." While he was speaking this word to me, I stood trembling. Then he said to me, "Do not fear, Daniel, for from the first day that you set your heart to understand, and to humble yourself before your God, your words were heard; and I have come because of your words. But the prince of the kingdom of Persia withstood me twenty-one days; and behold, Michael, one of the chief princes, came to help me, for I had been left alone there with the kings of Persia. Now I have come to make you understand what will happen to your people in the latter days, for the vision refers to many days yet to come (Dan. 10:11-14).

When the angel finished delivering his message, he went on to tell Daniel: "Do you know why I have come to you? And now I must return to fight with the prince of Persia; and when I have gone forth, indeed the prince of Greece will come. But I will tell you what is noted in the Scripture of Truth" (Dan. 10:20, 21).

In this dramatic account, Scripture pulls back the veil to show us the spiritual opposition to genuine prayer and use of the Word of God. There is ample evidence as well, that in the area of witness and spreading the gospel, Satan stands as an adversary. When Jesus revealed His commission to Saul on the Damascus Road, our Lord underscored the spiritual conflict that would occasion the advance of the gospel: "I will deliver you from the Jewish people, as well as from the Gentiles, to whom I now send you, to open their eyes, and to turn them from darkness to light, and from the power of Satan to God, that they may receive forgiveness of sins and an inheritance among those who are sanctified by faith in Me" (Acts 26:17, 18). There is also the warning of 1 Peter 5:8,

"Be sober, be vigilant; because your adversary the devil walks about like a roaring lion, seeking whom he may devour." So in summary, while Satan and his forces are not afraid of prayer, Bible study, and bold witness when such fails to conform to Scripture, he does oppose these genuine exercises or privileges when they are done in "spirit and in truth."

So what is the "treacherous trade-off?" Any military strategist knows that an enemy will often give up ground to gain a greater victory. From the previous discussion, we noted the scriptural evidence that Satan opposes the genuine exercise of prayer, Scripture, and witness for the Lord Jesus Christ. He is most willing to pull back opposition on these fronts, to allow the believer to advance, if he can woo the believer into the realm of experiential "truth" over against propositional truth. If opposition to Bible study, prayer, and witness is removed, the believer will experience advances in these areas. The danger is that the believer will attribute these advances to the tongues experience or to some of the other experiential aspects of the charismatic movement. By giving some ground, the Adversary leads many believers into a greater deception. Support is gained for non-scriptural practices, confusion increases, and biblical authority is weakened.

There is another consideration. The believer who accepts the sign gifts and revelatory gifts, in essence, replaces biblical truth and authority with experiential authority. Moreover, such experiential concerns now color the spiritual exercises of prayer, Bible study, and witness. Instead of objective comparisons of Scripture with Scripture, the believer tends to view Scripture through the eyes of the experience. Interpretation of verses become heavily weighted toward vindicating this or that experience. Prayer becomes oriented to supporting the sign and revelatory gifts, and desiring these for others. The trade-off steals the true substance and focus of prayer, impoverishes the individual, and the church suffers.

While the believer may witness for Christ and share a genuine message of the gospel, such is also colored by testimony to the signs and revelatory gifts. People are genuinely saved and come into the kingdom; however, the deception grows as more and more accept the signs and wonders message. The basis for Christian fellowship no longer becomes the Word of God, but rather the common ground of experience. That is why Roman Catholics, liberal Protestants, heretics, and so-called evangelicals come together in charismatic fellowship—which is the basis for ecumenical unity. Ultimately, the very essence of the gospel is obscured or lost. The "narrow way" becomes the "broad way that leads to destruction." Deception brings forth damnation.

WE ARE ONE IN THE SPIRIT?

When I received the Lord Jesus Christ as my Savior, I knew He was leading me into full-time Christian service. I was finishing my last year in pre-law studies at a major university in the United States when I came to Christ. Putting aside law school, I began to seek theological studies. My own pastor informed me that the seminary at that particular university was renowned for its biblical and theological studies. Thus application and acceptance soon followed.

I entered seminary as a young Christian, only a few months old in the Lord. Soon, however, I found myself being indoctrinated in German rationalism. The writings of Bultmann, Brunner, Barth, and others became my constant companions. The seminary teachers ridiculed the Scriptures and denied the miracles of the Bible. As I talked with fellow students, I found that many of these did not believe in the deity of Christ, the inerrancy of Scripture, and some were not even sure of the existence of God or an afterlife. When I asked them, "What are you going to preach if you do not accept these basic truths?" they would reply, "We can preach the example of Jesus for we firmly believe that His teachings will bring about a better world?" The longer I stayed in that seminary the more burdened I became.

Gradually my eyes were opened to see that these fine, upstanding clergymen and teachers were lost and on their way to hell. They were the blind leading the blind. Many times they used the language of evangelical and fundamental Christianity, but like the classic political tale of deception, *Animal Farm*, they meant something entirely different.[77] They would speak in glowing terms of learning about the "historical Jesus." Oh, it sounded fine until you learned that they did not accept the Gospel accounts of Scripture as historical fact. For them, the Gospel accounts were mere myths; stories made up by a primitive and superstitious society. To find the "true Jesus" or the "real facts," one had to dig and compare and theorize to discern what really happened.

I'll never forget the first semester social for students and faculty. At the close, we all were instructed to join hands and sing the song, "We Are One in the Spirit, We Are One in the Lord." As I grasped the hands of those on either side, and joined in with the singing, a sense of uneasiness and sickness gripped my soul. My eyes fell upon the professor who just a few days before cursed and used God's name in vain; to my right was another teacher who had denied the miracle of the Exodus and Red

Sea crossing. As my eyes scanned the room, I saw the students who did not believe the Bible, or the deity of Christ, or the Resurrection. I saw those who believed in salvation by works rather than by faith in the shed blood of the Lamb. And there I was, a new Christian, grasping hands in fellowship with these and singing, "we are one in the Spirit, we are one in the Lord." Something was wrong.

Even though my evangelical pastor had recommended the school saying, "It will stretch you academically and strengthen your faith," I knew this was a charade. No, it was more serious than that. It was a blasphemous affront to a holy and righteous God. That was a turning point for my own heart. Soon I left that school amidst cries from the faculty that I was too narrow. Praise God, truth by definition is narrow! But as I look back, I thank the Lord for letting me see the faces of deception. The same type of fellowship that was practiced that evening—fellowship on the basis of experiential affinity, rather than truth—is the same type of fellowship being pushed in many charismatic circles today. When heretic and lost clergymen can grasp hands with true believers, giving praise to God, and glorying in a common experience, the Spirit of God must be greatly grieved.

Satan has everything to gain, and nothing to lose in allowing "positive" effects and advances to accompany charismatic phenomena in a believer's life. The foundation for a treacherous trade-off is being laid in the life of the believer. As spiritual opposition to prayer, Bible study, and witness is being called off, the believer is induced to give credit of his spiritual advance to the charismatic experience. Instead of giving credit to the Person of the Holy Spirit for all genuine advances in the spiritual life, the believer glorifies the experience itself. The assumption is made that the experience brought forth the advance in spiritual matters. *Impressions, hunches, intuition, signs, and new revelation become the focus of the Christian instead of moment-by-moment dependence upon Scripture. Soon, even the lines of Christian fellowship are determined by "common experiences" rather than biblical truth. It is a fine line, but what a great deception. Again, Satan is willing to give ground, to gain a greater advantage.*

Is there any biblical proof that Satan operates this way? Most assuredly! I have already given scriptural examples of the Pharisees' commitment to prayer, Bible study, and witness. Yet, all three spiritual exercises met with the rebuke of Jesus. Why? Because they were oriented away from the truth. Yes, but some may say, "These were unsaved people; they were deluded by their bent toward legalism and their desire to maintain the people in bondage. You cannot use their experience to say that the Lord would allow such deception in believers." In response, I would remind the reader of Peter's emotional outburst of love which brought the greatest rebuke by Jesus (cf. Matt. 16:21ff.). Satan helped induce this expression of loyalty to Christ, but Peter didn't even know what was happening. What seemed like a positive expression of love was actually colored by the designs of the devil. And it brought forth a stern rebuke from Christ. Should Peter have known better? Most definitely, because just prior to his outburst, Jesus revealed the plan and purposes of God to the disciples. He must go to the Cross!

There are other biblical examples of Satan willing to give spiritual ground in order to gain spiritual advantages. What about his offer of the kingdoms of the world to Jesus in exchange for worship from the Lord (Matt. 4:8-10)? That stands of one of the greatest attempts at spiritual treachery. Then, too, there is the account of the possessed girl in Acts 16:16-18. This girl followed Paul around declaring, "These men are the servants of the Most High God, who proclaim to us the way of salvation" (v. 17). Was this girl proclaiming the truth? Most assuredly! Was she announcing that salvation was being proclaimed through the Apostle Paul? Yes! Satan was willing to have one of his spirits prompt the proclamation of the truth so that the gospel could be connected to an occultic source. Paul recognized the danger and thus commanded the spirit to come out of the girl (v. 18). Indeed, there is ample biblical proof that when it comes to spiritual realities, treacherous trade-offs are orchestrated and presented to believers. Only the Scripture can assist the believer in discerning the forces at work in any given situation. While it is gloriously truth that "He who is in you is greater than he who is in the world" (1 John. 4:4), the believer has the choice of glorifying God by submitting to Scripture or going with the leading of emotion and human intuition.

THE LONGING FOR GOD'S
POWER TO BE UNLEASHED

As Western Christianity settles into and absorbs the pagan world system, the hearts of many Christians cry out for revival. This is the way it should be. If ever believers needed to go to their knees and seek God's face, it is today. The principles embodied in God's exhortation to Israel continue to apply to Christians worldwide.

If My people who are called by My name will humble themselves, and pray and seek My face, and turn from their wicked ways, then I will hear from heaven, and will forgive their sin and heal their land (2 Chron. 7:14).

But are we prepared for the kind of revival that would create such a work in the hearts of believers that we would indeed be viewed as separate from the world? Are we prepared for the themes of holiness, sanctification, separation, and commitment to once again grip the pulpits of our churches? Do we dare challenge those who would "market" Christianity and truth at any price?

In many churches, the lighthouse has been replaced by a weather vane—instead of lighting the way in the darkness, churches merely turn with the whims of society. They follow whatever wind is blowing at the time. Indeed, where the cry of eagles was once heard from pulpits across the land, one hears only the peep of rabbits or a brood of quails gathering for afternoon tea. Such will not do for this crucial hour in our history.

There will always be forces to fill the vacuum created by squandered privilege or opportunity. When churches failed to preach the doctrine of the Second Coming of Christ, the cults were ready to advance. And so they did, from the mid-to-late nineteenth century until today. The Jehovah's Witnesses, Mormons, Armstrong's Worldwide Church of God, Children of God, and a host of others seized the opportunity and invaded Christian congregations to gain their converts. Now, as we approach the end of the twentieth century, Christianity is reaping its own neglect.

There is a vacuum in evangelical and fundamentalist circles today. Maybe it has been occasioned partly by the up-market stance and acceptance which the world has now accorded these groups. Maybe it is because churches have neglected preaching on the Holy Spirit, sanctification, the call to holiness, the Spirit-filled life, the gifts of the Spirit. No longer are evangelicals and fundamentalists on the defensive; but neither are they on the spiritual offensive. They once were the "movers and the shakers" of this generation of Christianity. Yet, in the midst of our disintegrating culture, many wonder: "What is being moved, and what is being shaken?"

For some reason, the Cross and the gospel are being wrapped and marketed in tinsel. They are no longer an offense to a degenerate world. Self-actualization and awareness, human potential, and personal quests for "power" have replaced concern for sin, condemnation, hell, salvation, holiness, and genuine revival. Christianity has been packaged and sold with *Fun and Excitement!* labels splashed all over the wrapping. Indeed, Christianity seems to be throwing a party and even those who choose to deny the Scriptures have a part in leading the program. The real substance of our faith lies hidden beneath the shallow jargon and frills. Yes, true Christianity DOES bring joy, and happiness, and fun, and excitement; but there is the flip side also—the daily challenge of taking up the cross, the warfare, the struggles, and the pressing on. Conversely, those who ardently defend the essentials of the faith often rest in their doctrinal purity while carnality abounds. Forms of godliness replace vibrant love and submission to the Savior.

So what is filling this vacuum? Counterfeit revival, self-induced spiritism, and unscriptural practices that come in the name of the Holy Spirit. The Lord is working even in the midst of this development, for He has never had a perfect church on this side of glory. He still works primarily in the midst of those who are "poor in spirit" and thirst after the things of God. Yet, such does not relieve the church of the responsibility of purging foreign elements from its heart.

There is a fine line across the heart of believers when it comes to longing for a display of God's power. If the desire is for God's power to be active in one's life so others may be reached for the kingdom, then such is in line with Scripture. If the desire for revival springs from prayers that the Lord's name may be revered throughout one's community, and indeed the world, then such is a noble desire. However, if the quest for power is primarily for personal gain, for personal edification, for personal acceptance with similar peer groups, then one joins the ranks of Eve (Gen. 3:6) and Simon (Acts 8:18, 19). And such stands under the condemnation of God. This latter motivation runs through the hearts of many today who seek the sign and revelatory gifts. Many are wanting short cuts to sanctification and the Spirit-filled life; and many are finding cheap substitutes that do not conform to Scripture. Be careful to follow the instruction of Proverbs 4:23, "Keep your heart with all diligence, for out of it spring the issues of life."

SIGNS, MIRACLES, AND REVIVAL: ALWAYS HAND IN HAND?

Is such always the case? Does the presence of signs, wonders, and revelatory gifts in the midst of believers mean that hearts are right? We have already seen that much of what is called the work of God is not that at all. Yet, our God is working among believers today through miracles, healings, and movements of His Spirit. We do not deny this, but stress that such comes as a sovereign act of God or as a result of corporate prayer, not the personal gifts of individuals dispensing to the needy. But again, does the presence of the miraculous mean God's people are what they should be?

Just take a journey back to the time when Israel was experiencing deliverance from Egypt. If any group of people were in a high-powered Bible seminar, they were! They saw the power of God displayed as few people on earth have seen it. A number of their group actually "saw" God and ate before Him (Exod. 24:9-11). The nation heard His voice and witnessed His majesty (Exod. 19). They witnessed the glory cloud, the parting of the Red Sea, the manna, the water from the rock, and supernatural victory over enemies. You would have thought with all that exposure to the one true God, the hearts of the Israelites would have been bursting with adoration and devotion for the Lord. Not so! Scripture records the following evaluation:

> Nevertheless they flattered Him with their mouth, and they lied to Him with their tongue; for their heart was not steadfast with Him, nor were they faithful in His covenant. . . . How often they provoked Him in the wilderness, and grieved Him in the desert! Yes, again and again they tempted God, and limited the Holy One of Israel (Ps. 78:36, 37, 40, 41).

With all that exposure to God, to His presence, to His revelation, and to His miracles, the hearts of the people were still far from Him. They honored the Lord with their mouths, but their hearts were full of sin and unbelief. You see the same mistake can be made today. Some may think because there is talk of miraculous signs and miracles that such automatically means they are in the presence of revival. Not so. All experiences and all movements must be filtered through Scripture to see if God is really at work. And even then, one must not assume that because God is at work that hearts are abiding in His power.

CENTER STAGE: THE HOLY SPIRIT?

Error always arises when a vacuum is created by neglected truth. As already noted, many evangelical and fundamental churches failed throughout the years to properly present the ministry of the Holy Spirit. Maybe this default occurred because we became smug in the growing respectability accorded to us by the world; maybe, knowledge of the doctrine and ministry of the Holy Spirit became assumed because of the ever increasing list of converts on membership rolls— after all, we could boast that while liberal churches and denominations were losing their members, we were growing; maybe, we just felt at ease in our doctrinal correctness regarding the Word of God and in our various checklists of what constituted a "faithful" and valuable worker for the kingdom. Whatever the reason, the dynamic power of the Lord in individual lives and a daily expectation of a vibrant walk with God became lost in the hustle and bustle of programs, ministry, seminars, and the like.

I have seen too many defections from the truth, too many people groping blindly for that special experience that will fill the void of the inner heart. *The answer is NOT the charismatic movement with its error and heresy. The answer is a return to biblical emphases and daily dependency upon the ministry of the Holy Spirit in leading believers to glorify the Lord.*

At the same time, balance is needed. The Holy Spirit never intended to occupy the center stage in the life of the church. Yes, He is the dynamic behind every Christian life. That is His role; that is His ministry (cf. Acts 1:8; 2 Cor. 3:18; Eph. 5:18). However, when He is thrust into the limelight by man, such is not in accord with the will of God as revealed in Scripture. Our Lord Jesus Christ is to have the preeminence in all things (cf. Col. 1:13-18). The Spirit's ministry focuses upon revealing the Lord Jesus Christ and in exalting Jesus before all (cf. John 15:26; 16:13-15).

> But when the Helper comes, whom I shall send to you from the Father, the Spirit of truth who proceeds from the Father, *He will testify of Me* (John 15:26; italics mine).

> However, when He, the Spirit of truth, has come, He will guide you into all truth; for He will not speak on His own authority, but whatever He hears He will speak; and He will tell you things to come. *He will glorify Me, for He will take of what is Mine and declare it to you.* All things that the Father has are Mine. Therefore I said that He will take of Mine and declare it to you (John 16:13-15; italics mine).

When people talk more about the Spirit than the Lord Jesus Christ, such an orientation points to error in the church.

While we must all seek the filling of the Spirit in our lives (Eph. 5:18), the Lord Jesus Christ must always occupy the center stage (Col.

1:18). Such must be true in our private meditation as well as in our public ministry. Why? Because this emphasis parallels the emphasis of Scripture and glorifies God.

REVIEW OF KEY CONCEPTS

1. From Genesis to Revelation one sees the pattern of Satan countering the Word of God. His first recorded words in Scripture are, "Has God really said . . ." (Gen. 3:1). Yet, he is not adverse to using Scripture, even quoting it, to promote error and sin (cf. Matt. 4).

2. In Jesus' earthly life, He gave preeminence to the Scriptures. Throughout the Gospel accounts, one hears Jesus using the phrase, "It is written," again and again.

3. The power of deception is seen in Jesus' rebuke of Peter in the region of Caesarea Philippi. When Jesus revealed for the first time that He was going to suffer, go to the Cross, and be raised, Peter took Jesus aside and rebuked Him. To Peter and to the other apostles, this expression of love was no doubt an admirable display of loyalty to Christ. However, Jesus saw the sinister hand of Satan intertwined in Peter's emotional outburst and rebuked him (Matt. 16: 21ff.). It takes more than logic or feelings to discern spiritual realities; it takes the Sword of the Spirit. Many charismatics are on dangerous grounds when they embrace experiences that "feel" right, or seem to be right, without filtering them through Scripture.

4. Every true believer has the power of the Holy Spirit. The issue of powerless Christians can be attributed to believers failing to surrender totally to the Lordship of Christ. The Spirit-filled life or the abiding life in Christ does not work on a "storage battery" principle, but rather, on a "contact principle." The analogy of a tram "abiding" in its power source illustrates the principle. Jesus uses the term "abide" to stress continual dependency. Moreover, He links the process of abiding in Him to that of the Scriptures abiding in the believer (John 8:31, 32; John 15:4, 5, 7; 1 John 3:24).

5. While "spring cleaning" may be required for a believer to be filled with the Spirit of God, the "abiding" process can only be maintained

through prayer and through conscious dependency upon the Word of God. The believer is challenged to be transformed by the renewing of the mind, to bring every thought into obedience to Christ. How is this done? How is this realized? Through filling our hearts and minds with the Word and with God-centered mediation (Josh. 1:8; Ps. 1; Ps. 19:14; Ps. 119:97; Isa. 26:3; Rom. 12:1, 2; Phil. 4:8; 2 Cor. 10:4, 5). As one seeks to internalize the Word of God, contact and communion with the Lord become a vibrant reality. Remember that with the heart, one trusts in Christ unto salvation; with the will, one obeys; with the mind, one abides.

The Scriptures also give the believer a practical checklist with which to measure one's abiding. The verse in Galatians 5:22 has most often been viewed as merely a descriptive account of what constitutes the fruit of the Spirit. The verse is meant to be more than descriptive; it is meant to be USED as a spiritual tool. It is a divine checklist. If at any point in one's Christian life, all of the nine manifestations of the fruit are not present, then that is evidence that that person is not Spirit-filled. Inventory needs to be taken moment-by-moment throughout the course of a day. Such discipline parallels the admonition of 2 Corinthians 10:5. Is all of this merely a self-help process? No, for the Lord gets all the credit. After all He is the One who instills the desire to even seek spiritual things (Phil. 2:12, 13).

6. Living the Christian life is often described in the Bible with words and phrases such as: "warfare," "fight," "run the race," "yield not," "work out," and "press on." The Christian life is a disciplined life of constant vigilance, of taking up the cross daily. There are no short-cuts. The spiritual conflict will continue till we step on the other side of glory. Many today are embracing superficial and shallow experiences which promise instant spirituality. Such is the nature of our times, but such is not the nature of true life in the Spirit.

7. What some believers view as positive advances in their Christian life following certain charismatic experiences are not really positive after all. Satan is not afraid of increased zeal for Bible study, prayer, or witness. He is only afraid of such if these exercises conform to the will of God. We know Satan opposes genuine use of the Word of God (Gen. 3:1; Eph. 6:17), prayer (Dan. 10:11-14), and witness (1 Pet. 5:8; Acts 26:18). Yet, he enjoys and even promotes these spiritual exercises when they deviate from the revealed Word of God. The

example of the religious leaders of Israel (cf. Matt. 6:5, 7; John 5:39; Matt. 23:15) and the cults of today prove that.

There is a treacherous trade-off which Satan is willing to make. He will give ground on some spiritual fronts, if he can gain greater advancement of his purposes. Satan's offer of the kingdoms of the world to Jesus in exchange for worship (Matt. 4:8-10); his operation in Peter's heart to express love and loyalty to Christ, though such was used to keep Jesus from the Cross (Matt. 16:21ff.); his working through the possessed slave girl to proclaim the truth concerning the mission of Paul, but intertwining the gospel message with an occultic source (Acts 16:16-18), all point to his willingness to give up ground in order to gain a greater advantage. Thus, when believers experience the false sign and revelatory gifts of today, Satan merely pulls back opposition to prayer, Bible study, and witness. The believer then attributes genuine advance to the false experience rather than to the Holy Spirit who would inspire growth anyway. Often, the experience colors further Bible study, prayer, and witness. Indeed, the believer begins to depend upon signs, wonders, and new revelations gained through impressions, intuition, hunches, visions, or dreams. This undermines the AUTHORITY and the SUFFICIENCY of Scripture.

The deception grows as others are proselyted into these views. Moreover, Christianity is weakened as a whole when fellowship no longer is based on biblical truth or doctrine, but rather on common experience. In this manner, floodgates are opened wide for heretics and unbelievers to join the ranks of so-called evangelicals in common fellowship and worship. Ultimately the essence of the gospel is obscured or lost. Deception then leads to damnation.

Studies show that Roman Catholics who are part of the charismatic renewal gain even greater zeal for the teachings of the church and for unbiblical doctrines such as papal authority, the sacraments, confession, devotion to Mary and to other "officially" recognized saints. The charismatic renewal thus becomes a great "reversal" of biblical doctrine and the gospel itself. That works against responsible faith.

All of the aforementioned points explain why the "god of this age" is willing to make trade-offs with those seeking the sensational. He will give ground, enhancing "positive" growth in the believer, in order to induce allegiance to a growing deception.

Question Four

If the sign and revelatory gifts being experienced today are not from God, why are the charismatic churches the fastest growing churches in the world?

The question is a fair one. Statistics show that charismatic churches are leading the church growth charts around the world—especially in Latin America, Africa, and Asia. Although the percentage growth rates have markedly decreased over the past decade compared to growth rates in the seventies and eighties,[78] the influence and impact of the movement continues to grow exponentially. A sampling of data from the *New International Dictionary of Pentecostal-Charismatic Movements* (2002) reveals the following:

> The Pentecostals, Charismatics, and Neocharismatics who make up this Renewal today number 27.7 percent of organized global Christianity. . . . All three waves are continuing to surge in. Massive expansion and growth continue at a current rate of 9 million new members a year—over 25,000 a day. One-third of this expansion is purely demographic (births minus deaths in the Pentecostal/Charismatic community); two-thirds converts and other new members.

> In the early days of all three waves, annual rates of growth were enormous; now they have declined gradually to 2.7 percent per year for Pentecostals, 2.4 percent for Charismatics, 3.0 percent per year for Neocharismatics and 3.2 percent per year for the Renewal as a whole.[79]

> Another indication of its dynamic is the disproportionately high Pentecostal/Charismatic penetration of the media. Charismatics in particular have seized the global initiative in radio, television, movies, audio, video, publishing, literature, magazines, citywide evangelistic campaigns (eight hundred each year), and so on. Virtually all varieties of ministries engaged in by institutionalized Christianity worldwide have now been penetrated by stalwarts of the Renewal.

141

Over one-third of the world's full-time Christian workers (38 percent) are
Pentecostals/Charismatics/Neocharismatics. . . . A majority of the fifty or so
mega-churches—the world's largest single congregations, each with over fifty
thousand members—are Pentecostal/Charismatic/Neocharismatic.[80]

I have already acknowledged that many people are genuinely being
reached for Christ through charismatic churches. However, it is important that one realize numerical growth is not synonymous with God's
stamp of approval. The Mormons, Jehovah Witnesses, and many other
cult groups can boast of phenomenal growth statistics. Such does not
mean that their doctrines, practices, or growth are of the Lord. Indeed,
in their case, they are servants and slaves to the kingdom of darkness.

Yet, what of those charismatic churches which hold to the fundamentals of the faith? Doesn't their growth argue for God's stamp of
approval? They are not in the same category as the cults or more
heretical elements of the charismatic movement. They are our brothers
and sisters in Christ. In response, one must remember that in the
parables of the Wheat and Tares (Matt. 13:24-30, 36-43), the Mustard
Seed (Matt. 13:31, 32), and the Leaven (Matt. 13:33), Jesus prophesied
of growth in the visible kingdom of God. Yet, Jesus also revealed that this
outward growth would be accompanied by growth in evil influences
from within.

The same basic principle noted above applies to churches genuinely
committed to the fundamentals of the faith—i.e., numerical growth
does not mean God's stamp of approval rests upon *all* doctrines and
practices of a particular church. As one studies the pages of Scripture,
one of the principles that emerges is that numerical growth, even by way
of genuine conversions, can occur amidst error and unscriptural practices. Again, the Lord never has had a perfect church on this side of
glory. He will use and bless those, however, who have a genuine thirst
for Him—even amidst error.

THE EARLY CHURCH SCENE

Let's take a quick spiritual inventory of the early church experience in
the first century. What would you have observed as you moved about
with the apostles? As you visited brethren in the Galatians churches, the
churches at Corinth, the church at Colossae, the church at Thessalonica,

the church at Jerusalem, and other fellowships, what would you have found? Most of these churches were bursting at the seams with new converts and growth. Yet, amidst the blessings of the Lord, amidst the numerical growth in conversions, were there any errors or heresies that needed to be addressed? Let us see.

The Apostles and the Jerusalem Church

The apostles had a special anointing from the Lord for their ministry. They were the companions of Christ in His earthly ministry. They were the stewards upon whose shoulders would rest the establishment and instruction of the churches which were to follow. Theirs was an awesome responsibility. As they moved about prior to the Lord's crucifixion, God's power was evident in their lives. The sick were healed, demons took flight, and their preaching saw results as souls came into the kingdom. Yet, throughout their earthly association with Jesus, the apostles were beset by jealousy. Even as the hour of Jesus' greatest trial was approaching, they were arguing over who was the greatest among them. Jesus had to deal with this issue on several occasions (cf. Luke 22:24-30; John 13:1-20; John 21:18-22).

Following the resurrection of Jesus, our Lord met with the apostles for forty days teaching them spiritual truths concerning the kingdom of God (Acts 1:1-3). It was during this time that the Lord gave the Great Commission to these men (Matt. 28:18-20; Mark 16:15-18; Luke 24:44-49; John 20:19-23; Acts 1:8). They were to take the gospel to every creature, Jew and Gentile alike. All nations were to be touched by the gospel (Luke 24:47). Scripture records that the apostles received the commission with great joy (Luke 24:52). *Yet, Scripture also records that the apostles and the church at Jerusalem, in its early days, failed to carry out the Great Commission.*

The Lord had to allow persecution to burst forth upon the church, to scatter believers, so that the gospel would go to Gentile as well as Jew. Note the testimony of Scripture regarding the mind-set of these early Christians from the church in Jerusalem: "Now those who were scattered after the persecution that arose over Stephen travelled as far as Phoenicia, Cyprus, and Antioch, preaching the word to no one but the Jews only" (Acts 11:19). Do not miss the fact that the common practice of these early Christians was to preach to "Jews only." This narrow approach to the gospel was in direct disobedience to the revealed will of God.

Consider also the Lord's personal instruction to Peter as recorded in Acts 10. Three times the Lord had to speak to Peter through the vision of the clean and unclean animals (Acts 10:10-17). This was necessary in order for the apostle to finally grasp that it was permissible for the Gentiles to be received into the kingdom on the same grounds as the Jew. WAS GROWTH TAKING PLACE IN THE CHURCHES OF THAT DAY? YES! WERE CONVERTS SWELLING THE RANKS OF CHRISTIANS? YES! HOWEVER, WAS THERE A MAJOR ERROR WHICH HAD TO BE ADDRESSED? MOST ASSUREDLY!

It is significant that the Lord continued to bless the Jerusalem church, to multiply its ministry even amidst a failure of the church to correct its doctrine and practice. The same was true for the personal ministry of Peter. All of this took direct intervention from God to correct. As one follows the history of the Jerusalem church in the book of Acts, one finds that the intermingling of Old Testament practices continued to color that assembly for decades after the Cross. When Paul concluded his third missionary journey, James and the elders of the church implored Paul to pay the expenses of four men who would be offering sacrifices in recognition of the successful completion of a Nazarite vow (Acts 21:23-26; cf. Num. 6:13-18). What is amazing is that the ceremony included the offering of a blood sacrifice.[81] One can see that Jewish elements in the early church took some time to lose their influence.

Error Amidst Blessing and Growth in Other Churches

As one follows the advance of Christianity throughout the book of Acts and the epistles, the same pattern of growth amidst error occurs. On Paul's first missionary journey, the apostle witnessed the establishment of many churches in southern Galatia (Acts 13-14). However, just a short time after his departure from the region, these churches became embroiled in heresy. Jewish legalists appeared in their midst maintaining that faith in the Lord Jesus Christ was not enough to secure salvation. According to these false teachers, one had to be circumcised and continue to observe Jewish ceremony and laws in order to move on to perfection. Such heresy occasioned the Galatians letter (cf. Gal. 1:6-10; 2:11-21; 3:1-9). Were there growth and conversions in Galatia? Yes, but error had to be addressed, and it had to be addressed decisively.

The Thessalonian Christians were commended by Paul for their faithfulness and for their evangelistic zeal.

> For our gospel did not come to you in word only, but also in power, and in the Holy Spirit and in much assurance, as you know what kind of men we were among you for your sake. And you became followers of us and of the Lord, having received the word in much affliction, with joy of the Holy Spirit, so that you became examples to all in Macedonia and Achaia who believe. For from you the word of the Lord has sounded forth, not only in Macedonia and Achaia, but also in every place. Your faith toward God has gone out , so that we do not need to say anything (1 Thess. 1:5-8).

Amidst persecution and growing hostility, the Thessalonian Christians had remained steadfast in the faith and were spreading the gospel abroad. Theirs was a growing fellowship as new converts turned from idols to embrace the living God (1 Thess. 1:9, 10). Nevertheless, doctrinal error arose over the Second Coming of Christ. This occasioned Paul's Second Letter to the Thessalonians. Some were confused over the judgments preceding the coming of Christ; others had stopped working in anticipation of the Lord's coming (2 Thess. 2:1-12; 3:6-15). Despite the Lord's evident and continued blessings upon this church, doctrinal error had occurred. It needed to be addressed, and it was.

Discussion has already been put forth regarding the Corinthian church. Paul spent eighteen months in Corinth. We know from the testimony of Scripture that this church experienced great growth through conversions (cf. 18:8-11). Nevertheless, the Holy Spirit regarded the Corinthian church as a carnal assembly by the Holy Spirit and a fellowship beset by error on every side: divisions, immorality, legal disputes among believers, misuse of spiritual gifts, desecration of the Lord's Table, and false teaching regarding the resurrection of believers. Did the Lord stop using the Christians in Corinth? No! Souls continued to be saved; growth continued to characterize the assembly. Nevertheless, the Holy Spirit moved Paul to correct the errors lest the testimony of the church be severely hindered.

Why would the Lord continue to bless the assembly with converts and growth when error touched some aspects of their Christian experience? The answer is simple. Although every believer is commanded of the Lord to strive for perfection, such will not be experientially attained in this life. While the believer is positionally perfect before God, having the righteousness of Christ imputed to him, and while the believer

experiences "perfection" in the sense of being filled with the Spirit, the
permanent state of perfection must await glory. Thus, the Lord will still
bless an imperfect believer, or assembly. Yet, He cannot condone error
and will address it when it surfaces.

Further mention could be made of the heresies influencing the
churches at Colossae and Philippi. Ryrie well summarizes the problem
at Colossae:

> It was syncretistic, fusing Jewish legalism, Greek philosophic speculation, and
> Oriental mysticism. Specifics included dietary and Sabbath observances and
> circumcision rites (2:11, 16), the worship of angels (2:18), and the practice
> of asceticism, which stemmed from the belief that the body was inherently evil
> (2:21-23). In combating this heresy, Paul emphasizes the cosmic significance
> of Christ as Lord of creation and Head of the Church. Any teaching, practice,
> or intermediary that detracts from the uniqueness and centrality of Christ is
> against the faith.[82]

Indications are that the church at Philippi suffered from both the
heresies of the Jewish legalists and the libertines (cf. Phil. 3:1-7, 18, 19).
Again, the Lord continued to build His church despite the encroachment of doctrinal error or human failure to uphold the truths of God.
While the ideal is both doctrinal purity and evangelistic zeal, Scripture
shows numerical growth in first century churches occurred even amidst
serious doctrinal errors.

The Final Commentary of Christ on the Churches of Asia

The previous discussion sheds some light on how the Lord can continue
to bless charismatic churches which condone unscriptural doctrines and
practices. He has never had a perfect church to work with on earth. He
will use those who have a hunger for the things of God and a humility
before the Word of God.

Not every charismatic church fits that description, for many main-
line denominational churches and independents which embrace charismatic practices are heretical. Many of the pastors of these churches are
like those whom I encountered in my seminary days. They sound like
evangelicals; they employ glowing and dramatic oratory on the teachings
of Christ; but corner them on the inerrancy of Scripture, the historical
accuracy of Genesis 1-11, the factual nature of Jonah's entombment in

the belly of a fish, the scientific accuracy of a literal creation week, and they will begin to backpeddle. Some will even deny the Virgin Birth, the reality of Hell, the deity of Christ, the Resurrection, and the gospel itself. This group of heretics are to be distinguished from the faithful Assembly of God and Pentecostal churches that have for decades held to scriptural authority. I am not talking about the Lord working with those who are complete heretics and wolves in sheeps' clothing.

Probably no better passage of Scripture exists to explain the Lord's dealing with His churches than the letters to the seven churches of Asia (Rev. 2-3). The Apostle John was instructed by the Lord to write to these seven churches: Ephesus, Smyrna, Pergamum, Thyatira, Sardis, Philadelphia, and Laodicea. Five out of the seven churches were publicly rebuked by the Lord in Scripture. While the Lord commended the majority of these churches for their positive traits—good works, faithfulness in tribulation, patience, love, and service—He rebuked their doctrinal errors, lack of true devotion, immorality, idolatry, apostasy, and called upon them to repent. *Amidst the commendation and rebuke, He still continued to use these churches to reach souls for the kingdom.* That underscores once again the principle that while the Lord uses an imperfect church, He does not hesitate to publicly rebuke error.

When one considers the great soldiers of the faith on the pages of Scripture, one sees the same principles unfold. There is Peter, used of the Lord in a mighty way at Pentecost and during the early days of the church. Nevertheless, he drifted off into doctrinal heresy by withdrawing from the Gentiles (Gal. 2:11-21). Paul had to confront him publicly, especially since his error was affecting other brethren. Moreover, Paul was led of the Holy Spirit to put his rebuke of Peter in a circular letter to the Galatians churches. The Lord used Peter, but did not hesitate to publicly rebuke him when his doctrinal heresy became a public issue. And what of John Mark and his defection from the first missionary journey? Everything in Scripture points to doctrinal differences with Paul and Barnabas over direct outreach to the Gentiles (cf. Acts 13:1-3, 13; 15:36-40). The Jerusalem Council settled the question of the ministry to the Gentiles in John Mark's heart; yet Paul would not allow him on the second missionary journey. Later, Paul would commend John Mark for his effectiveness in the ministry (2 Tim. 4:11). Loving rebuke and the Lord's blessing go hand in hand in dynamic faith

Some may charge writers like Peter Masters, John MacArthur, David Hunt, Tal Brooke, Norman Geisler, and others are being unloving in publicly rebuking the charismatic movement. However, the example of our Lord in the letters to the churches of Asia stands as the biblical foundation for such action. In actuality, such mirrors the highest expression of love for the brethren. Error must be addressed, even when it occurs in a portion of a movement that is genuinely being used of the Lord. *And that is the answer to the main question of this chapter.*

Many standing under the charismatic umbrella are deluded heretics, or knowing adversaries of the faith dressed in sheeps' clothing. Remember that much of the growth of the charismatic movement is through *assimilation* and attraction of others who already claim the Christian banner. Heretics and well-meaning saints alike are being drawn into the movement. Moreover, because many churches associated with the charismatic movement place little emphasis on sound doctrine, this breeds an atmosphere of acceptance which further undergirds numerical growth. It is interesting that when charismatic phenomena occur in a local church setting, such usually weakens those churches committed to the fundamentals of the faith, while it energizes those who would push ecumenical heresy, liberal theology, and affiliations with the pagan world system about us.

Growth does occur through assimilation. Did not the Holy Spirit warn that the time would come when true doctrine would be replaced by "soothing sessions" where teachers would appeal to preferences of man? Second Timothy 4:3, 4 states it plainly: "For the time will come when they will not endure sound doctrine, but according to their own desires, because they have itching ears, they will heap up for themselves teachers; and they will turn their ears away from the truth, and be turned aside to fables."

Nevertheless, there are many dedicated saints in the charismatic movement being used of the Lord. They are still in serious error when they embrace the false sign and revelatory gifts. Yet, the Lord still works through them because of their genuine love for the Savior, their high regard for Scripture (even though they do not realize the revelatory gifts undermine the authority of Scripture), their fervent dedication to prayer, their burden to reach the lost, and their faith.

With apostasy growing in many denominational structures and independent fellowships, who is the Lord going to use? He will use those who bow humbly before His Word and who have a heart reflecting the primary concerns of heaven. Many charismatic churches fit that description.

While the openness of charismatics helps to foster growing amounts of deception, non-charismatics in fundamental and evangelical ranks cannot sit smugly on the sidelines and cast stones. Being doctrinally right does not make one right with the Lord. Many a fundamental or evangelical assembly is gripped by false pride, legalism, divisions, carnality, immorality, and sin. It is just not out in the open for all to see. The yearning for genuine revival needs to grip the hearts of charismatics and non-charismatics alike.

BALANCING LOVE AND TRUTH

As mentioned in an earlier portion of our study, one often hears people say: "Why not just love the Lord and one another; does the Lord want us to put so much emphasis on doctrine that division occurs between the saints?" Francis Schaeffer issued a warning in 1984 against the growing trend in evangelical circles of sacrificing biblical truth on the slave block of human love. His work, *The Great Evangelical Disaster*, stands as a Christian classic and continues to call believers back to a biblical balance between love and truth.[83] In decrying the relativism that pervades evangelical Christianity, and underscoring the absolute authority of the Scripture, Schaeffer writes:

> Here is the great evangelical disaster—the failure of the evangelical world to stand for truth as truth. There is only one word for this— namely *accommodation:* the evangelical church has accommodated to the world spirit of the age. First, there has been accommodation on Scripture, so that many who call themselves evangelicals hold a weakened view of the Bible and no longer affirm the truth of all the Bible teaches—truth not only in religious matters but in the areas of science and history and morality. . . . This accommodation has been costly, first in destroying the power of the Scriptures to confront the spirit of our age; second, in allowing the further slide of our culture. Thus we must say with tears that it is the evangelical accommodation to the world spirit around us, to the wisdom of this age, which removes the evangelical church from standing against the breakdown of our culture.[84]

While Schaeffer laments the encroachment of higher criticism and rationalistic thinking upon the evangelical mind, the principle of accommodation to the spirit of the age applies to our present study. Biblical authority is being undercut through the clamor for new revelation and through the acceptance of wolves into the evangelical fold in the name of "Christian unity." Schaeffer's work sounds an alarm that the Scriptures are being destroyed by "theological infiltration and compromise," and by "cultural infiltration and compromise."[85] I would add a third concern: "cosmic and experiential infiltration"—i.e., new revelation and false sign gifts. Schaeffer's plea is even more needed today than when it was first issued:

> I call for Christian radicals, and especially young Christian radicals, to stand up in loving confrontation, but confrontation—looking to the living Christ moment-by-moment for strength—in loving confrontation with all that is wrong and destructive in the church, our culture, and the state.[86]

You see truth always defines love. One cannot reverse the order. That is why Jesus said, "If you love Me, keep my commandments" (John 14:15; cf. 14:19-24; 15:10). The Scriptures define the nature of the love expressed. That is why the Lord also prayed that the Father would sanctify believers through His truth, the Word (John. 17:17), before He prayed that believers would be one (John 17:21). Again, Scripture defines love and true unity. Martin Luther well summarized the responsibility of believers to confront error. He is quoted by Schaeffer:

> Martin Luther said, "If I profess with the loudest voice and clearest exposition every portion of the truth of God except precisely that little point which the world and the devil are at the moment attacking, I am not confessing Christ, however boldly I may be professing Christ. Where the battle rages, there the loyalty of the soldier is proved and to be steady on all the battle front besides, is mere flight and disgrace if he flinches at that point."[87]

There is a battle raging today for the hearts and minds of Christians. The battle pits the Scriptures against an invasion of revelatory phenomena. This is no little issue. It is a worldwide development, literally, a cosmic development. The stakes are high. Thus, to disregard or diminish what is going on would not only be a travesty of truth, but the quenching of biblical love that demands confrontation.[88]

WHAT THEN MUST WE DO?

The question needs to be pondered by charismatic and non-charismatic alike. Indeed, what must we do in light of the present hour? What must we do when the Lord is definitely using many in the charismatic churches to reach people for Christ, but at the same time calling brethren to forsake unscriptural practices that contribute to a growing deception? What must we do when faced with the pride and spiritual vacuum existing in many fundamental and evangelical churches today—when many wrongly assume that to "be right" makes one right with God? What must we do when seasoned Bible teachers, men of international acclaim, leave the moorings of scriptural exposition and take anecdotal arguments or personal experience and logic as their guide in reaching a verdict on spiritual realities? What must we do when we see heretic and true believer joining hands under the banner of unity and Christian fellowship?

For the Charismatic Who Is a Genuine Believer

The answer lies in getting back to Scripture. Keep those elements of your faith which conform to biblical reality, which meet the test of Scripture. Your enthusiasm, your burden for souls, your willingness to trust the Lord and step out in faith, your sacrificial spirit, and your willingness to praise the Lord without concern for societal expectations or the traditions of men. All these are to be commended.

However, getting back to Scripture also means that you *reexamine, renounce,* and purge many of the practices which do not conform to the revealed will of God. Then, too, rediscover the biblical guidelines for fellowship—that such is to be done on the basis of truth. *Realize* that separation from those who do not hold to the teachings of the Bible is a biblical doctrine and mandate (cf. Rom. 16:17). *Reaffirm* that those who fail to preach salvation by grace through faith, those who deny the inerrancy of Scripture or the fundamentals of the faith, stand under the judgment of God and should not be recognized as brethren (Gal. 1:6-10). Finally, *recommit* yourself to bringing every thought, every experience in life into conformity with Scripture. All of this should be done with the understanding that letting oneself "flow" with impulses, intuition, visions, prophecies, and dreams endangers dependency upon the Word of God. Such undercuts the authority and sufficiency of Scripture. Only by exercising this kind of vigilance can one's abiding glorify the Lord.

The thirst for the presence and power of God is an admirable spiritual quality. If ever western Christianity needed revival, it is now.

However, this longing for the movement of God among His people must also conform to Scripture. There are no shortcuts to spiritual fruitfulness. Such is only gained through day-by-day, and moment-by-moment, commitment to abiding in Christ. Should the Lord grant a genuine movement of His Spirit, He will bring forth the two aspects that He highlighted in Job's life: righteousness evidenced in reverential fear and communion with God; but also the conscious shunning of evil—whether it takes the form of doctrinal error or sin in the Christian walk (cf. Job 2:8).

For the Non-Charismatic Who Is a Genuine Believer

We, too, need to seek God's face as never before. We need to realize that although we may disagree with the charismatic interpretation of the sign and revelatory gifts, the Lord is using many of these dear brethren to reach others for the kingdom. Those charismatics who hold to inerrancy of Scripture and the fundamentals of the faith are our brothers and sisters in Christ. We must reaffirm with a loud voice that God is indeed still doing miracles today: that He gives miraculous answers to prayer; that He can heal in response to the corporate prayers of God's people. Does that mean we should hesitate to expose and rebuke the errors of the charismatic movement? No. I have already demonstrated from Scripture that true love for the brethren requires public rebuke when error surfaces. Nevertheless, such rebuke needs to be accompanied by a sense of humility (Gal. 6:1-3). There is no place for arrogance or spiritual pride. To be right doctrinally does not mean that one's heart is right, it does not mean that there is a consuming love for the Lord Jesus Christ.

Many fundamentalist and evangelical churches which hold the line doctrinally have lost their zeal and compassion for the lost. While we sit in our stained-glass foxholes amidst soothing organ music, the battle rages about us for the souls of men and women, boys and girls. The Lord will not excuse our lack of compassion or care. A "holding" mentality will not do. We are charged by our Master to advance against the forces of hell. Complacency and false satisfaction must also be purged. One need only look around at our society to see the conflict that awaits committed soldiers of the Lord Jesus.

Those charismatic churches which hold to the fundamentals of the faith and which take the offensive in proclaiming the gospel stand as a positive challenge to many a cold, orthodox, and non-charismatic church. Many of the following emphases of charismatic churches are biblically based and need to be embraced by those in the service of the Lord Jesus Christ:

1. *The Focus on Jesus As Lord.* Believers are continually challenged to yield every aspect of their lives to the Lord Jesus and to seek a deeper commitment to Him. Charismatics are bold in their proclamation of the Lordship of Jesus Christ and the practical application of such to the individual life.

2. *The Focus on Praise and Worship.* The prayer life of most Christians centers upon thanksgiving, confession, and intercession for others. While these are essential elements, the most neglected aspect is that of praise: praise to the Lord for his Person and marvellous attributes; praise to the Lord for His wondrous ways and actions. The Psalms teach us the same lesson. While not all elements of charismatic worship conform to biblical standards, their call to praise the Lord and to deepen one's awareness of worship is a positive challenge to all believers.

3. *The Focus on Evangelism and Outreach.* Charismatic boldness in this area is well attested, whether through media, person-to-person witness, or church related programs. An aggressive church in the area of evangelism parallels the New Testament model. While some churches embrace solely "friendship evangelism" and "lifestyle evangelism," the more fundamental charismatic churches are reminding believers of the joy and fruit which comes through "encounter evangelism." What is "encounter evangelism?" Such involves DIRECT outreach through surveys, door-to-door visitation, gospel tract distribution, and witnessing encounters. In the same way that Jesus shared the gospel through "encounters" with Nicodemus, the Woman at the Well, Zacchaeus, and many others, so believers are exhorted to do the same. Both models of "friendship evangelism" and "encounter evangelism" are biblical and should not be practiced at the exclusion of the other.

4. *The Focus on Spiritual Sensitivity.* Most of the charismatic churches speak openly of spiritual conflict, the need for the spirit-filled walk with Christ, and spiritual gifts. Again, while many of their emphases

extend into error, their overall call to spiritual awareness needs to be heard by a sleeping and complacent church.

5. *The Focus on Sacrificial Service and Giving.* This is not to say that such is found only within charismatic circles. However, it is a fact that traditional Pentecostals and the more fundamental charismatic churches minister to and draw from the poor sectors of society. This trend is changing with the growing emphasis on the *Prosperity Gospel*; nevertheless, Pentecostals and charismatic groups are often seen spearheading evangelistic thrusts into urban slums, neglected ethnic groups, and lower class areas. This is true in cross cultural mission contexts as well. Such stands as a challenge to all churches to move out of the "comfort zone" to reach the people of the worl through intensified evangelism and ministry.

6. *The Focus on Trained Laity.* Seminars, programs, and training sessions abound in many charismatic churches to train laypeople in the ministry. Indeed, this "in-house" approach to training explains why many people move into paid staff positions without attending formal Bible college or seminary training. While the right kind of formal theological education certainly enhances one's ministry, the charismatic churches serve to challenge believers with the truth that personal surrender to the lordship of Christ and to the Bible are the primary prerequisites for service in the kingdom of God.

7. *The Focus on Strong Pastoral Leadership.* While excesses of authority certainly exist, most fundamental charismatic churches demand a strong pastoral leader or team of pastors. This emphasis on strong leadership balances the commitment to training people for ministry in the context of the local church. Many churches fear strong leadership either because of the vested interests of some within the fellowship or because of the excesses which may arise. However, church growth studies indicate that whether one addresses a charismatic or non-charismatic context, strong leadership is vital to a growing church.

Again, these aforementioned emphases are not the sole possession of conservative and fundamental charismatic churches. However, they do reflect a dominant trend within these circles. So, before we non-charismatic believers accord *only* criticism to the more fundamental and conservative charismatics, let us check our own condition: (1) Do we express our love for the Lord through enthusiastic and dedicated service? (2) Are we really burdened for the lost souls about us and are we *actively* engaged in reaching people for the Lord Jesus Christ? (3) Are we seeing lives changed, believers maturing in their faith, and people coming to know the Lord? (4) Does our own church foster an environment where believers experience and evidence the lordship of Christ in their lives, where praise and worship go beyond mere formality, where the power of the Holy Spirit transforms and becomes a living reality to all?

Praise the Lord, many fundamental and evangelical churches which do not embrace the charismatic stance are on fire for the Lord. A great multitude of souls do come into the kingdom through the witness of these faithful brethren. And indeed, when one speaks of miracles, none is greater than that of bringing lost souls from darkness into light, from the power of Satan into the kingdom of Christ! Many of these churches do give evidence of a membership who hunger for the Lord, walk in the Spirit, display the gifts, and minister in a myriad of ways. Yet again, so much more needs to be done. May the burden of revival weigh upon our hearts even more as we approach the day of our Lord's return.

In closing this section, I am reminded of my early seminary days when I sat in the class of Dr. Robert L. Hughes—missionary, church planter, scholar, and author. He was and still is a mighty soldier of the Cross. Many of us referred to him as "the gentle lion," for he was a unique combination of compassion, zeal, and boldness for Christ. Time and again, he would pause in his lectures, look out at "his" batch of young preachers and say:

> Men there are three kinds of orthodoxy: orthodoxy of belief, orthodoxy of life, and orthodoxy of service. You must be faithful in all three, or you are a heretic in the service of Jesus. . . . You see you can believe the right things, live an impeccable personal life, but if you have not a compassion for souls, then you are a heretic. On the other hand, you can live a good life, witness to people of the gospel, but if you fail to believe the fundamentals of the faith, you are a heretic. And then, you can believe the right things, reach others for Christ, but have an impure heart—if that is the case you are a heretic.

Then he would urge us in his firm, yet gentle way, to live for Jesus in spirit and in truth. May that be so in your life and in mine as we enter "the age of revelation.

REVIEW OF KEY CONCEPTS

1. Why does the Lord continue to bless charismatic churches if their acceptance of the sign and revelatory gifts is wrong? Scripture demonstrates that although the Lord does not have a perfect church this side of glory, He still blesses even in the midst of doctrinal error. The key is a humility before God, a high regard for His Word, and a consuming desire to see souls touched for the kingdom.

2. The early church scene of the first century affirms the above. The apostles were anointed of God in special ways, yet they had problems with jealousy. Even though the early church was commissioned to take the gospel to every creature, they disobeyed that command— preaching to Jews only (cf. Acts 11:19; Acts 10). It took direct intervention by God to correct the error. The Jerusalem church continued to be influenced by Old Testament ceremony and legalism. The instruction by James and the elders to Paul to pay for the offerings associated with a Nazarite vow prove this (Acts 21:23-26).

3. As one follows the advance of the gospel through the Scriptures, one sees that numerical growth characterized these early churches. The Lord's blessings upon the churches were evident. However, amidst the blessings, there were doctrinal errors which needed to be addressed. Such occasioned the writing of the letters to the churches of Galatia, Corinth, Thessalonica, Colossae, and others. The biblical principle emerges: the Lord will continue to use and bless imperfect churches to reach others for Christ; yet, He will not overlook doctrinal error and sin. Such public transgression brings public rebuke. The personal examples of Peter and John Mark further confirm this (cf. Gal. 2:11-21; Acts 15:36ff.).

4. The last words of Jesus Christ to the church are recorded in the Book of Revelation. In Chapters 2 and 3, the Lord instructed the Apostle John to write to seven churches in Asia. The letters were a call to repentance. Five out of the seven churches the Lord rebuked

publicly. He also commended them. Did the Lord stop blessing these churches? No, He continued to use the majority of them to reach souls for the kingdom. Nevertheless, He did not hesitate to rebuke error and sin. Such an example of our Lord stands as a mandate for brethren to publicly commend faithfulness, but also to expose and rebuke error.

5. Even though the charismatic movement has seriously erred in promoting false sign and revelatory gifts, many of these churches are committed to the inerrancy of Scripture and to the fundamentals of the faith. They just fail to realize that embracing new revelation and false signs undermines the AUTHORITY and the SUFFICIENCY of Scripture. This is a serious matter. Yet, because many in the charismatic churches have a humble and hungering heart before God, He is blessing them in spite of their error. Furthermore, many liberal and neo-evangelical churches are pastored by men who deny the Scriptures and have no compassion for the lost. Who is the Lord going to use? He has never had a perfect church on earth; thus, He will use those who have a high regard for Scripture, a humble heart before God, and a commitment for spreading the gospel to an unbelieving world. Many charismatic churches fit that description.

6. Truth defines biblical love. That is always the scriptural order (cf. John 17:17, 21; John. 14:15). The authority of Scripture is being eroded in three ways: theological infiltration and compromise; cultural infiltration and compromise; and cosmic and experiential infiltration (i.e., new revelation and false sign gifts). What must we do? Subject every thought, action, and experience in life to the Scriptures. Realize that genuine revival will always foster a high regard for Scripture.

7. This study stands as a call to charismatics to reexamine and renounce those doctrines and practices that run counter to Scripture. Nevertheless, our charismatic brethren are urged to hold fast to their zeal and those things which are honoring to the Lord. The challenge for non-charismatic believers is that of seeking genuine revival while holding forth the Truth. One must ever be reminded that to be right on doctrine does not mean one is right with the Lord. Orthodoxy touches doctrine, life, and a heart in tune with the compassion of heaven for the lost. That is important to the Christian faith.

Conclusion

Years ago, I had the joy of being a part of one of the largest churches in America. It wasn't the size that captured my attention, but the fervent spirit that prevailed in that fellowship. The church had founded a seminary. Even though the school was just getting off the ground, it had a motto: *Scriptural Scholarship Aflame for Christ and Souls!* When I first heard of the motto, I almost shouted, "Hallelujah, that's it, that's it . . . that's what I'm looking for!" Not just scholarship, for that alone can kill; not just shallow emotionalism, for that can open the door to deception; not just an inward look, for we must be channels to the world—vessels from whom rivers of living water would flow (John 7: 37-39). Praise the Lord, the emphasis was *scriptural scholarship*; praise the Lord, the emphasis was upon a heart *aflame for Christ*; and yes, both of these emphases were to lead us to reach out to a lost world—souls .

Those days were precious days. It seemed like every service was a revival. The praise, the prayers, and the proclamation of the Word all resounded with a touch of heaven. Moreover, the Spirit's movement upon lives was so apparent. Miraculous answers to prayer became an everyday experience. We literally combed the community with the gospel and many souls were born into the kingdom of God. Through it all, I never forgot the balance of *scriptural scholarship aflame for Christ and souls.*

As the world enters the last half of the final decade of this millennium, those who name the name of Christ face unparalleled opportunities to spread the gospel to every person. Yet, at the same time, Christianity is being besieged by deception. The onslaught already has grown to global proportions. A cosmic contest is unfolding on planet earth between the formulations of truth contained in the Bible and new revelations and wonders orchestrated by the "god of this age" (2 Cor. 4:4)—the "prince of the power of the air" (Eph. 2:2). The sovereign and Almighty God is in full control. His triumph over the kingdom of darkness is already won. Indeed, it was won in the timeless counsels of the Trinity and enacted in time and space upon Golgotha's hill. One day, the Lord Jesus Christ will put down all opposing rule, and power, and authority (1 Cor. 15:20-28). When that day arrives, and He delivers up the kingdom to God the Father, God's program in history will then be complete.

Until that time, however, the Lord allows His children the freedom to serve and obey Him. He gives us the desires and the promptings to do His good pleasure (Phil. 2:12, 13; Heb. 13:20, 21), but He allows us the choice to follow His bidding. He does not insulate us from the devices of Satan; but He does give us the armor and weapons to gain the victory in our personal lives. If one chooses to put down the Sword of the Spirit or to let it lie on a shelf, if one chooses to walk in the halls of the heart without the sound of Scripture filling the air, then our God will allow this. But He is grieved. Why? Because the Lord Jesus Christ exhorted believers to abide in Him and to allow His Word to abide in them (John 8:31, 32; 15:1-7).

Today, in ever increasing numbers, many Christians are making trade-offs: biblical authority and sufficiency for new revelations; moment-by-moment abiding in the Word and the Spirit for artificial dependency on those wielding the promise of spiritual highs. May the trade-offs cease. May believers committed to the authority of Scripture fulfill the command of bringing every thought unto the captivity of Christ (2 Cor. 10:4, 5). To do that is not easy. And yes, to "be right" does not mean one "is right" with God.

What is required? It will mean everything in life must be subjected to *scriptural scholarship*. Oh, I do not necessarily mean the kind found in a theological seminary; for all believers are commanded to study to show themselves approved unto God. And that takes work (2 Tim. 2:15)! But at the same time, our Lord requires a heart *aflame* with love and devotion for Him (Matt. 22:37; Luke 14:25-33; John 14:19-24). Finally, a heart *aflame for Christ* will produce a heart *aflame for souls* (Matt. 22:39; John 3:16; John 20:21-23). Why? Because such is the mind of Christ.

Scripture affirms, "we have the mind of Christ" (1 Cor. 2:16); but this is only true when we are in accord with *His revealed will, when we abide in His Word*. Only Scripture can serve as a lamp unto our feet and a light unto our path (Psalm 119:105). For those who choose another path; for those who are content to open themselves up to the universe, to revelations which have no verifiable source, theirs is a dangerous course. One may discover that the "mind of Christ" has been replaced by the manipulative devices of the "god of this age."

The two paths confront every believer. Again, the stakes are high. Which choice will you make?

Appendices

Appendix A
Additional Questions

Appendix B
Tongues (Glossai)

Appendix C
Jesus Christ: God's Supreme Revelation

Appendix D
Faith in the Melting Pot: WCC Slides into Syncretism

Appendix A
Additional Questions

Question 1: *In your study, you made reference to the passing of the Apostolic Office. You also noted that some teach the sign gifts were the exclusive ministry of the apostles. Can you comment on this "exclusive" position in light of Mark 9:38-41 and the apparent non-restrictive implications of Mark 16:17-20 and 1 Corinthians 12:1-31?*

Response: The biblical evidence supports the position that the sign gifts primarily authenticated the apostles and their appointed representatives: John 15:27; 1 Corinthians 9:1; 2 Corinthians 12:11, 12; Acts 2:43; 4:33; 5:12; 8; 10; 19; Hebrews 2:3, 4; Acts 6:8-10 (Stephen); Acts 8:5-8 (Philip); and Acts 13:50-14:3 (Barnabas). Nevertheless, there are those instances where others were involved in miracles and sign gifts who did not hold the status of an apostle.

The seventy witnesses who were sent out by Jesus also possessed the power and authority to perform miracles (cf. Luke 10). They were "apostles" in the sense that they were "sent ones" who proclaimed the message of the kingdom; however, they did not hold the office of apostle. The account in Mark 9:38-41 clearly shows that others outside the apostolic band could invoke the name of Jesus in casting out demons. Moreover, they met with the approval of Jesus.

> Now John answered Him, saying, "Teacher, we saw someone who does not follow us casting out demons in Your name, and we forbade him because he does not follow us." But Jesus said, "Do not forbid him, for no one who works a miracle in My name can soon afterward speak evil of Me. For he who is not against us is on our side. For whoever gives you a cup of water to drink in My name, because you belong to Christ, assuredly, I say to you, he will by no means lose his reward."

How is one to explain this situation? Exegetical gymnastics cannot erase the approval which Jesus gave to this miracle worker. If the sign and rev-elatory gifts were given exclusively to the apostles (and their representa-tives) to vindicate their ministry and message, why did Jesus condone the miraculous activities of one outside the apostolic band? Moreover, does such an incident suggests a growing pattern that would carry over into the rest of the New Testament era?

First of all, neither the seventy witnesses of Luke 10 nor the account in Mark 9:38-41 suggests a post-Cross pattern. The Lord Jesus Christ at that time was still on earth personally directing the kingdom program. The day would come, however, when He would go to the Cross, die, be raised, and ascend into heaven. *Then* the apostles would become the stewards of the church. Thus, while Luke 10 and Mark 9:38-41 show that miracles were performed by those outside apostolic circles, these passages do not establish the fact that such became the pattern after the Lord ascended into heaven.

The passages in Mark 16:17-20 and 1 Corinthians 12:1-31, how-ever, present some interesting considerations. If one fails to read the entire context of Mark 16:9-20, one may receive the immediate impression that the sign gifts noted in verses 17 and 18 apply to *all believers*. However, a strong case can be made for these verses applying *only to the apostles*.

In Mark 16:14 one sees that Jesus is addressing only the eleven apostles and is rebuking them for their unbelief concerning the resur-rection: "Afterward He appeared to the eleven as they sat at the table; and He rebuked their unbelief and hardness of heart, because they did not believe those who had seen Him after He had risen." Following the rebuke, Jesus then gives the apostles their commission to preach the gospel to every creature (Mark 16:15, 16). Once the commission is given, it is indeed possible that Jesus returns to His immediate audience when He says: "And these signs will follow those who believe" (i.e., those of *you* who believe—those whom Jesus had just rebuked a few moments earlier for their unbelief). This interpretation is further bol-stered by the clear reference to the eleven apostles in verse 20: "And they went out and preached everywhere, the Lord working with them and confirming the word through the accompanying signs. Amen."

While the overall context seems to favor the restricted application to the apostles, such an interpretation is far from conclusive. Indeed, it is also possible that the "they" in verses 17 and 18 could apply to believers at large. In other words, those who will be able to perform the signs are those who have believed through the preaching of the apostles. Certainly the apostles would be included in the group who employ the sign gifts to confirm the gospel—the apostles' initiation of the process accounts for their mention in verse 20. Other passages in the New Testament seem to favor the non-restrictive interpretation. The fact that one of the sign gifts, tongues, appears outside the experience of the apostles argues for the wider reference. Moreover, the listing of the gifts of healing and tongues in 1 Corinthians 12 also points to a wider sphere than the apostles. Paul testifies in 1 Corinthians 1:7 that the Corinthian church was not lacking in any gift. So what is the final conclusion? BOTH the restrictive interpretation of Mark 16:17-20 (i.e., applying only to the apostles) and the non-restrictive position (i.e., applying to all believers) enjoy scriptural support. While I personally favor the non-restrictive interpretation, neither position alters the ultimate case regarding the cessation of the sign gifts. Why?

Remember the purpose of the sign gifts and the pattern that governs their use throughout Scripture. Earlier in our study, we focused on three distinct periods of biblical history when signs and wonders flooded human experience: the Exodus; the divided kingdom and the ministries of Elijah and Elisha; and the ministry of Jesus and the apostles. One may scan the entire biblical record and find only these three periods of history when continuous manifestation of signs and wonders became the order of the day. Granted, other periods of biblical history experienced miraculous interventions of God; yet, again, God reserved three distinct periods of time to unveil His signs. Moreover, these periods marked monumental advances in the kingdom of God on earth:

1. The Exodus————————> Establishment of the Nation of Israel

2. The Divided Kingdom (Elijah and Elisha)> Preservation of Israel

3. Jesus and the Apostles————————> Institution of the Church

Each of these periods, so characterized by **signs and wonders**, was also characterized by **new revelation and prophecy**. These two aspects are highlighted by a number of Scriptures. Note the following:

> But since then there has not arisen in Israel a prophet like Moses, whom the Lord knew face to face, in all the signs and wonders which the Lord sent him to do in the land of Egypt, before Pharaoh, before all his servants, and in all his land, and by all that mighty power and all the great terror which Moses

performed in the sight of all Israel (Deut. 34:10-12; cf. Exod. 4:1-9; Deut.
4:33-40; Ps. 78:1-8).

And it came to pass, at the time of the offering of the evening sacrifice, that
Elijah the prophet came near and said, "Lord God of Abraham, Isaac, and
Israel, let it be known this day that You are God in Israel, and that I am Your
servant, and that I have done all these things at Your word. "Hear me, O Lord,
hear me, that this people may know that You are the Lord God, and that You
have turned their hearts back to You again." Then the fire of the Lord fell and
consumed the burnt sacrifice, and the wood and the stones and the dust, and
it licked up the water that was in the trench. Now when all the people saw it,
they fell on their faces; and they said, "The Lord, He is God! The Lord, He is
God" (1 Kings 18:36-39; cf. 2 Kings 5:8)!

O God, why have You cast us off forever? Why does Your anger smoke
against the sheep of Your pasture? . . . *We do not see our SIGNS; There is no
longer any PROPHET; Nor is there any among us who knows how long* (Ps. 74:1,
9; italics mine).

Then those men, when they had seen the sign that Jesus did, said, "This is
truly the Prophet who is to come into the world" (John 6:14; cf. Deut. 18:15;
John 10:37, 38).

For I will not dare to speak of any of those things which Christ has not accomplished through me, in word and deed, to make the Gentiles obedient—in
mighty signs and wonders, by the power of the Spirit of God, so that from
Jerusalem and round about to Illyricum I have fully preached the gospel of
Christ (Rom.15:18, 19; cf. 2 Cor. 12:12).

For if the word spoken through angels proved steadfast, and every transgression and disobedience received a just reward, how shall we escape if we
neglect so great a salvation, which at the first began to be spoken by the Lord,
and was confirmed to us by those who heard Him, God also bearing witness
both with signs and wonders, with various miracles, and gifts of the Holy
Spirit, according to His own will (Heb. 2:2-4)?

In this brief sampling of Scriptures, one sees the vital connection between
signs and prophecy. When signs, wonders, and miracles become the
order of the day, new revelation also pours forth from heaven. Such a
striking connection forms the basis for the cry of Psalm 74:9.

The significance of Ephesians 2:19, 20 bears repeating. When the Apostle John penned the last words of the book of Revelation, not only did Scripture come to a close, but the era of the apostles and prophets also came to an end. Furthermore, because of the vital connection between prophecy and signs, the need for the sign gifts ceased. Again, note the force of the Ephesian passage: "Now, therefore, you are no longer strangers and foreigners, but fellow citizens with the saints and members of the household of God, having been built on the foundation of the apostles and prophets, Jesus Christ Himself being the chief cornerstone. . . ." *One only needs to lay a foundation once.* With the passing of the apostles, prophecy also passed. Why? Because the Scripture stood complete. Moreover, with the completion of Scripture, the need for signs confirming the Word of God passed as well. God still intervenes to do miraculous works on behalf of His children, but the sign gifts are no more.

The miracles which attested to the ministry and message of Jesus and the apostles have become part of the Word of God. They live today. The clear teaching of John 20:30, 31 would have to be torn from Scripture if signs and wonders were still needed to confirm the preaching of the gospel. Prayerfully note the force of these verses: "And truly Jesus did many other signs in the presence of His disciples, which are not written in this book; but these are written that you may believe that Jesus is the Christ, the Son of God, and that believing you may have life in His name."

Question 2: *You have stated that error and truth can go hand in hand; that God can still be working even where elements of error and satanic opposition are present. Can you give any further biblical support for this position? How or why would God allow error to persist in settings where the Spirit is blessing? Isn't God stronger than that?*

Response: In answering the question, let us refer to an incident which occurred in the life of our Lord. You will find the incident recorded in Mark 1:21-28.

Then they went into Capernaum, and immediately on the Sabbath He entered the synagogue and taught. And they were astonished at His teaching, for He taught them as one having authority, and not as the scribes. Now there was a man in their synagogue with an unclean spirit. And he cried out, saying, "Let us alone! What have we to do with You, Jesus of Nazareth? Did You come to destroy us? I know who You are—the Holy One of God!" But Jesus rebuked him, saying, "Be quiet, and come out of him!" And when the unclean spirit had convulsed him and cried out with a loud voice, he came out of him. Then they were all amazed, so that they questioned among themselves, saying, "What is this? What new doctrine is this? For with authority He commands even the unclean spirits, and they obey Him." And immediately His fame spread throughout all the region around Galilee.

This is an amazing account! Here you have the Son of God involved in a teaching ministry. He is proclaiming the Word of God in the synagogue on the Sabbath. Such would parallel a service today in our churches where the Word of God is being taught. Right in the middle of the "service," Jesus is interrupted by a demon-possessed man. He rebukes the spirit and the man is delivered.

Do not miss the implications of this incident. During the teaching session conducted by the Lord Jesus Christ (God Incarnate), He is challenged by demonic forces. Even while the Word of God is being taught and proclaimed, Satan is at work in that very setting! Yes, Satan is overcome in this incident because his devices are unmasked and his corrupting influence rebuked. **The trouble with many Christians today is that they assume because God is blessing in a particular setting, all aspects of that setting glorify Him.** It is naive to hold such a view. If satanic activity could characterize the very service wherein our Lord Jesus was ministering, then the same activity could be present in the most heart-inspiring service.

Many of our charismatic brothers and sisters assume that because God is blessing lives through various ministries, then all aspects of the ministry, doctrine, and practices also bear the Lord's stamp of approval. This is simply not so! How then is one to identify those elements which are from God and those which have other sources? The only true measure is Scripture. Jesus could perceive the nature of the disruption because of His Person and spiritual sensitivity. Though believers do possess spiritual discernment, such only operates in conjunction with the Scriptures which are authored by the Spirit. They never contradict or conflict with each other.

Non-charismatics can make the same mistake and assumptions as well. All aspects of ministry must be examined under the searchlight of the Scriptures. Only then, will any corrupting aspects be revealed and rebuked.

Again, why would God allow such to occur in the synagogue as recorded in Mark 1:21-28? The Scriptures give us the reason: so that Jesus' claim to messiahship would be vindicated by signs and wonders—and these included His power over the demonic realm. Why does God allow Satan to operate in the same fashion today? A number of reasons may be put forth:

1. To allow our faith and dependency on the Lord and His Word to be exercised (cf. James 1:12).

2. To give opportunities for His saints to exercise their rights and powers as soldiers in the kingdom of God (cf. 2 Cor. 10:4, 5; Eph. 6:10-18; James 4:7).

3. To display the riches and power of God's grace even amidst spiritual conflict—which ultimately brings glory to God (Eph. 3:8-12; 2:4-7; 1 Cor. 15:22-28).

4. To show that ultimate triumph in this life and in the life to come is always attained through the operation of and submission to God's Word (Matt. 28:20; John 14:15, 23; John 15:7-10).

One final thought on this subject. If, even after his rebellion, Satan could still have access to heaven—and he does (cf. Job 1, 2; Rev. 12:7-12)—surely his activities would be most pronounced in those places seeking to uphold the name of the Lord Jesus Christ. That is why spiritual discernment, governed by the Word of God, needs special undergirding in the hearts of those who really seek to do the Lord's will. Without the guidelines of Scripture, even the most dedicated saint is open to deception. Be careful in condoning all aspects of a ministry or particular worship service.

Question 3: *Is not there a legitimate parallel between much of the phenomena occurring in charismatic circles today and phenomena which characterized the great revivals of the past? In condemning the charismatic movement, are you not also condemning the mighty movements of God in these past revivals as well?*

Response: First, I would like to correct the inference that I am condemning all aspects of the charismatic movement. The deception, error, satanic activity, and excesses which characterize much of the movement have been addressed. I do not hesitate to point out that charismatic ranks are filled with apostates, heretics, and enemies of the gospel—the Catholic Charismatic Renewal being one major source of error. Nevertheless, I have also maintained that many elements which characterize the conservative and fundamental Pentecostal churches mirror biblical emphases.

Now regarding the nature of past revivals, a parallel does seem to exist between some phenomena present then and phenomena occurring within various charismatic circles. While parallels may exist, such does not mean that all aspects of a service, ministry, movement, or work reflect the hand of God (cf. Mark 1:21-28). Please remember our previous discussion under the second question in this Appendix.

John White, in his book *When the Spirit Comes With Power* (InterVarsity Press, 1988), goes to great lengths to establish a connection between God's movement in past revivals and current phenomena being experienced in charismatic circles and in Wimber's Vineyard Movement. He draws upon experiences associated with the Welsh Revival (1904/5), the Great Awakening in New England (mid-1700s), the Wesleyan Revival (mid-1700s), the camp meetings in Cane Ridge, Kentucky (1801), and the ministries of Moody, Finney, Whitefield, and others. From this historical perspective, White draws up a list of phenomena which characterized these meetings: fear of God; grief and mourning over sin; trembling and shaking; uncontrollable weeping; unspeakable joy; falling; and manifestations of the miraculous intervention of God (White, pp. 84-102). Additional writers report that these revivals and others throughout history also involve visions, instances of tongues, healings, deliverance from demons, sounds of rushing wind, miracles, and similar phenomena.

The implications from such a comparative analysis are obvious. The reasoning goes something like this: (1) All agree that the Lord moved mightily in these revivals; (2) thus, if the same phenomena present then are present now within charismatic and Third Wave circles, then such vindicates these movements. They must be of God! In response, I would caution against this simplistic equation.

The Holy Spirit does intervene in special ways and in special times. This is readily acknowledged. Moreover, none of the phenomena which White lists counter biblical revelation. There is nothing biblically inconsistent with people being burdened over sin, fearing the Lord, and crying uncontrollably or trembling when confronted with the reality of the living God (cf. Neh. 8-10). Indeed, many a church needs a powerful movement of God to rid the assembly of false pride, human formalities, a "programming and performance mentality," and a sense of self-sufficiency. The sound of weeping is a beautiful sound when such proceeds from a broken heart seeking to draw near to Almighty God. As stated earlier, many churches have become museums where people go to be seen rather than being spiritual hospitals where people go to worship, serve, and receive ministry from the Great Physician. Moreover, if in the midst of revival, our Sovereign God chooses to manifest His power through healings, miracles, or unusual phenomena, then this also does not run counter to biblical revelation. God must not be put into a box constructed by human experience or human expectation. The same God who made an axe head swim (2 Kings 6:1-7) can and does do the unusual. The critical issue is whether such an incident *transgresses* Scripture. To state it another way, the key is to discern which parallel elements are biblical and which are not.

D. Martyn Lloyd-Jones cites the case of Evan Roberts who was used so mightily by God in the Welsh Revival, but who eventually crossed a line and moved into unscriptural practices (*Prove All Things*; Kingsway Publications, 1985, p. 93). Roberts became the catalyst for the Welsh Revival when he gave himself to prayer for revival. The Lord used his example and kindled a growing flame in the hearts of many which swept innumerable souls into the kingdom. However, Roberts later digressed into a state where he would not do anything without direct guidance from the Spirit. Such introspection touched on the smallest decisions. Eventually he had a nervous breakdown which led to other health complications. Somewhere along the way, a biblically-based burden became replaced by unscriptural emphases. What became true in Evans' life has parallels in both the history of revivals and current charismatic practices. Again, the issue revolves around which elements or phenomena meet with biblical approval and which do not. (Note: Evan Roberts later co-authored a book with Jesse Penn-Lewis entitled *War on the Saints*. Reflecting on the Welsh Revival and the events following, Roberts and Lewis identified and categorized deceptive and false manifestations of the Spirit which appeared in the very midst of revival blessings.)

A vast difference exists between much of the phenomena associated with past revivals and current charismatic practices.

Past Revivals: Healings, casting out of demons, and miracles did occur in some revivals, but not in all; however, where healings and the like occurred such were accomplished through and in response to the corporate prayers of God's people. Those who claimed to have the "gifts" of healing or special "ministries of deliverance" were shunned. Miracles and healings were never viewed as essential to the powerful proclamation of the gospel.

Current Charismatic Phenomena: People claim to possess the same sign gifts as the apostles. Wimber and others stress that individuals can receive the gift of tongues, healing, miracles, and individual ministries of deliverance. Many such as Wimber use phrases like "power encounters" to stress that the gospel must be undergirded by signs and wonders to be effective. (See the article by Ken L. Sarles, "An Appraisal of the Signs and Wonders Movement," *Bibliotheca Sacra*, January-March, 1988, pp. 57-82.)

Past Revivals: There are documented cases of people being overcome by the reality of the Spirit's power: fear of God; grief and mourning over sin; and shaking, trembling, and falling down. Such is viewed as a sovereign act of God whereby He so moves upon people through the Spirit.

Current Charismatic Phenomena: People claim to have the individual gift and power to "slay people in the Spirit." Such has no biblical basis whatsoever. Any appeal to the experiences of Daniel (Dan. 8:16-27), the disciples on the Mount of Transfiguration (Matt. 17:1-7), John on the Isle of Patmos (Rev. 1:17), Ezekiel (Ezek. 2:1-3), or the multitude in the Garden when confronted by Jesus (John 18:1-6) will not do. Why? Because in each one of these incidents, people fell to the ground because of direct contact with God or a heavenly representative. Again, there is no biblical basis for a person having the "gift" or power to "slay others in the Spirit."

Past Revivals: While reported cases of visions, prophecies, and tongues do exist, these phenomena were neither endorsed nor embraced by those leading the revivals. In many cases, these phenomena were repudiated. Preeminence was always given to the Scriptures.

Current Charismatic Phenomena: Charismatics encourage prophecies and tongues. They are open to new revelation coming in the form of visions and dreams. This openness to new revelation stands as one of the more serious errors confronting charismatics. As increasing preeminence is given to tongues, prophecies, and other revelatory phenomena, the authority and sufficiency of Scripture is undermined.

In view of the preceding, some parallels do exist between the great revivals (past and present) and *certain elements* within charismatic circles. However, such parallels do not establish a common Source. Similar parallels may be drawn between these revivals and phenomena occurring in non-charismatic groups. One must remember that *major differences* exist as well. One, therefore, cannot use parallels with God-given revivals to vindicate the signs and wonders movement. Some elements parallel, but some do not. In fact, when one goes beyond superficial observations, the differences outweigh the similarities.

Question 4: *You seem to leave no place for the ministry of the Holy Spirit to lead and direct the Christian life in a personal way. Do you feel that Scripture precludes any direct communication between the Spirit and an individual?*

Response: The answer to the question rests upon what one means by the phrase "direct communication." If by direct communication one means the same type of communication as that which occurred throughout the New Testament era, the answer is "no." Please note the precise nature of the Spirit's communication in those times prior to the completion of Scripture:

> While Peter thought about the vision, the Spirit said to him, "Behold, three men are seeking you. Arise therefore, go down and go with them, doubting nothing; for I have sent them" (Acts 10:19, 20; cf. Acts 8:29; 1 Tim. 4:1-4).

This verse and other Scriptures point to a word-for-word communication by the Spirit of God. Directions and revelations were not general, but specific. These were not "leadings" or "impressions" but the revelation of the Word of God.

Certainly all true believers receive communication and guidance from the Holy Spirit. However, this communication does not take the form of the word-for-word pattern highlighting both the Old and New Testaments. Why? Again, Scripture serves as a "lamp" and a "light" to guide the believer (Ps. 119:105). In the Scriptures, the completed revelation of God, we have all things that pertain to life and godliness (2 Pet. 1:2-4). The Spirit has already spoken "word-for-word" in the Scriptures. He still speaks to individuals. Yet, this communication comes through leadings, impressions, assurances, and inward peace, as we seek to live out the revelation of Scripture (cf. Gal. 5:22,23 with Phil. 4:4-7).

Allow me to illustrate. One of the manifestations of the fruit of the Spirit is "peace" (Gal. 5:22). Philippians 4:7 contains a promise that the "peace of God" will guard our hearts and minds through Christ Jesus. What is the practical application? In the normal course of decision-making, whenever that "peace" is not present, one should be very careful to evaluate any given situation, circumstance, or choice. The Spirit assists the believer through this means. No doubt there have been times in your life when this very scenario has played itself out.

Other times arise when the believer seeks guidance and wisdom from the Lord over a certain matter. Through prayer and living out the principles of Proverbs 3:5, 6, the answer or guidance comes. Sometimes such occurs through the quiet inner voice of the Spirit—not a word-for-word command, but a leading so clear, so shrouded in peace, that you know it is the Spirit's leading. Other avenues may also be used of God to bring the answer: a passage of Scripture accompanied by personal application of the divine principles revealed; circumstances; open and closed doors; and the wisdom of consecrated friends. Of course, the Lord may sometimes miraculously intervene.

Does the Spirit speak directly to individuals today? The answer is "yes!" The key consideration focuses on the manner in which the Spirit communicates. Because the Spirit has completed His work of giving to us the word-for-word revelation of God—the Scriptures (cf. Prov. 30:5, 6; 2 Pet. 1:19-21; 2 Tim. 3:16), He speaks through the Word and through general impressions upon the heart. Yes, there may be specific leadings, but these do not assume the character of a word-for-word revelation.

Question 5: *In warning of the excesses and errors of the charismatic movement, you highlight concern over ecumenical affiliations and the emphases on new revelation. Do you view these as the most serious developments within the charismatic movement?*

Response: I will never forget a Bible conference I attended during the early seventies. The keynote speaker focused his message on the Second Coming of the Lord Jesus Christ. In laying the foundation for his sermon, he addressed forces and developments on the world scene which he felt had prophetical significance. Remember, this was in the early seventies.

I was stunned when the speaker stated something similar to the following: "I am convinced that the charismatic movement will be used to bring about unprecedented ecumenical unity and that this movement will lay the foundation for and usher in the harlot church of Revelation 17—the worldwide church which will be part of mystery Babylon."

At that time I did not even know the meaning of "mystery Babylon" or its significance in Revelation 17. However, I did know that the general scheme of prophecy outlined the emergence of an apostate church, bearing the name of Christ, but giving loyalty to the very Antichrist who is yet to appear (cf. 2 Thess. 2:1-12; 2 Tim. 4:1-5; 2 Tim. 3:1-7; Rev. 3:14-22; Rev. 13 and 17). I recoiled from the force of the speaker's assertions. Quick evaluations began to fill my thoughts: "He's just trying to be sensational. He's going too far with his predictions. There are no sinister elements in the charismatic movement. There are some dear saints with whom I disagree on the matter of tongues, but no sinister elements. His judgments are too harsh."

The only charismatics I knew at that time were dedicated saints in some local Assembly of God churches. I felt it was wrong to lay such a heavy accusation on dedicated servants of God. *I later would learn that the words of the speaker were not directed at these dear saints, but rather at the forces working on the international scene to link the charismatic movement with the ecumenical movement.*

The coming years would prove the speaker to be correct and the naive, first-year seminary student wrong. I did not know then that ties between Catholic and Pentecostal representatives had been strengthening for ten years. I did not know of David du Plessis' visits to the Vatican in the early sixties; of his discussions with three pontiffs; of his reception at the third session of Vatican II; and of his growing status in the World Council of Churches. I did not know that this leading Pentecostal representative was giving lectures at Yale, Princeton, Colgate, and other universities. No one informed me of Vatican II's statements on both the ecumenical and charismatic movements. News was just breaking in 1972 of the Roman Catholic Church establishing the International Communications Office—later to become the International Catholic Charismatic Renewal Office (ICCRO). And few noticed that by 1973 the first national charismatic conferences were being held by Roman Catholics, Episcopalians, Lutherans, Mennonites, Methodists, and Presbyterians.

Recent history well documents the fact that what was emerging in embryonic form in the early seventies has now taken on global proportions of monumental significance. Francis Schaeffer saw the trends building and raised an alarm in 1984. In his *The Great Evangelical Disaster*, he warned the Christian community against trading biblical truth for the false euphoria of ecumenical "love" and fellowship. Sadly, a "paradigm shift" has already taken place within evangelical circles. On March 29, 1994, some of the leaders of evangelical and conservative Christianity issued a declaration titled *Evangelicals and Catholics Together: The Christian Mission in the Third Millennium*. Among their ranks were the following: Chuck Colson, J. I. Packer, Bill Bright, Pat Robertson, Richard Land, and Larry Lewis of the Southern Baptist Convention. The twenty-five page document called upon evangelicals to accept Roman Catholics as brethren and to work together in social and evangelistic causes.[89] While differences were noted, the signatories of the document failed to stress that true Christians come to salvation by faith in Christ, and faith *alone*.

Joining a growing chorus of concerned Christians, John MacArthur directly addressed the document in his book *Reckless Faith*.[90] Later, MacArthur, D. James Kennedy, and R. C. Sproul met with some of the signatories and tried to get them to recant. While clarifying their own commitment to the basic tenets of the Reformation, the evangelical framers of this ECT document allowed it to stand as written. How tragic! Note just one section from the document:

> There are, then, differences between us that cannot be resolved here. But on this we are resolved: All authentic witness must be aimed at conversion to God in Christ by the power of the Spirit. Those converted—whether understood as having received the new birth for the first time or as having experienced the *reawakening of the new birth originally bestowed in the sacrament of baptism*—must be given full freedom and respect as they discern and decide the community in which they will live their new life in Christ.[91]

Through this document—even with its new addendum—"*the great evangelical disaster*" continues. Such further sets the stage for a growing deception that is sweeping planet earth. As doctrine is swept aside to make way for unity, the climate is enhanced for new revelations and close encounters of the "spiritual kind."

While the charismatic movement does have under its umbrella well-meaning saints who hold to the basic tenets of the faith, sinister elements do exist. To repeat a thought used earlier in our study, in many places *the sheep are beginning to howl as never before* (cf. Acts 20:28-30). And true sheep, as any good shepherd knows, do not howl!

So, in answer to the question, "YES, the ecumenical and revelatory aspects of the charismatic movement are most disturbing." Mention has already been made of the New Age Movement. The platform for the New Age Movement parallels much of what characterizes the emphases of the ecumenical movement—unity, peace, love, at the expense of truth and doctrine. New revelations to the inward man play a major role in New Age thought. That is why the New Agers plug themselves into occult phenomena, not caring who the "higher entities" or "masters" are who "channel forth" new revelations for the coming New World Order. No need to check out the source of these new revelations. That, too, accounts for the alarm being sounded within Christian circles over the rush of many to experience some new vision, some new prophecy, some new tongue, some new revelation. And again, no one pauses to check out the source. Just open yourself up to the universe, and the truth will come and transform.[92] Sensational? You better believe it. And you had better heed the warnings of Scripture to test the spirits, for the spirits are on the move as never before (cf. 1 John 4:1).

Question 6: *You have attributed much of charismatic growth to the planning and support of the Roman Catholic Office for Charismatic Renewal. You further state that "the gospel which a Roman Catholic priest would preach is not the gospel of Scripture." In your opinion, are there true Christians within the Roman Catholic Church, or are we to regard every Roman Catholic as an apostate or heretic?*

Response: In another seminar, I was once asked the following question: "Who is the God of a Roman Catholic?" The person asking the question was no doubt seeking a similar clarification. My answer on that occasion went something like this: "The god of Roman Catholic doctrine is not the God of the Bible; therefore, that leaves only one alternative, the "god of this age" (2 Cor. 4:4). Thus, the vast majority of those in the Roman Catholic Church are lost. However, those in Roman Catholic churches who have trusted in the Lord Jesus Christ *alone* and do not embrace the teachings of the Roman Catholic Church in their heart may be saved."

Some of these people who are genuinely born again within the Roman Catholic Church may remain in the church because of limited spiritual discernment or growth. Some may stay with the church because of family ties. I would quickly add that given time, if a person is truly born again, the Spirit of God will lead that person to see the error of remaining in a system which promotes a false gospel and holds so many in spiritual bondage. In time, these true Christians will disassociate from the heretical system.

One only has to talk to a converted Roman Catholic to learn of the spiritual bondage fostered by that system. The mass, the sacraments, the works doctrine, allegiance to Mary, and papal authority are not just insignificant "extras"—they stand as a perversion of the true message of salvation.[93]

Question 7: *We know of prophecies and revelations that have come true. Some of these were uttered as a "word from the Lord" and others came through interpretations of tongues. Why should we question their source when they have proven to be true?*

Response: All of the previous discussion which we have given on prophecy and tongues would answer the question. Biblical prophecy and tongues are no longer operative today in view of the completed Scriptures (cf. 1 Cor. 13:8ff. with James 1:22-25). This evidence alone governs any evaluation of a particular revelation. New revelation is to be rejected regardless of its outcome. A true prediction does not automatically point to a divine source. The source could just as easily be demonic.

Scripture sets forth the test of a true prophet. What is the test? That which is prophesied must come to pass—i.e., one hundred percent accuracy (cf. Deut. 18:15ff.; Ezek. 13:1-7; Jer. 23:25-40). *However, the tests of true prophecy comprise more than the single consideration of accuracy.* The prophecy must comply with the total testimony of Scripture. Deuteronomy 13:1-3 (cf. 2 Thess. 2:9) is instructive on these matters:

> If there arises among you a prophet or a dreamer of dreams, and he gives you a sign or a wonder, and the sign or the wonder comes to pass, of which he spoke to you, saying, "Let us go after other gods which you have not known, and let us serve them," you shall not listen to the words of that prophet or that dreamer of dreams, for the Lord your God is testing you to know whether you love the Lord your God with all your heart and with all your soul.

If a prophecy or sign comes to pass, but the total revelation of the prophecy conflicts with God's revelation of Himself, His will, or His program, the prophecy and the prophet are to be rejected.

Applying these principles to the question at hand, even true prophecies which may be given today are not to be viewed as having God as their source. Why? Because such stands against the program of God as revealed in Ephesians 2:20, 1 Corinthians 13:8-12 (with James 1:22-25), and Revelation 22:18, 19.

One must also remember that Satan quoted Scripture to Jesus (Matt. 4). He knows how to tailor a given prophecy to conform to circumstances as well as meet the apparent guidelines of Scripture. While Satan is not omniscient, his network of henchmen do have access to a phenomenal amount of information. No wonder then that occult prophets can approach accuracies of seventy percent or more in their pronouncements. Nevertheless, false prophets and any occult contact with spirit entities come under the condemnation of God (cf. Lev. 19:31; 20:6, 27; Deut. 18:11; 2 Kings 21:6, 23:24; Isa. 8:19; Isa. 47:12-14; Ezek. 13:1-7; Jer. 23:25-40). So again, be careful in accepting the validity of prophets or prophecies claiming God as their source (cf. Matt. 24:24; Mark 13:22).

Question 8: *In view of the innumerable testimonies of people who claim to have seen the Lord Jesus Christ, how do you know that such is not possible? You cited Peter Wagner's report of the young Cambodian girl, Kham Put, who was led through the jungle by the mysterious "guide" shrouded in an aura of light. Later a picture of Jesus in a refugee camp revealed the identity of her "guide" as being the Lord. In what way are this report and others contrary to Scripture? Did not Jesus personally appear to Paul on several occasions?*

Response: Let us take the case of Kham Put first. One must remember the instruction of 2 Corinthians 11:13-15:

> For such are false apostles, deceitful workers, transforming themselves into apostles of Christ. And no wonder! For Satan himself transforms himself into an angel of light. Therefore it is no great thing if his ministers also transform themselves into ministers of righteousness, whose end will be according to their works.

Satan is able to transform himself into a messenger of light. Was the messenger in the Cambodian jungle the Lord Jesus Christ? No! How can one be so sure? If the "guide" *was* the Lord Jesus Christ, such an appearance counters clear biblical revelation.

Before going to the Cross, Jesus prayed to the Father: "And now, O Father, glorify Me together with Yourself, with the glory which I had with You before the world was" (John 17:5; cf. John 7:37-39). In this high priestly prayer, Jesus was appealing to the Father to restore the glory that was veiled or laid aside in the incarnation (cf. Phil. 2:5-11). That glory had only been evidenced fully on the Mount of Transfiguration (Matt. 17:1-8; cf. 2 Pet. 1:16-21; John 1:14 with 1 Tim. 6:13-16). After the resurrection and ascension, the Lord Jesus Christ assumed His rightful position of authority at the right hand of the Father (Ps. 110:1; Acts 2:33-35; 7:55, 56; Rom. 8:34; Eph. 1:20; Col. 3:1; Heb. 1:13; 8:1; 10:12; 12:2). The glory that was His before the foundation of the world shown forth in full majesty. That is why every post-ascension description of Jesus presents Him in full majesty, arrayed in light brighter than the sun (Acts 9:3-8; 22:6-11; 26:12-18; Rev. 1:12-20; Rev. 21:9-11, 23; 22:5). *The Lord Jesus Christ will not veil his glory again; thus, any manifestation of Christ must parallel the full majesty of His Person as detailed in the aforementioned Scriptures.*

In the account of Kham Put, the "guide" was arrayed in an aura of light, but the aura came from hundreds of "fire flies" which seemed to surround the man. Such hardly parallels the glory of the Lord Jesus as revealed in Scripture. The Lord's glory is brighter than the sun; the Lord's glory will give light to the New Jerusalem and to earthly Jerusalem (cf. Rev. 21:9-11, 23; Isa. 60:1-3). When Jesus comes in great glory to rule upon the earth, His appearing shall be as lightning filling the heavens (Matt. 24:27-30; 25:30, 31). Our Lord warned believers in the first century that some would claim secret appearances of Christ:

> Then if anyone says to you, "Look, here is the Christ!" or "There!" do not believe it. For false christs and false prophets will arise and show great signs and wonders, so as to deceive, if possible, even the elect. See, I have told you beforehand. Therefore if they say to you, "Look, He is in the desert!" do not go out; or "Look, He is in the inner rooms!" do not believe it. For as the lightning comes from the east and flashes to the west, so also will the coming of the Son of Man be (Matt. 24:23-27).

While admittedly, the time frame of these warnings relates to the tribulation period just prior to the Second Coming of Christ, the prophecy still reinforces the fact that the risen Christ now appears in glory! Any supposed appearance of the Lord Jesus Christ, or any supposed vision of Jesus, which does not manifest His full glory, fails the test of Scripture.

Could the "guide" have been an angel sent from the Lord? Possibly. Yet, why would God send an angel whose appearance matched the likeness of Jesus on the poster in the refugee camp? In view of the warning of Exodus 20:4, 5, certain questions arise. Whether the "guide" was an angel from God or demonic deceiver, one will never know. However, one thing is sure: the "guide" was not the Lord Jesus Christ.

Some may be thinking: "Did not the Lord Jesus appear to the Apostle Paul even after the Lord was glorified?" (cf. Acts 9:3-8; 18:9, 10; 22:17-21; 23:11; 2 Tim. 4:17); "Did not Paul claim to have seen the Lord Jesus?" (1 Cor. 9:1); "Did not Stephen have a vision of the glorified Lord Jesus?" (Acts 7:55, 56); "And what of Ananias in Acts 9:10-16?" If such appearances were made to these saints after Jesus' ascension, why could not Jesus appear to saints today?

The Scriptures which have just been cited vindicate the position put forth earlier. One must remember that Jesus is *positionally* seated at the right hand of the Father (Ps. 110:1; Col. 3:1; Heb. 8:1; 10:12; 12:2). From that enthroned position He ministers as our High Priest. This requires a *localized* ministry. Of the scriptural instances noted above, where Jesus appeared to certain individuals, the majority were visions. While there were localized phenomena when Paul encountered Jesus on the Damascus Road (Acts 9:3-8; 22:4-11; 26:9-18), Paul never testified that He saw Jesus there in a localized sense. Granted, he saw the aura of glory and was blinded; granted, he heard the voice of Jesus; but, again, Paul gave no testimony of a localized appearance of the Lord. Although the Lord is seated at the right hand of the Father, His voice and glory may be manifested or projected into space-time realities. Paul was granted that privilege of seeing the Lord in the later visions (Acts 18:9, 10; 22:17-21).

Yes, but what about the Scripture passages in Acts 23:11 and 2 Timothy 4:17 which attest to the fact that the Lord "stood by" Paul and spoke to Him or strengthened him? Surely these passages strongly point to a localized appearance of the Lord Jesus on the earth.

We are not "splitting hairs" here. In view of the declarations of Jesus in Matthew 24:23-27 and that of the angels in Acts 1:9-11 (cf. Zech. 12:10-14:8), this is an important issue. Such becomes all the more important when leading evangelicals are claiming personal appearances of Christ and the imparting of new revelation.

Remember that Jesus presently assumes a *localized* ministry in heaven for the saints. We have already noted numerous Scriptures to support this position. Stephen's vision in Acts 7:55, 56 presents the key elements of a revelation of Jesus Christ which meet the biblical criteria: (1) Jesus is seen in glory; (2) He is seen in His authoritative position at the right hand of the Father. We are concerned with those who claim localized appearances of Jesus on earth, or with those who testify of visions of Jesus which do not mirror scriptural realities—i.e., a failure to manifest the Lord's full majesty or the imparting of new revelation.

But let us return to the question at hand. Do not the references in Acts 23:11 and 2 Timothy 4:17 point to localized appearances of the Lord on the earth? Although both passages stress that the Lord "stood by" or "stood with" Paul, the verses do not detail the *manner* in which Christ made His presence felt. We know He verbally communicated to Paul; we know He encouraged and strengthened Paul by imparting new revelation. However, did Jesus leave His localized ministry in heaven, the position at the right hand of the Father, to personally minister to Paul? The burden of proof rests upon those who would demand such an interpretation. The Greek words translated stood by or "stood with" also carry the following meanings: *to approach; to come to; to come near; to appear*. Thus, the phrases "stood by" or "stood with" could merely be metaphorical in their intent to show the Lord's support of Paul in his times of trial. Again, these verses do not suggest that the Lord left His place in glory to appear personally to Paul. *Even the Damascus road appearance, though localized, was a manifestation of Jesus' glory and His voice, not His full presence.*

The warnings in Scripture against secret appearances of Jesus still stand. These warnings become even more serious in view of the completion of Scripture and the passing of the Apostolic Office. Moreover, in view of the present "Age of Revelation" and the coming New World Order, Christians need to be especially careful to identify and resist deception. Even the most thrilling encounter with an apparent manifestation of Christ needs to be tested by Scripture. If the Apostle Paul only experienced four brief encounters with the resurrected Christ—and these encounters affected the course of Christianity down through the ages, one must question the reason why Jesus would grant appearances to certain saints today.

Question 9: *Are not you limiting the work of the Holy Spirit in light of Peter's proclamations on the Day of Pentecost? After all, in Acts 2:16-21, Peter testified that Joel's prophecy was being fulfilled. Indeed, the Spirit was being poured out on all flesh. Peter, like Joel, declared that men and women would experience visions, dreams, and would prophesy.*

Response: First of all, JOEL'S PROPHECY WAS NOT FULFILLED AT PENTECOST; MOREOVER, IT WAS NOT EVEN PARTIALLY FULFILLED. As we proceed with our discussion this will become quite evident.

The setting and timing of Joel's prophecy is crucial to the matters before us. As one studies the Book of Joel, one will find the key focus to be the *Day of the Lord*. In the first chapter, Joel makes reference to an actual locust plague that previously engulfed the land. This locust plague becomes a historical parallel for a future invasion described in Chapter Two. Yet, this future invasion does not involve locusts; rather, it involves a northern army which ravages Israel. Even though this army is called the "Lord's army" in Joel 2:11, one must not confuse this army with the people of God. The pagan king, Cyrus of Persia, was named of the Lord decades before his birth; he was called the Lord's "shepherd," the Lord's "anointed," because he would fulfill the purposes of God (cf. Isa. 44:28-45:7). In the same way, the northern army in Joel 2 refers to hostile forces which come against Israel in the last days. They are referred to as the Lord's army because they fulfill His sovereign purposes in history.

One of the most important statements of Joel's prophecy occurs in Joel 2:18-20. In these verses the Lord reveals that He will destroy the northern army and drive them from the land of Israel (cf. Ezek. 38 and 39). When one compares these verses with those in Ezekiel, one comes to understand that the destruction of the northern army occurs during the tribulation period, just prior to the Second Coming of Jesus. Even the term "Day of the Lord" has primary reference in the Old Testament to the terrible times on the earth just prior to the coming of the Lord (cf. Zeph. 1:7, 14-18; 3:8; Zech. 14).

What is the significance of all this? *The portion of Joel's prophecy quoted by Peter at Pentecost relates to the time AFTER the destruction of the northern army. That means that Joel's entire prophecy will only be fulfilled during the Tribulation. Please note the time frame which Joel gives for the prophecy:*

> And it shall come to pass **afterward** that I will pour out My Spirit on all flesh; Your sons and your daughters shall prophesy, Your old men shall dream dreams, Your young men shall see visions; And also on My menservants and on My maidservants I will pour out My Spirit in those days. And I will show wonders in the heavens and in the earth; blood and fire and pillars of smoke. The sun shall be turned into darkness, and the moon into blood, before the coming of the great and terrible day of the Lord. And it shall come to pass

that whoever calls on the name of the Lord shall be saved (Joel 2:28-32; boldface mine).

Do not miss the introduction to this portion of Joel's prophecy. The context clearly reveals that all of the manifestations of Joel's prophecy occur after the invasion and destruction of the northern army (Joel 2:1-27). The prophecy thrusts us right into the tribulation period just prior to Jesus' Second coming. When one compares the prophecy here with Jesus' description of the Tribulation in Matthew 24:29, the parallels are unmistakable.

The *pouring out of the Spirit* is seen again in Ezekiel 39:29, *"'And I will not hide My face from them anymore; for I shall have poured out My Spirit on the house of Israel,' says the Lord God."* What is the context here in Ezekiel? It is the same as that in Joel: that is, the Spirit will be poured out after the destruction of the northern army (cf. Ezek. 39:1-15; Ezek. 38:23).

None of the latter signs of Joel's prophecy were fulfilled at Pentecost—i.e., the wonders in the heavens and in the earth; the blood, the fire, the smoke, and the darkening of the sun and moon. Why not? Again, because the entire prophecy of Joel refers to the time after the destruction of the northern army. Such is the clear context of Joel's prophecy. This means that none of the elements of Joel's prophecy was fulfilled at Pentecost. They must all await a future fulfillment.

What then did Peter mean by his statement: *"But this is what was spoken by the prophet Joel. . ."*? Obviously, he was referring to the miracle of tongues which had just occurred. Was he saying that the phenomenon of tongues was fulfilling the prophecy of Joel? No! He simply meant, "THE 'AGE OF THE SPIRIT' HAS ARRIVED; THE SAME SPIRIT WHO WILL BRING MARVELLOUS BLESSINGS WHEN JOEL'S PROPHECY UNFOLDS IS ALREADY HERE AND MANIFESTING HIMSELF." Peter did not declare that Joel's prophecy was fulfilled; but he certainly related what was happening at Pentecost to similar phenomena and to the same Source as Joel's prophecy.

A simple illustration is in order here. Let us suppose we are in an area that receives little or no snow during the year. And let us further suppose that we have never seen snow. The news forecast warns us of an unusual weather pattern which makes a blizzard very likely in two days. As we are walking down the street conversing about this approaching anomaly, all of a sudden we see a few snowflakes falling. Remember, for the sake of the illustration, we have never really seen snow. Upon seeing the snowflakes, one of us exclaims, "This is that which was spoken of by

Robert the weatherman!" Notice, the testimony is not saying that the "prophecy" concerning the blizzard is now unfolding. All that is being said is that the snowflakes now falling are the same kind of phenomena forecast to come at a later date. Such is the force of Peter's pronouncement at Pentecost. He was merely declaring that the "Age of the Spirit" had arrived and such was akin to the power behind Joel's prophecy.

Thus, for those who wish to find in Joel 2 support for the current emphasis on visions, dreams, or prophecies, no biblical support exists. The entire prophecy of Joel relates to the tribulation period when just before the return of Christ, there will be signs and wonders in the heavens and a mighty outpouring of the Spirit of God. Such will occur in the Day of the Lord.

Peter quoted Joel to emphasize that a special ministry of the Spirit had begun. He also quoted Joel because Joel's prophecy builds to the statement, "whoever calls on the name of the Lord shall be saved" (Joel 2:32; Acts 2:21). That invitational phrase was well known to the Jews. It first appears in Genesis 4:26 and occurs a number of times in the Old Testament. In that invitation, Peter sees the doorway for the redemption of the nation. Paul would later employ the same phrase in Romans 10:13 and apply it to salvation. Thus, even though Pentecost did not even partially fulfill Joel's prophecy, there are some parallels which occasioned its use.

Question 10: *In Acts 8:1-17, Scripture records that many of the people in Samaria accepted the Lord Jesus Christ when they heard the gospel. Those who believed were baptized (8:12, 13). However, it was not until the apostles came from Jerusalem and laid hands on the new converts that they received the Holy Spirit. Why the delay in believers receiving the Holy Spirit? Could not this point to a second work of grace which many speak about today?*

Response: Normally, the Holy Spirit baptizes, indwells, and seals a believer at the moment of faith (Eph. 1:13, 14; Rom. 8:9; 1 Cor. 12:13). Indeed, the teaching of Romans 8:9 is very clear: "Now if anyone does not have the Spirit of Christ, he is not His." Yet, here in Acts 8 there was a delay in some believers receiving the Spirit. The text seems to imply that it was necessary for an apostle to be present at the coming of the Holy Spirit to indwell believers in Samaria. One must remember that the apostles were stewards of the early church during its infancy. The coming of the Spirit through them not only vindicated their ministry, but also served both to vindicate Philip's ministry and to underscore the *unity* between what was happening in Jerusalem and in Samaria. In essence, Peter and John's prayer that the Samaritan believers would receive the Spirit, and the imparting of the Spirit through the laying on of hands: (1) confirmed the apostles' authority over the Samaritan work; (2) prevented any schism from occurring in the early church—this because of the long-standing animosity between the Jews and Samaritans; now, the Samaritan believers were on equal standing with their brothers in Jerusalem, and all had both the testimony of Peter and John, and the Holy Spirit (cf. Luke 9:52-54); (3) confirmed Philip's ministry in Samaria; (4) and confirmed the advance and message of the kingdom of God—the Spirit's coming indicating the presence of the interim kingdom (cf. Acts 8:12; Jer. 31:31-34; Ezek. 36:23-27; Joel 2:28-32; Matt. 21:43; 1 Pet. 2:9).

In view of the evidence, one should not view Acts 8 as setting forth a pattern for the church today. The same may be said for the account in Acts 19:1-7. Why? Because many aspects and practices of the early church were *transitional* in nature. In other words, with time, certain practices, institutions, phenomena, and emphases would pass away. As the early church grew out of its Jewish mold, as the Spirit incorporated Gentiles into the Body of Christ, and as new revelation came forth in the form of Scripture, new patterns would establish themselves under the guidance of the Spirit. What were some of these transitional elements which passed away with time? In addition to the delay of the Spirit coming to indwell some believers (Acts 2, 8), the following were also transitional elements:

1. *The continued observance of Jewish practices* by these early Christians. Even Paul was willing to assist Jewish believers execute a Nazarite vow by paying for the offering of blood sacrifices (Acts 21:18-26; cf. Num. 6; Acts 3:1; 18:18; 20:16; 21:15-26). Even though the early church knew it was to take the gospel to every creature, some time elapsed before the Jewish prejudices were broken (cf. Acts 10; 11:1-18, especially 11:19; 15:1-35). With the Lord revealing through Paul the "mystery" of the Body of Christ, and the New Man (Eph. 1-3), and with the destruction of Jerusalem by Roman forces in A.D. 70, the trappings of Judaism which so influenced the church faded away.

2. *The community of goods* (Acts 4:33-37). While such is not demanded today, the example of care and sacrifice shared by all believers serves

as a worthy model to emulate (cf. Acts 6:1-7; 1 Tim. 5:9, 10).

3. *The instant judgment upon sin* (Acts 5:1-11). Purity was essential for the infant church. Purity is still essential and the Lord judges His children even today (1 Cor. 11:29-32; Heb. 12:1-11; 1 John 5:16,17). However, the decisiveness and severity of the judgment in Acts 5 does not serve as the common pattern for today.

4. *The Apostolic Office* (Rev. 21:14). More than sufficient discussion has been devoted to the transitional nature of this office.

5. *The sign and revelatory gifts* (Mark 16:20; Eph. 2:20). Again, much discussion and considerable scriptural evidence have been presented to underscore the transitional nature of these phenomena.

6. *The "Old Testament saints"* caught in transition brought into the Body of Christ (Acts 19:1-8). This was an essential part of the ministry of the Spirit in the early church.

7. *The giving of Scripture* (1 Thess. 2:13; 2 Tim. 3:16; Rev. 1:1 with 22:18, 19). The time would come when Scripture would be complete.

Question 11: *You have noted that a number of well known and credible evangelical scholars have recently endorsed the charismatic movement. Moreover, you have stated that this trend is continuing. How do you explain this? Isn't it a bit arrogant to assume that these dedicated men who have done so much for the cause of Christ are wrong in their assessments? In responding to the charismatic movement, should not we follow the advice given by Gamaliel to the Jews of his day regarding the advance of Christianity, lest we find ourselves fighting against God (cf. Acts 5:38, 39)?*

Response: Your question really poses a number of critical considerations. You have correctly understood the fact that there is a growing trend within evangelical scholarship to endorse the charismatic movement. Let me quickly add, however, that a host of fundamental and conservative scholars still hold to their basic critique of the movement. Nevertheless, you ask the question, "How can so many credible evangelical leaders, of long-standing reputation, endorse the charismatic movement if it is wrong?"

One cannot offer an explanation that will satisfy everyone. Many of these now endorsing aspects of the charismatic movement have been used of the Lord in times past to enrich all our lives. They have studied biblical exegesis. They know the rules of biblical interpretation. Their intent and motives are no doubt to glorify the Lord and to promote "truth" as they see it. However, a proven track record is no insurance against error. Even Solomon, who had a divine gift of wisdom and wrote Scripture, failed to order his later life by Scripture (cf. Deut. 17:14-20; 1 Kings 3:1-11). This is not to suggest that every evangelical scholar endorsing the charismatic movement falls into this category or knowingly departs from Scripture.

Some, however, have allowed personal experience and their own evaluation of reported spiritual phenomena to influence their assessment of Scripture. We all approach Scripture with certain presuppositions. None of us is truly objective in the purest sense. However, the test of spiritual realities must always be Scripture. And Scripture will interpret Scripture. This must be reaffirmed continually, regardless of how long one has served the Lord Jesus Christ and regardless of the status one holds.

Some have made the mistake of asserting that the miracles, signs, and wonders which God IS DOING in some areas of the world should be the norm for every believer or every church setting. They have failed to understand that those people groups which do not have access to Scripture are in an "ACTS SITUATION." God can and will do supernatural acts and use unique avenues to break into those cultures which do not have Scripture. However, it is a mistake to take what God is doing to bring forth an infant church and demand that such be the common experience for all Christians in all settings.

Relationships also enter into the picture. Friendship ties grow as our circle of ministry grows. As one is exposed to an ever broadening sphere of ministry, one comes to see that our marvellous God is a God of diversity. He displays His power and His programs amidst many patterns of ministry and worship. As friendship ties are made, the pressure to be "open" to possible alternatives of God's workings also grows. In the midst of these relational considerations, objective adherence to Scripture is sometimes put aside—not knowingly; it just happens.

So, whether one grapples with personal experiences, confirmed reports of miracles, fulfilled prophecies, signs and wonders, broadened horizons of ministry, deepened relationships and appreciation for the diversity within the Body of Christ and the program of God, all must be subjected to Scripture. This takes a daily renewed commitment.

Let us return once again to the example of Solomon and what may be termed the "**Solomon Syndrome.**" What in the world is the "Solomon Syndrome?" Please stay tuned.

In Deuteronomy 17, the setting is very moving. Moses is addressing a new generation of Israelites who shall go in and possess the promised land. As he gazes into the eyes of this new generation, Moses is led of God to give instruction regarding the future of the nation. Specifically, he gives guidelines which any future king of Israel should follow:

> When you come to the land which the Lord your God is giving you, and possess it and dwell in it, and say, "I will set a king over me like all the nations that are around me," you shall surely set a king over you whom the Lord your God chooses; one from among your brethren you shall set as king over you; you may not set a foreigner over you, who is not your brother, *But he shall not multiply horses for himself,* nor cause the people to return to *Egypt* to multiply horses, for the Lord has said to you, "You shall not return that way again." *Neither shall he multiply wives for himself,* lest his heart turn away; *nor shall he greatly multiply silver and gold for himself.* Also it shall be, when he sits on the throne of his kingdom, that *he shall write for himself a copy of this law in a book,* from the one before the priests, the Levites. And it shall be with him, and *he shall read it all the days of his life, that he may learn to fear the Lord his God and be careful to observe all the words of this law and these statutes,* that his heart may not be lifted above his brethren, that he may not turn aside from the commandment to the right hand or to the left, and that he may prolong his days in his kingdom, he and his children in the midst of Israel" (Deut. 17:14-20; italics mine).

Do not miss the four great prohibitions for Israel's future king; and do not overlook the one great positive exhortation. Let us summarize:

Prohibitions:

1. *Do not multiply horses for yourself.* Why? In those days, horses and chariots were the state-of-the-arts military hardware. Israel's king was to place his confidence in God, not military might.

2. *Do not make alliances with Egypt*—whether to buy horses or for any

other means. Egypt represents everything the world offers in rebellion to God. Israel's king and Israel's population were to have nothing to do with Egypt.

3. *Do not multiply wives to yourself.* Why? Not only does such destroy God's original model for marriage (cf. Gen. 2:24), but pagan wives could affect the heart of the king and his loyalty to God. *Relationships can become the doorway for doctrinal defections.*

4. *Do not multiply gold or silver to yourself.* Why? Because such could focus the kings heart upon earthly treasures rather than upon the glory of God. The glory of God is always to be preferred to the glory and praise of men.

Positive Exhortation: *Copy and read the Word of God continually so that you will always observe to do all that is written in these commands.*

Again, these were the instructions for Israel's future king. Now for the "Solomon Syndrome."

Most Bible students are well aware of the fact that Solomon was blessed by God in many wonderful ways. He was given special wisdom by God; he was promised prosperity; he was promised peace; he was given the right to build a temple in honor of God's name; and he would even be given the privilege of being used of the Spirit to write Scripture (cf. 1 Kings 3-11). In essence, he had it all: wisdom, wealth, and world acclaim. YET, IN THE MIDST OF ALL THIS BLESSING, HE BROKE EVERY ONE OF THE FOUR PROHIBITIONS SET FORTH BY MOSES IN THE WORD OF GOD.

Solomon multiplied horses to himself—indeed, he had forty thousand stalls of horses for his chariots (1 Kings 4:26; cf. 10:26-29). He married Pharoah's daughter and thus opened avenues of contact between himself and the former enemy of the people of God (1 Kings 11:1). He multiplied wives unto himself; and through their influence, Solomon's heart was turned to embrace false gods (1 Kings 11:1-14). Solomon also multiplied gold and silver to himself (1 Kings 10:14-25). To adorn the temple of God with gold served as an act of adoration; however, to accumulate gold for his own possession transgressed the clear commands of Scripture.

If you had served in the court of Solomon for a number of years, if you had witnessed firsthand Solomon's wisdom, the filling of the temple with the glory of God, the foreign emissaries coming to view the splendor of Solomon's reign, how would you respond if some charged that Solomon had begun to drift away from God in his latter years. You might have been tempted to respond: "Remember what he has done, what he has accomplished, and how God has mightily used him; Israel is respected throughout the world because of Solomon and there is peace and prosperity; even though images of foreign gods are present in Jerusalem, Yahweh is still honored throughout the land and the temple is magnificent!" You might be tempted to point out that his contributions to the cause of Yahweh have far outweighed his present deficiencies. Nevertheless, the deficiencies would have to be addressed by any true prophet in the land.

Why did Solomon stray so far? Again, he possessed a special portion of wisdom from the Lord. He was used of the Lord to write Scripture. Why? And again, why? The answer is simple. HE NEGLECTED THE POSITIVE EXHORTATION OF MOSES REGARDING THE WORD OF GOD. Remember that the future king of Israel was not only to personally copy the Word of God, he was to ABIDE in the Word of God. *Even a supernatural gift of wisdom could not supplant daily dependency on the Word of God.* That is why Solomon moved away from the truth and eventually went into error.

The "Solomon Syndrome" may be summarized in the following way: one may serve the Lord faithfully for a number of years; one may make tremendous contributions on behalf of the kingdom of God on earth; one may be divinely endowed with special gifts and wisdom; and yet, in the latter years of one's walk with God, one may allow presumption, relationships, and the failure to internalize the Word of God to lead one away from the truth. Only a commitment to the Word of God, lived out in daily dependence and obedience to God, can assure faithfulness to Him to the end.

Many of the leading evangelical scholars of our day have endorsed the charismatic movement. Could their endorsements be right? No! And again, NO! The scriptural evidence, the errors and excesses of the charismatic movement, the "mixed multitude" which is gathering under the charismatic umbrella, all point to a growing deception. Why then do these good men join the chorus for acceptance? For *some*, the answer is the "Solomon Syndrome." *They have allowed relationships and a false concept of love and tolerance to lead them away.*

Again, Francis A. Schaeffer, in his *The Great Evangelical Disaster*, applies the same type of analysis to evangelical defections in general. Relationships and a false understanding of biblical unity and love can become doorways for doctrinal defection. If such could happen to the gifted Solomon, it could happen to anyone. And it is happening. Gifted men who have been a blessing to the Body of Christ and who are regarded as leading evangelicals are promoting associations that go against Scripture and grieve the Spirit of God. (See J. I. Packer, *Keep in Step With the Spirit*, pp. 170-199; also Charles Colson, *Loving God* [Grand Rapids, Michigan: Zondervan Publishing Company, 1987], pp. 125-129; *Kingdoms in Conflict* [London: Hodder and Stoughton, 1987], pp. 193-197, 318-328). When these true brethren embrace leading figures in the Roman Catholic Church as "brothers," the distinction between evangelical and heretic becomes blurred. (See the booklet *The Charismatic Challenge* by Seamus Milligan [Belfast: E.P.S., 1985].)

Years after the destruction of Solomon's temple and the dispersion of the Jewish nation, a Jewish remnant returned to Jerusalem to rebuild the temple. They came under the leadership of Zerubbabel and Joshua. With great expectation and joy, they laid the foundation of the new temple (cf. Ezra 3). Even though they were as a mere island in a pagan sea, the people of God were once again establishing a witness to Yahweh through the temple effort. Yet, as they continued to build, they were approached by their neighbors who offered assistance. These people who practiced a syncretic form of religion falsely claimed that they worshiped the Lord just like the Jews. Note the scriptural account:

> Now when the adversaries of Judah and Benjamin heard that the descendants of the captivity were building the temple of the Lord God of Israel, they came to Zerubbabel and the heads of the fathers' houses, and said to them, *"Let us build with you, for we seek your God as you do; and we have sacrificed to Him since the days of Esarhaddon king of Assyria, who brought us here."* But Zerubbabel and Jeshua and the rest of the heads of the fathers' houses of Israel said to them, "You may do nothing with us to build a house for our God; but we alone will build to the Lord God of Israel, as King Cyrus the king of Persia has commanded us" (Ezra 4:1-3; italics mine).

It would have been very easy for Zerubbabel and the leaders of Israel to have positively responded to these overtures. Yet, they knew the value of truth; they knew the prohibitions of Scripture and the disastrous effects of the *Solomon Syndrome*. Therefore, they risked war and offense to their neighbors in order to be faithful to the Word of God and to their Lord. May their example be lived out in similar situations facing the church today. Christians everywhere must remain faithful to God's claims.

Question 12: *Why do we have to go into such intricate and complicated studies to know the answers on these charismatic issues? Why can't we just approach the Scriptures as a child looking in faith to our Father for the answers?*

Response: The Bible is like an ocean. Some parts allow us to stand in the shallows and see the bottom. Some things are very clear and very definite at first glance. Yet, other portions of the Bible lead to depths which will take an eternity to fully explore. Even the Apostle Peter recognized this when he wrote the following concerning Paul's writings:

> Therefore, beloved, looking forward to these things, be diligent to be found by Him in peace, without spot and blameless; and account that the longsuffering of our Lord is salvation—as also our beloved brother Paul, according to the wisdom given to him, has written to you, as also in all his epistles, speaking in them of these things, *in which are some things hard to understand*, which those who are untaught and unstable twist to their own destruction, as they do also the rest of the Scriptures (2 Pet. 3:14-16; italics mine).

If such was an admission of Peter, then we too need to realize that there are portions of Scripture which require study and work. While we accept the Scriptures and reverently submit to them in child-like faith, we must labor diligently with those controversial areas to discern the truth. Remember the admonition of Paul in 2 Timothy 2:15, "Be diligent to present yourself approved to God, a worker who does not need to be ashamed, rightly dividing the word of truth."

Part of the problem of the Corinthian church was their contentment with immaturity. Paul calls them "babes in Christ" and "carnal" (1 Cor. 3:1). Paul went on to declare that because of their immaturity they could not even understand further spiritual food (1 Cor. 3:2, 3). He used the same rebuke to the Corinthians on the issue of tongues—that is, they were approaching the issue in a state of immaturity (cf. 1 Cor. 14:20). Throughout the Scriptures the Spirit exhorts believers to approach the Word of God with maturity (2 Tim. 2:15; Heb. 6:1-3). If one rejects this, one may commit the same interpretive errors as the Corinthians.

Years ago, just a few weeks prior to entering seminary training, I met a "retired" Baptist preacher. He was in his eighties and had served the Lord faithfully for years. As a matter of fact, he still held revivals in the city in which we lived. When he learned I was headed for seminary, he tried to dissuade me from going. His reasoning went something like this:

"Son, you have the Holy Spirit of God living within you; you don't need other men to tell you what the Scriptures mean. Didn't Jesus say in John 16:13 that His Spirit would lead you into all truth; didn't the Lord say in 1 Corinthians 2:10 that it is the Spirit who searches and reveals the deep things of God. Son, you just stick with the Bible and the Spirit of God, and preach the Word. You don't need men to tell what to believe."

To a new Christian such arguments sounded pretty persuasive. On the one hand, I knew there was much more for me to learn about the Bible; yet, on the other hand, I did not want to diminish the role of the Holy Spirit in my life. This man's arguments both challenged and disturbed me.

I wrestled with these words until another good friend reminded me that the same Lord Jesus who spoke the words of John 16:13 gave teachers to the church. He pointed out a number of passages that underscored the need for teachers—and these words were just as much from the Holy Spirit as the words recorded in 1 Corinthians 2:10 (cf. Eph. 4:11-16; 1 Cor. 12:28-31; 1 Tim. 3:2; 2 Tim. 2:1, 2). Praise the Lord! What a relief and joy to find the balance.

Yes, the Spirit of God does reveal the deeper things of God in the Word; but there is also a place for teachers to impart the lessons which they have been taught. Moreover, there is a special gift of teaching where one's teaching is especially anointed of the Lord. This does not mean that believers should sit passively just absorbing everything which a teacher may impart. Believers are to be like the Bereans who received the preaching and teaching of Paul, but tested them by the Scriptures (Acts 17:11). Any true teacher from the Lord will invite and encourage believers to test the teaching by Scripture.

So, in summary, why should we not just accept the Scriptures as we read them—much like a child? We do accept their authority, inerrancy, and sufficiency. We do admit our dependency upon the Holy Spirit to reveal the precious truths of God's Word. Nevertheless, in the area of biblical interpretation we acknowledge that some portions of Scripture will require work and mature labor (2 Tim. 2:15; 1 Cor. 14:20); some portions will be hard to understand (2 Pet. 3:14-16; Heb. 6:1-3; 1 Cor. 3:1-3); and we acknowledge that the Lord has given teachers to the Body of Christ to assist in that perfecting work of the saints so that they will not be tossed about by every wind of doctrine or the trickery of men (Eph. 4:11-16).

Question 13: *You referred to "ministries of deliverance" with reservation.*

Why the reservation? Do you feel that there is no place for such ministries in the church today; and if so, do you base that on the cessation of the sign gifts of Mark 16:17-20?

Response: One must remember that the sign gifts were given to individuals to confirm the spoken Word of God (Mark 16:20). There were some sign gifts which by their very nature had parallels in the corporate ministry of the Church. For instance, in James 5:13-16 the church is called upon to corporately pray for the sick. Even though the sign gift of healing ceased with the completion of Scripture, the ministry of believers praying for the sick continues. GOD STILL HEALS TODAY, BUT HE DOES SO IN RESPONSE TO THE PRAYERS OF HIS PEOPLE AND IN ACCORDANCE WITH HIS SOVEREIGN GRACE. One does not possess the gift of healing today. One, however, may have greater faith and surrender to pray for healing in this area than others—but this greater faith does not equate with the sign gift of Mark 16.

Deliverance ministries would follow the same pattern. The sign gift of casting out demons was also given to individuals to confirm the spoken Word. While this gift is no longer operative today, believers do have the power through prayer to effect deliverance from demonic oppression and possession. Again, such occurs through the power of the Lord Jesus and the prayers of God's saints, not because someone has the gift of exorcism. As stated earlier, the power and prayers for deliverance are not the property of a few, but the possession of every believer.

Granted, only a few saints venture into this area. Maybe this is so because the direct confrontation with the powers of darkness requires so much spiritual consecration on the part of believers. I would refer the reader to Mark I. Bubeck's excellent work, *The Adversary: The Christian Versus Demonic Activity* (Chicago: Moody Press, 1975). While I do not endorse all aspects of Bubeck's book, I do feel he approaches the issues regarding deliverance from a sound biblical perspective. Thus, his book is certainly worth reading.

While there may arise those occasions in the ministry to pray over those who are demon possessed or oppressed, it is important to establish, *in the individual,* direct dependency upon the Lord Jesus Christ. How is this done? The individual should be encouraged to confess and renounce any claims of sin or the powers of darkness, and appeal personally to the Lord. The oppressed or possessed individual needs to realize that his deliverance comes from the Lord Jesus Christ. If he or she prays for salvation or deliverance, such sets the pattern for future problems which may arise. Instead of depending upon human agency or looking to others for ministries of deliverance, the individual looks to the Lord Jesus Christ. The promise of James 4:7 holds for every Christian: "Therefore submit to God. Resist the devil and he will flee from you."

One final word is in order. Those who engage in "ministries of deliverance" must be very careful to avoid leading one into a morbid inward spiral. I have personally counselled those who were damaged spiritually through the counsel of some in deliverance ministries. Instead of focusing upon the Lord Jesus Christ, believers struggling with sin were told to make a list of every negative or non-spiritual aspect which appeared in their life. They were then to renounce the demon associated with such activity. In many cases, everyday struggle with one's own sin nature has been confused with demonic activity. While all of us no doubt need to have our discernment and sensitivity to spiritual warfare increased, preoccupation with the power of Christ must have the preeminence.

Question 14: *How do you explain the FACT that some people are genuinely healed at charismatic meetings? I attended a meeting on one occasion and personally witnessed a miraculous healing as the speaker prayed for the sick. How can you say the speaker did not possess the gift of healing, when one was healed in response to his prayers?*

Response: I would agree that in some charismatic meetings, genuine healings do take place. Again, I would stress that such does not occur because the speaker or healer has the gift of healing (see previous question). God is sovereign and merciful, and He will step into our lives at times to heal—even in the midst of charismatic error.

Put yourself in the position of a Christian that has come to such a meeting. Maybe this person has lived with an infirmity for years. In the context of a meeting which stresses God's miraculous power to heal and to touch lives, that particular individual's heart is at a point of surrender and openness to God as never before. Prayers pour forth in petition and praise. Even though the "healer" or speaker is praying for the sick, so the individual is praying as well—and so are many others. God is not restricted by any setting. He may heal that individual in response to surrender and in accordance with His will. However, God does not heal because the speaker has the gift of healing. Thus, I would respectfully differ with those who maintain that all healings in charismatic circles are spurious; many certainly appear to be authentic.

You see, the crucial point comes after the healing takes place in such a context. The healed person faces the temptation of focusing on (1) the man or speaker, (2) the method employed, or (3) the message preached. The person may view the healing as vindicating the ministry of the "healer." That is the danger. Instead, one should focus on the *majesty* of God and then *measure* the entire experience by the Word of God. Remember, if God allowed Samuel to appear in the context of an occult encounter (cf. 1 Sam. 28:3-25), God can heal in the midst of error.

As John Wimber, Jack Deere, and the Vineyard Ministries have fostered much of the current emphases on healing, their teachings need to be assessed. In March of 1990, John Wimber and Jack Deere led a "Spiritual Warfare Conference" in Sydney, Australia. Over 5,500 people attended from various parts of the country. During the conference, John Wimber and Jack Deere were interviewed by leading evangelicals in the Sydney area. In planning for the discussions, the men informed John Wimber and Jack Deere that their responses would be made available for later publication. Accounts of the conference and the discussions formed the substance of a special double issue in the Anglican magazine *The Briefing* (Issue #45/46, April 24, 1990). Please remember that at that time, John Wimber and Jack Deere spearheaded the Vineyard Movement which sponsored seminars to teach people "to minister like Jesus."

At every session of the conference, there was a call for healing. Most of the disorders were of the following nature:

1. Bad backs, necks
2. Problem with left great toe
3. Nervous disorders
4. Unequal leg lengths
5. Breathing problems
6. Barrenness

As one can see, most of these conditions which were prayed over hardly compare to the disorders which Jesus and the apostles healed.

Nevertheless, the Vineyard Movement still maintains that it can teach people "to minister like Jesus." Because John Wimber was aware of the special scrutiny being accorded the conference, he seemed to tone down claims which were so bold at other conferences. He even stated in one session, "many or most aren't healed"; and at another time, "healing sometimes happens, more often than not it doesn't." Wimber then proceeded to explain the reason why the majority of people are not healed: "because we are not mature enough in faith." ("Spiritual Warfare: Medical Reflections" by Dr. Philip Selden in *The Briefing*, p. 19, used by permission.)

When John Wimber was asked about healings regarding Down's syndrome children—a genetic disease which cannot be healed by psychosomatic factors—the response was startling. John Wimber claimed to have prayed over more than two hundred children with Down syndrome. According to his own testimony, only one child evidenced signs of healing. Yet, when pressed on this point, Wimber admitted that this child still had many of the symptoms of his problem (i.e., visual features), but had been able to reach the lower end of educational attainments. Since many Down's syndrome children reach the lower levels of educational attainments, one may conclude that in regard to this disease there were no genuine healings by Wimber and his team. Such lends question to the entire credibility of Wimber's ministry and the claims that surround the movement. ("John Wimber Changes His Mind," by Phillip D. Jensen in *The Briefing*, p. 4, used by permission.)

Jack Deere tried to salvage some of the credibility of Wimber's movement by suggesting that the team was not ministering in the context of apostolic power, but rather in the power associated with the gifts of 1 Corinthians 12. Basing his arguments on John 14:12 and Revelation 11:3, Deere shared his expectation for a coming age of apostolic power. He viewed the Vineyard Movement as the forerunner for this coming age of power. All that was needed, according to Deere, was apostolic understanding of suffering and apostolic character. ("Spiritual Warfare: The Signs and Wonders Gospel," by Graham Banister in *The Briefing*, p. 15, used by permission.) The following account of Philip Jensen testifies to the shift that has taken place in the Vineyard Movement:

> Given the very low percentage of healings, we asked John Wimber if he considered that his healings were like Jesus' or the apostles. He quickly and rightly saw that they were quite radically different. We asked about the claims of his books and his previous teaching that the powerlessness of evangelicals lay in their failure to pray for and claim the Signs and Wonders of the Kingdom seen in Jesus and the Apostles. He replied that thanks to the advice of Jack Deere he had come to understand that the current miracles fit into the New Testament not at the point of Jesus and the Apostles and the coming of the Kingdom, but in 1 Cor. 12-14 and the gifts of healing.
>
> This change of mind seriously compromises the stance of the previous Signs

and Wonders conferences, Vineyard Ministries and John Wimber's books. He was asked if he would be explaining this change of mind to the Sydney conference, but he declined. ("John Wimber Changes His Mind" by Phillip D. Jensen in The Briefing, p. 4, used by permission.)

Although Wimber admitted that his earlier writings on Power Evangelism contained error and did not reflect his true position, he was not willing to publicly repudiate the thesis of the book. The inconsistencies of Wimber's position hardly reflect one who faithfully represents the work of the Spirit to a needy world.

Question 15: *Can God raise people from the dead today?*

Response: Certainly the Lord in His sovereignty could raise the dead today. One must balance this question with another question. Why in light of Luke 16:31 would God raise the dead? If the Scriptures are already in place and accessible to a people group, such seems to go against the instruction of Luke 16:31. However, where one is in an Acts situation the Lord could step in through such a display of power. Scripturally, nothing prevents this.

A few additional words of caution should be given. During the Indonesian Revival, numerous reports attested to the dead being raised. George W. Peters in his book, *Indonesia Revival: Focus on Timor* (Zondervan Publishing House, 1973), recorded his personal investigation into these reports. He found that the nationals had varying "definitions" for what constituted death. For some, if a person was unconscious, that person was termed "dead." For others, if a person ceased breathing, that person was "dead." After examining numerous cases, Peters could not find one instance of resurrection from the dead. He concluded: "I went away satisfied that according to *their usage* of the word *death*, and their concept of death, they had experienced resuscitation. According to my concept of death, no such miracles happened" (Peters, p. 83). So, while our Lord may raise the dead, even today, such must meet with the biblical considerations of Luke 16:31 and be thoroughly documented. Again, in an Acts situation—i.e., where people do not have access to the Scriptures—our God will often step in and do the miraculous to undergird the spoken Word.

Question 16: *You have given a number of reasons why prophecy and new revelation ceased with the completion of Scripture: (1) the apostles and prophets were the foundation of the church and the church needs only one* *foundation (cf. Eph. 2:20); (2) the Lord Jesus Christ is the highest revelation of God and the Book of Revelation serves as a capstone on all revelation—any further revelation would diminish the preeminence of Christ and His role in revealing the Father; (3) the Scriptures give us all the guidelines that pertain to life and godliness (cf. 2 Pet. 1:2-4). If this is all true, why do we read in Scripture that in the time just prior to Christ's return, men and women will prophesy (cf. Joel 2:28-32; Rev. 11:3)? Does not this new revelation lend question to your overall argument?*

Response: First of all, Scripture does assert that during the Tribulation period just prior to the coming of the Lord Jesus Christ, men and women will prophesy. To be a bit more specific, Joel states that men and women will "dream dreams," "see visions," and "prophesy." What then is the content of this new revelation? The Scripture does not tell us directly. However, the close of Joel's prophecy holds a clue.

Joel's prophecy ends with the phrase, *"whoever calls on the name of the Lord shall be saved"* (Joel 2:32). This phrase ("call on the name of the Lord") reaches all the way back to Genesis 4:26. The context in which this phrase first appears in the Bible is significant. In the midst of a rising pagan world order, God made provision for anyone in any location to call upon Him. In the Tribulation, when the Antichrist will be waging war against the saints (cf. Dan. 7:25; 13:7, 8), the same invitation extends to all mankind—people all over the earth may call upon the name of the Lord. The nature of the tribulation period and the context of Joel's prophecy would suggest that the content of those visions, dreams, and prophecies would *not be new revelation*. Rather they would be filled with the proclamation of revelation previously given regarding the Lord Jesus Christ, salvation, and the invitation to call upon the name of the Lord.

One must remember that in the Book of Daniel, Antiochus Epiphanes IV is described in detail in chapters eight and eleven (cf. Dan. 8:23-27; 11:21-35). He serves as a type of the Antichrist who is to come. History confirms that Antiochus tried to eradicate the Jewish faith from Palestine. He ordered copies of the Scriptures to be destroyed and erected a statue of Zeus in the Holy of Holies in Jerusalem. Because Scripture presents Antiochus as a preview of the coming Antichrist, one could well imagine the Antichrist trying to rid the earth of Christians, Jews, and the Word of God (cf. Rev. 13:7, 8; Rev. 12:13-17). Thus, there would be the need for proclamation of the gospel as never before. Prophecy has two elements: that which foretells future events and that which "forthtells" in power the revelations of God previously given. The content of these visions, dreams, and prophecies seem to reflect the revelation of God already given and lead people to call upon the name of the Lord.

Question 17: *In your discussion of the "perfect" of 1 Corinthians 13:8-12, you make much of the parallel between this passage and the passage in James 1:22-25. Because the words "face," "mirror," and "perfect" occur in the same basic forms in both passages, you see a definite connection. Moreover, you stated that the "perfect" (i.e., completed Scriptures) was to be equated with the "mirror" in which believers see their own reflection. Thus, the phrase "face to face" in 1 Corinthians 13:12 refers to seeing one's own reflection in the Word of God, not seeing Christ "face to face" at His coming. If this interpretation is correct, how do you explain the imagery of 2 Corinthians 3:18 where the context clearly seems to equate looking into the "mirror" with beholding the glory of Christ? In other words, we see Christ's reflection in the mirror, not our own.*

Response: The term "face to face" throughout both the Old and New Testaments most often refers to seeing or speaking with another person. Note the following examples:

> And Jacob called the name of the place Peniel: "For I have seen God face to face, and my life is preserved" (Gen. 32:30).

> So the Lord spoke to Moses face to face, as a man speaks to his friend (Exod. 33:11).

> They have heard that You, Lord, are among these people; that You, Lord, are seen face to face and that Your cloud stands above them; and You go before them in a pillar of cloud by day and in a pillar of fire by night (Num. 14:14).

> Now Gideon perceived that He was the Angel of the Lord. So Gideon said, "Alas, O Lord God! For I have seen the Angel of the Lord face to face" (Judg. 6:22).

> To them I answered, "It is not the custom of the Romans to deliver any man to destruction before the accused meets the accusers face to face, and has opportunity to answer for himself concerning the charge against him" (Acts 25:16).

> Having many things to write to you, I did not wish to do so with paper and

ink; but I hope to come to you and speak face to face, that our joy may be full
(2 John 1:12).

Thus, the very nature of the phrase "face to face" would seem to make
1 Corinthians 13:12 a reference to our meeting with the Lord Jesus in
the perfected state: *"For now we see in a mirror, dimly, but then face to face."*
Other verses in Scripture point to the time when we will behold the
Lord's face in glory:

As for me, *I will see Your face* in righteousness; I shall be satisfied when I awake
in Your likeness (Ps. 17:15; italics mine).

They shall see His face, and His name shall be on their foreheads (Rev. 22:4;
italics mine).

Again, in view of these and other verses, 1 Corinthians 13:12 seems to
be making reference to beholding the Lord "face to face" in glory.

One major consideration, however, alters the aforementioned interpretation of the phrase "face to face"—that is, THE INTRODUCTION
OF THE "MIRROR" CONCEPT. In the James passage (1:22-25) the
"mirror" is clearly equated with the Word of God and with one seeing
his *own* reflection. The overall context of 1 Corinthians 13:8-12 deals
with unfolding revelation. This context would also support the imagery
of the "mirror" in verse 12 as referring to Scripture. But what about the
passage in 2 Corinthians 3:18: *"But we all with unveiled face, beholding as
in a mirror the glory of the Lord, are being transformed into the same image
from glory to glory, just as by the Spirit of the Lord."* The verse seems to say
that we see the Lord's glory when we look into the "mirror" and that one
day we will bear that same image. Is the "mirror" here in this verse to be
equated with the Scriptures? Most certainly.

When one views the immediate context of the verse, one will see the
contrast between the unbelieving Jews who cannot discern the truth of
Scripture and believers who can look into Scripture and behold the
truth. The former have a veil of unbelief over the heart which prevents
them from seeing the Lord Jesus Christ in Scripture; the latter have the
veil removed in redemption and thus behold the glory of the Lord, *as in
a mirror.* Moreover, there is also the contrast between the fleeting glory
which Moses reflected under the law, and the permanent glory which is
the possession of every believer. The glory of the Lord Jesus Christ,
which the Christian sees in Scripture (the mirror), transforms us into the

same image in conjunction with the ministry of the Spirit. Thus, in essence, the Lord's reflection is also the possession of the believer. The Spirit thus works through the Word of God (the mirror), showing us the glory of Christ, and He also works in us transforming us into that very same image.

> But if the ministry of death, written and engraved on stones, was glorious, so that the children of Israel could not look steadily at the face of Moses because of the glory of his countenance, which glory was passing away, *how will the ministry of the Spirit not be more glorious?* For if the ministry of condemnation had glory, the ministry of righteousness exceeds much more in glory. For even what was made glorious had no glory in this respect, because of the glory that excels. *For if what is passing away was glorious, what remains is much more glorious.* Therefore, since we have such hope, we use great boldness of speech— unlike Moses, who put a veil over his face so that the children of Israel could not look steadily at the end of what was passing away. But their minds were hardened. *For until this day the same veil remains unlifted in the reading of the Old Testament, because the veil is taken away in Christ. But even to this day, when Moses is read, a veil lies on their heart. Nevertheless when one turns to the Lord, the veil is taken away. Now the Lord is the Spirit; and where the Spirit of the Lord is, there is liberty. But we all, with unveiled face, beholding as in a mirror the glory of the Lord, are being transformed into the same image from glory to glory, just as by the Spirit of the Lord* (2 Cor. 3:7-18; italics mine).

The observations of Charles Hodge are instructive on this verse. Commenting on the phrase "beholding as in a mirror," and the structure of the verb, Hodge observes the following:

> . . . The active voice, means to "show in a mirror," and *in the middle (the form here used), it generally means,* "to see one's self in a mirror." This is its constant use in the classics. But in Philo it is used to express the idea of seeing by means of a mirror. As this sense is perfectly suited to this passage it is generally adopted by commentators, because the other explanations given to the word are either contrary to usage or to the context. Some render it simply beholding. But to this it is objected that it overlooks the special etymological signification of the word. . . . Besides, this interpretation loses sight of the figure involved in the passage. It is an image we see, and therefore we see, as it were, by reflection, or as in a glass. . . . We are transformed into the image of the Lord by beholding it, not by reflecting it. The common interpretation is therefore to be preferred: "beholding as in a mirror. . . ." It is not the immediate, beatific

vision of the glory of the Lord, which is only enjoyed in heaven, but it is that manifestation of his glory which is made *in his word and by his Spirit, whose office it is to glorify Christ by revealing him to us* (John 16:14; italics mine).[94]

Hodge goes on to emphasize the causal relationship between beholding the glory of the Lord in Scripture and our own transformation into the image of Christ: "The conformity to the image of Christ, as it arises from beholding his glory, must of course begin here. It is the vision of that glory, although only as in a glass, which has this transforming power" (Hodge, p. 76). Thus again, the image of Christ seen in Scripture becomes the image of the believer as the Word of God and the Spirit of God exercise their transforming power.

One can safely say that the "mirror" in 2 Corinthians 3:18 refers to the Scriptures. The immediate context establishes this. Moreover, when we look into the mirror we see the "glory of the Lord." Yet, the "glory of the Lord" which is seen in the mirror is also that which is shining through the believer. As we look into the mirror (the Word), we are able to see and discern the measure or degree of the Lord's glory which is shining through in us (cf. James 1:22-25). And unlike Moses' glory, which was temporal and fleeting, our glory will never pass away. Through the Word of God and the ministry of the Spirit of God, we are being transformed into the image of Christ (cf. Rom. 8:29). We will take on His likeness (cf. 1 John 3:2). Indeed, one day His image shall be our image; His reflection in the Word shall be our reflection.

With the completion of Scripture, there was a completion of the portrait of Christ that reflected His glory. What was "dim" at the writing of 1 Corinthians 13:12 became clear at the completion of Scripture so that believers could see the Lord and their own changing likeness to Him "face to face." Thus, the passage in 2 Corinthians 3:18 complements and is consistent with the interpretations offered regarding 1 Corinthians 13:8-12 and James 1:22-25.

Question 18: *I can understand why God would allow believers to grapple with the issue of deception and testing. However, I still find it difficult to believe that the Lord would allow His children, especially dedicated saints, to CONTINUE in error and deception to their hurt or spiritual detriment. Can you comment further on this point.*

Response: The account in 1 Kings 13 helps us to deal with the question at hand. Here, Scripture reveals that even a dedicated and fearless prophet of God must suffer the consequences when he chooses deception over the clear *revelation* of God.

You may remember the story. An unnamed "man of God" was sent to Bethel "by the word of the Lord" to prophesy against King Jeroboam and the idolatrous practices promoted by the King (vv. 1-3). When the King tried to arrest the prophet, the King's hand withered (vv. 4, 5). He entreated the man of God to intercede. The man of God complied with the request and the King's hand was restored (v. 6). Yet, when the King offered the prophet a reward, the man of God refused:

> Then the king said to the man of God, "Come home with me and refresh yourself, and I will give you a reward." But the man of God said to the king, "If you were to give me half your house, I would not go in with you; nor would I eat bread nor drink water in this place. For so it was commanded me by the word of the LORD, saying, 'You shall not eat bread, nor drink water, nor return by the same way you came.'" So he went another way and did not return by the way he came to Bethel (1 Kings 13:7-10).

Why the refusal? The prophet refused because the clear revelation of God forbade him from receiving food, or drink, or retracing his steps. So far, this prophet, this man of God, was walking in perfect obedience to the Word of God.

He had overcome the *test of fear and compromise*, for he had boldly carried out his mission of proclaiming the Word of the Lord to the king. He had not allowed the threats of the king to destroy a merciful heart, and thus had passed the *test of compassion*. There was no "getting even," or spirit of revenge in this prophet when he had prayed for the physical restoration of the king. Then, too, in turning down the overtures of Jeroboam, the man of God had testified that his ministry was gratuitous and that faithfulness to the Word of God was his primary concern. The *test of faithfulness to God over human favor* had been overcome. BUT THERE WAS ONE MORE TEST: *the test of deception*. And when it came to this test, the man of God failed to cling to the previous revelation which God had so clearly given. Moreover, it cost the prophet his life.

There was an old prophet in the land who heard about the fearless stand of this man of God. Having lived in compromise for some time in Bethel, the old prophet sought the man of God and entreated him to come home with him and dine (vv. 11-15). When the man of God told the old prophet that he was under strict orders from God not to eat, or drink, or retrace his steps, the old prophet said the following words:

I too am a prophet as you are, and an angel spoke to me by the word of the
LORD, saying, "Bring him back with you to your house, that he may eat bread
and drink water" (1 Kings 13:18).

However, we read the ominous words in Scripture: "But he lied to
him" (v. 18). We are not told why the old prophet lied. Maybe he was
moved by envy over seeing a true prophet faithfully discharge his respon-
sibilities, when the old prophet had lived in compromise; maybe he was
captured by malice and a convicted conscience; whatever the reason, he
claimed *new revelation* from God. And all of this brought the true man of
God to a crossroads. Would he accept at face value the *new revelation*?
Would he continue to cling to the previous revelation of God and seek
God's wisdom directly? Which way would the man of God go?

Sadly, the man of God, the once fearless and faithful prophet, suc-
cumbed to deception. AND GOD ALLOWED THIS TO HAPPEN TO A
DEDICATED SAINT! Why? Because in our pilgrimage on earth, there
will always be the choice to follow the clear teaching of God or to sub-
stitute the shallow promises, prophecies, and deceptions of man. The
man of God retraced his steps back to the home of the old prophet and
ate with him. Over the meal, the old prophet revealed that because the
man of God had disobeyed the Word of God, he would die. And that is
exactly what happened (vv. 19-26).

In conclusion, if a dedicated prophet of God was allowed to choose
between the clear teaching of the Lord and deception, it is not inconsistent to maintain that the Lord will allow this even today. Multitudes of
Christians suffer impoverished spiritual lives because they trade the
Word of God for teachers who prophecy or give new revelation after their
own spirit. And if someone should say, "Why doesn't God step in and
chastise His children and woo them back into obedience?" (cf. Heb. 12),
the answer comes quickly: the Spirit and the Word of God continually
call the believer to faithfulness and obedience (cf. Phil. 2:12, 13).
Moreover, deception and impoverishment are the bitter fruit of turning
away from the Word of God. And sometimes God will allow his children
to remain in such a state as a condition of chastisement—until they turn
once again in submission to the Word of God. Their relationship with
God is secure through the blood of the Lord Jesus Christ; they may serve
the Lord faithfully in other areas and indeed be used by Him; but they
will forfeit the blessings which come through total submission and obedience.

The Lord will allow his children the choice of whether to glorify Him through submission and obedience to Scripture, or not. For those believers—even dedicated servants of God—who put aside the clear revelation of God and embrace new prophecies and new revelations, there will be deception and impoverishment in this life and loss of rewards at the Judgment Seat of Christ (2 Cor. 5:10).

Question 19: *How can one best respond to those who claim tongues is the only sign that we have the Holy Spirit or are filled by Him? Indeed, what is the evidence that we are filled with the Spirit?*

Response: The force of 1 Corinthians 12:29-31 both grammatically and contextually rules out the application of these verses to all believers. In the early church, all were not apostles; all were not teachers; all did not speak in tongues. The very fact that the Spirit of God distributes gifts as He wills (cf. 1 Cor. 12:7-10) further underscores the fact that tongues was not the possession of every believer. Therefore, tongues could not have been a sign that one had the Holy Spirit or was filled with the Spirit.

One must remember that Paul referred to the Corinthians as "babes" and "carnal" (1 Cor. 3:1-3), so their misuse of tongues was hardly an evidence of the Spirit-filled life. A carnal believer can still exercise his or her gift, but not accompanied with the eternal benefits and blessings of the Spirit of God which otherwise would follow a Spirit-filled vessel.

If one were to ask the average church congregation to paint a portrait of the Spirit-filled individual, most would probably point to Galatians 5:22, 23. That person would be characterized by all the manifestations of the fruit of the Spirit: love, joy, peace, longsuffering, kindness, goodness, faithfulness, gentleness, self-control. This indeed would be a true portrait.

However, we should also be reminded of John the Baptist and Jesus. Both conducted their ministries in the fullness of the Spirit's power. But certainly John the Baptist was not Spirit-filled? There he was, dressed like Elijah, calling the religious leaders of Israel "vipers" and challenging them publicly to bring forth spiritual fruit (Matt. 3:7). Certainly, John the Baptist was not showing love, and joy, and peace. He was not approaching differences of opinion with social and Christian graces or refinement. Spirit-filled? You better believe it! Scripture affirms that John was Spirit-filled from his mother's womb (Luke 1:15). Our contemporary world is not quite comfortable with that kind of Spirit-filled portrait. Yet, it is biblical. And although John would not have been welcome in the ministerial association of his day, he certainly was displaying the fruit of "faithfulness." You will find that in Galatians 5:22, 23.

And what of Jesus? He had compassion on people from various circumstances and stations in life: beggars, children, soldiers, tax collectors, prostitutes, lepers, demon possessed, the hungry, and the destitute. The list goes on and on. But there was one group that only received rebuke and scorn from the Lord Jesus Christ: the religious leaders of the day who distorted truth and misrepresented the way of salvation. The same Jesus who placed a child on His knee and extended love to the multitudes was the same Jesus who made a whip and cleansed the Temple. And Scripture refers to the Lord Jesus as the "faithful and true witness." So, again, the Spirit-filled life is not attested by tongues; rather such is attested by the fruit of Galatians 5:22, 23. Moreover, the lives of John the Baptist and the Lord Jesus Christ give further perspective and substance to the portrait of the Spirit-filled life; one that includes being a "faithful witness."

Question 20: *You stated in your discussion of the ISAIAH CONNECTION that tongues served as a sign of judgment to unbelieving Jews. Did tongues also serve as a sign to Gentiles and as a means of communicating the Gospel message in other languages?*

Response: As noted in previous discussion, many respected Bible teachers do hold to the exclusive position that tongues served as a sign **only** to unbelieving Jews. They would point to the presence of Jews at each recorded instance in the book of Acts where tongues were spoken (cf. Acts 2, 10, 19). They would also point to the Jewish argument used in 1 Corinthians 14:20-25 and distinguish between Jewish "unbelievers" in 14:22 and Gentile "unbelievers" in 14:23. This position has much to commend itself. However, several considerations would seem to counter this exclusive position.

1. The first mention of tongues occurs within a cluster of signs (cf. Mark 16:17-20). The other signs in this cluster were not restricted to Jewish experience, nor did they demand a Jewish presence. In other words, Gentile believers could cast out demons, heal the sick, and survive perilous encounters with snakes and poison. Significantly, 1 Corinthians 1:7 affirms that in the Corinthian church believers were lacking in no gift.

2. The account of Peter's visit to Cornelius' home would seem to

counter this exclusive position also (Acts 10). Scripture records that Peter travelled to Cornelius' home with some "brethren." Acts 10:45 and 11:12 indicate that these six men were believing Christian Jews. And while Acts 10:24 does record that Cornelius was waiting for Peter with his relatives and close friends, *nothing is said about the presence of unbelieving Jews in Cornelius' home*. Thus, when Peter and his company witnessed Gentiles speaking in tongues (cf. Acts 10:44-46 with 11:15), this occasion of tongues did not serve as a sign to unbelieving Jews. Indeed, such served as a sign to unbelieving Gentiles that the Gospel message and promises extended to them; and such also served to confirm to Peter and the other *Jewish Christians* that God showed no partiality regarding acceptance of Jew and Gentile (Acts 10:34-48).

3. Even though the context of 1 Corinthians 14:20-22 applies to a Jewish situation, the instruction regarding the sign purpose of tongues need not be restricted to Jewish unbelievers. One can argue from singular examples to general principles and such could be the intent of the passage. In other words, one could admit the restrictive Jewish sense of verse 14:21, 22 while embracing the broader application to include Gentile unbelievers—this by implication.

So, in summary, while tongues certainly served as a sign of judgment for *unbelieving Israel*, tongues were not restricted to this purpose. Tongues affirmed to *Jewish Christians* that God showed no partiality regarding acceptance of Jew and Gentile into the Body of Christ (Acts 10:34, 35; 11:17, 18). Moreover, they also became a means to communicate the wonders of God's grace to *Gentiles as well*.

Question 21: *What is your response to Jack Deere's book* Surprised by the Power of the Spirit *and its sequel. He seems to build a strong case for the sign and revelatory gifts and even documents a case that combines a true prophetic utterance with one being raised from the dead?*

Response: While the present format does not allow for a full response to Deere's more recent works, I would like to make some comments about his book *Surprised by the Power of the Spirit*. This particular book catalogues Deere's entrance into the charismatic movement and represents some of his primary arguments.

On a positive vein, Deere correctly identifies the vital need for

Christians to affirm their belief in a miracle-working God! As stated earlier in *Charismatic Challenge*, our God IS a miracle-working God: He still heals today; He still answers prayer in marvelous and miraculous ways; He still manifests Himself in supernatural power in those settings where people do not have access to the Scriptures (i.e., what has been termed an "Acts situation"). Deere's book issues a call for all believers to avail themselves of God's power. Of particular benefit are his sections entitled "Why Does God Heal," "Why God Doesn't Heal," and "A Passion for God." These sections will stir believers to do some personal inventory.

One will also appreciate the openness and genuine passion which characterizes Deere's presentation. His transparency regarding his own thoughts and feelings reveals a man who is seeking with an honest heart. He grapples with key questions on both the theological and personal level. Nevertheless, glaring deficiencies do characterize some of Deere's analysis and applications. Please note the following:

Three Periods of Signs and Wonders

Deere counters cessasionists regarding their claim that there were only three distinct periods in biblical history where signs and miracles were the order of the day (i.e., the times of Moses; Elijah and Elisha; and Jesus and the apostles). Through charts and discussion (pp. 253-266), he proves that miracles were not confined to three distinct periods; rather they were found throughout biblical history!

The amazing fact is that his own charts PROVE AND ESTABLISH the "three period thesis." Cessasionists—to use his term—readily accept that miracles have occurred throughout biblical history. Deere has **misrepresented** the "three period thesis" by failing to understand that cessasionists are referring to SIGNS and MIRACLES. When one speaks of signs and miracles during these periods, one is focusing upon miraculous events accomplished through human instrumentality. Concerning Moses, the Scriptures affirm, "But since then there has not arisen in Israel a prophet like Moses, whom the Lord knew face to face, *in all the signs and wonders which the Lord SENT HIM TO DO in the land of Egypt* . . ." (Deut. 34:10; italics mine); at the miraculous display of the Lord's power on Mt. Carmel, Elijah prayed: "O Lord, *HEAR ME*, that this people may know that You are the Lord God . . ." (1 Kings

18:36-39; italics mine); and Paul declared: "For I will not dare speak of any of those things which Christ has *not accomplished THROUGH ME*, in word and deed, to make the Gentiles obedient—in mighty signs and wonders, by the power of the Spirit of God . . ." (Rom. 15:18, 19; italics mine).

In Deere's chart on miracles throughout the Bible, he includes supernatural events such as: the creation, God confusing human language at the Tower of Babel, the Lord appearing to Abraham, angels blinding the men of Sodom, the glory of the Lord filling the temple, the Lord causing the sunlight to go back ten steps on the stairway of Ahaz, and a host of others. As one scans Deere's list, one will see that very FEW "signs and wonders" (accomplished through human instrumentality) are included. Miraculous and supernatural events? Yes! These DO occur throughout the biblical record and are not confined to specific periods of time. Signs and wonders involving human instrumentality— throughout the biblical record? No! Again, DEERE'S OWN CHART ESTABLISHES THE "THREE PERIOD THESIS."

The Limitations Regarding Jesus' Power to Heal

Deere notes three key passages that indicate Jesus could not heal *at His own discretion, every person, in any or every circumstance*: Luke 5:17; John 5:19; and Mark 6:5-6. He also makes reference to the inability of the apostles to heal—this incident recorded in Matthew 17:16 (pp. 60-64). He points out that the Father's will (i.e., His sovereign determination to withhold power to heal) and the unbelief of individuals explains why some were not healed. Deere declares that "It is our responsibility to listen for those directions [from God] and follow them, rather than to determine who gets healed" (p. 61).

Deere uses this reasoning to help explain why many in charismatic meetings are not healed or face reversals. His arguments, however, reveal a major flaw when applied to the contemporary scene. When Jesus DID pray over people, THEY WERE HEALED. Not so in many instances where those claiming the "gift" of healing pray for the sick. Of course, they could claim that they either "misread the directions" or failed to discern "unbelief" in those seeking help.

Even though the Scriptures record one incident where the apostles could not heal, the KIND of miracles and healings accomplished

through them, and the FREQUENCY of their success, have no comparison with today. YES, God still heals through the corporate prayers of
God's people; but Deere's claim that some possess the gift of healing,
just like the early Christians, does not hold up.

Cessasionists Argue from "Negative Experience"

All of us approach the Scriptures with certain presuppositions. We
would agree with this point. Yet, Deere paints "cessasionists" as those
who stifle the work of the Spirit: they do not believe in the miraculous;
limit manifestations of the Spirit's power; do not *really* pray for the sick;
would not ever think of confronting demonic powers; and shun displays
of emotion in worship services or group meetings. Deere maintains that
because of cessasionists' "negative experience," they are prone to justify
their scriptural position.

Sadly, Deere's caricature of the "cessasionist" grows out of his own
experience (or lack), rather than a factual understanding of the life and
heart of many non-charismatics. The "negative experience," of which
Deere speaks, may characterize some cessasionists, but not the majority.
I and many other non-charismatic believers teach, have participated in,
or know those who have participated in the following:

- praying over the sick and anointing with oil
- confronting demonic possession and oppression through prayer and
  victorious deliverance
- conducting services where people openly come forward to trust in Christ,
  weep over burdens, confess sin, seek deliverance from a myriad of
  situations
- special sessions of prayer where believers kneel and fall on their face before
  God in intercession
- fasting to "loose the bonds of wickedness, to undo heavy burdens, to let
  the oppressed go free, and to . . . break every yoke (Isa. 58:6).
- leadings of the Spirit through inner impressions, through the Scriptures,
  or through inclinations of the heart (cf. Phil. 4:5-7).

Many non-charismatics DO arrive at their position through a detailed
study of the Word of God. Many believe in God's power to heal in
response to the corporate prayers of God's people; many believe in

God's power to overcome demonic possession and oppression; many believe in divine manifestations of the Spirit of God as He sweeps over a congregation—convicting of sin, drawing people to their knees and faces in supplication, saving the lost. And many LIVE OUT THEIR BELIEFS by conducting their ministries after the above fashion. Yet, these same non-charismatics reject the claims of those who say they possess the "sign gifts and revelatory gifts."

Parallels with Past Revivals?

Deere, like so many charismatic writers, seeks to parallel what is occurring today in charismatic circles with displays of God's power in revivals of old. I will refer the reader to the section in *Charismatic Challenge* which counters this comparison. However, a few comments are in order. While great displays of God's power did characterize revivals of old, the manifestation of God's Spirit was accompanied by a reverence for the Word of God, a clear understanding of the message of salvation, and a dedication to holy living. Yet today, "counterfeit revival" finds people putting aside biblical doctrine and rolling in the aisles in laughter; heretics join hands with true believers singing "We are One in the Spirit, We are One in the Lord." Such is a far cry from revivals of old!

A Documented Account of
One Being Raised from the Dead

Deere tells of the miraculous story of Katshinyi who was raised from the dead on June 12, 1985 in Zaïre (pp. 203-206). His healing was accompanied by "word for word" instructions from the Holy Spirit and by a prophetic utterance from another preacher. Deere has seen the medical records and personally knows some of those involved. How is one to respond to this?

As expressed earlier in *Charismatic Challenge*, God still moves in power today. He may choose at times to raise the dead! Such is most likely to occur in an Acts *Situation* where people have little access to the Word of God. The situation in Zaïre may parallel just such an Acts *situation*, as opposed to a mere resuscitation. I know of Christian leaders who have brought similar reports out of China: people were raised from the dead and thousands were later saved. The common thread in these instances is that the people at large have no access to the Scriptures. Again, God CAN step in to raise the dead if He so chooses. He is the sovereign God. This does not mean, however, that one has the "gift" of healing.

A number of other points in Deere's book are disturbing: (1) he represents cessasionists as believing that "signs and wonders" confirmed the apostles and the Scriptures—when in fact, many non-charismatics feel the signs and wonders confirmed the SPOKEN Word of God (whether from the lips of apostles or believers at large); (2) he *partially reverses* his earlier position [Amen!] that the gospel NEEDS signs and wonders to be effective; yet, he seeks to transfer this qualification to cessasionists who claim the signs "confirmed" the gospel message; (3) he talks about "degrees of effectiveness" in regard to spiritual gifts—this to explain why some can "heal" more effectively than others possessing the SAME gift. Again, this format does not allow for a full response. Suffice it to say that Deere's book will generate both enthusiasm and confusion in the ongoing debate before us.

Question 22: *Did not Jesus say in John 14:12 that those who believe in Him would do the same works as He, and even greater works than those which He did during His earthly ministry? In saying that individual Christians cannot exercise the same power and ministry as Jesus, are not you limiting God and denying the teaching of Jesus in this verse?*

Response: Let us take a brief survey of the miraculous works that Jesus did: *miracles of creation*—turning the water to wine (John 2:1-11), multiplying the loaves and fishes (Matt. 14:14-21); *innumerable healing miracles* involving the lame (John 5:1-9), lepers (Luke 17:11-19), blind (Matt. 9:27-31; 20:29-34), deaf (Mark 7:31-37), and others (Matt. 8:5-13; Luke 14:1-6); *casting out demons* (Mark 1:23-28; Matt. 8:28-34); *miracles displaying Jesus' control of nature*—stilling storms (Mark 4:35-41), cursing the fig tree (Matt. 21:18, 19), walking on water (John 6:16-21); *raising the dead* (Matt. 9:18-26; John 11:17-44; Luke 7:11-15).

Are there any documented cases of man creating, or displaying power over the natural and spiritual realms, or healing, or exercising power over the dead to the *same degree* as Jesus did? Obviously, the answer is "no!" Indeed, while a miraculous God still manifests Himself in the affairs of men, none can claim to work miracles greater than Jesus. *Those who try to use John 14:12 to support their claims just do not measure up.* In the realm of the miraculous, none comes close to the preeminence of Jesus.

What then is the meaning of John 14:12? Certainly Jesus was referring to the total ministry of believers in proclaiming the gospel to a lost world. At Pentecost and during the weeks which followed, believers would see more people embrace the Lord Jesus Christ and step into the kingdom of God than during the entire three-year ministry of Jesus on earth. While Jesus' earthly ministry was confined to Palestine, the gospel would go to the ends of the earth. These are the "greater works" which believers would do. Even though the signs and miracles would accompany the proclamation of the gospel (cf. Acts 14:1-3; Rom. 15:18, 19), they pointed to the message of salvation and the preeminence of the Lord Jesus Christ (cf. Luke 10:17-20; Acts 2:22-24; Heb. 2:1-4; Col. 1:13-18).

Appendix B

Tongues (Glossai)

Dr. Deane J. Woods
Principal of the Adelaide College of Ministries
Adelaide, Australia

A definition of terms is vital to achieve meaningful communication and interaction in any discussion. The present study on the *Charismatic Challenge* is no exception. A clear definition and analysis is in order so as to substantiate the author's claim that ". . . the biblical tongues of the first century were *known languages*. . . ."

To achieve such goals, it will be helpful to trace the meaning of the term from classical Greek times to the way it was used in the New Testament era.

HISTORICAL (DIACHRONIC) STUDY

The term *glossa* ("tongue") was used in classical Greek in three ways. Firstly, it was used to refer to the *physical organ itself*.[95] Secondly, the term was used in describing *something shaped like a tongue*. The reed of an instrument or a shoe latchet are but two examples.[96] Thirdly, it was employed in a wider sense to refer to a *language* or *dialect*.[97]

When one consults the Septuagint, or LXX (the Greek translation of the Hebrew Old Testament), one finds these same three characteristics. In Exodus 1:7, Joshua 10:21, and Zechariah 14:12, the reference is to tongue as a *physical organ*. In Genesis 10:5 and 11:7, *language* or *dialect* is the intended meaning. In Joshua 7:21 and Isaiah 11:15, anything shaped like a tongue is connoted.

In comparing the Septuagint usage with the classical Greek usage, it is quite obvious that there is no distinction whatever. The same three basic understandings are employed in all the sources.

SYNCHRONIC STUDY

The Greek spoken during the first century A.D. was known as Koine ("common") Greek. It was widespread across the Mediterranean world. It was the language of trade between people from diverse nations, cultures, and practices.

The term *glossa* was used for the tongue as a *physical organ* by Galenus in the second century A.D.[98] Plutarch used the term in the sense of *dialect*.[99] Appianus (second century A.D.) used it with the idea of anything *shaped like a tongue*.[100] There are other sources which substantiate these usages. In particular, attention is drawn to the papyrical evidence.[101]

Thus the Koine usage, when compared with the way the term was employed in the classical and Septuagint sources, is seen to be "parallel." The same three usages are in evidence.

But what about the New Testament? Again, these same three usages are seen. The term is used with reference to the *physical organ* in Mark 7:33 and Luke 16:24. In Acts 2:4 it is used for a *language* or *dialect*, while in the preceding verse, Luke uses *glossai* for that which was *shaped like a tongue*.

The term is used forty-eight times in the New Testament. Paul uses it on twenty-four occasions,[102] only three of which are found outside 1 Corinthians 12-14.[103]

In the twenty-one instances where *glossa* is used in 1 Corinthians 12-14, the apostle employs it in terms of *language* or *speech*. Some have argued that because *glossa* was unintelligible even to the speaker (1 Corinthians 14:15, 19), it must refer to an ecstatic utterance.[104] But one needs to consider certain other significant factors, as Hoehner[105] and others[106] have argued. This is what Hoehner says:[107]

> However, it seems far better to take *glossa* to refer to an actual language. First, [it] is normally used to refer to an actual language. When it occurs in the plural form (*glossai*) it is an abbreviation of "different languages" (*gene glosson*) and refers to "different languages" (cf. 12:10, 28, 30).[108] Second, Paul states that tongues need to be interpreted (*hermeneia*). This word has the primary sense of "translation" of a foreign language.[109]

> Third, Paul's quotation of Isaiah 28:11-12 in 14:21 uses the word *heteroglossois*, which is translated "strange tongues." This word is counterpart of

glossai,[110] and when one looks in the context of Isaiah, the "strange tongues" refer to the actual language of the Assyrians. Fourth, in Acts 2:4, Luke states that the apostles "began to speak in other tongues" (*glossais*). Then in the next two verses Luke states that the Jews from various parts of the Roman Empire heard the apostles speaking in their own dialects, which indicates that the "tongues" were known foreign languages.

Fifth, Paul and Luke were companions and Paul does not say that the gift of tongues being experienced in Corinth was different from that experienced on the day of Pentecost. Likewise, Luke (who wrote after Paul) did not make any qualifications to indicate that the Pentecost situation was different from the Corinthian situation. Sixth, that Paul instructed the Corinthians to control the tongues by forbidding anyone to speak when there was no interpreter and by not allowing more than three to speak seems to indicate that the gift of tongues was not an uncontrollable ecstatic utterance (14:27-28). Thus it seems best to see tongues as a genuine human language that needs to be translated into another human language in order to be understood.[111]

MacArthur argues along similar lines.[112] He cites seven reasons. Firstly, he shows that *glossa* primarily means *human language* when used in Scripture. Secondly, he discusses *dialectos*[113] from which we get the English word *dialect* (Acts 2:6, 8). The point is made: "[classifications] like languages and dialects would never have been used if ecstatic speech had been presented."[114] Thirdly, he points out that the same term for language *glossa* is used in both Acts and 1 Corinthians 12-14. In Acts the plural is always used, indicating a *multiple of languages*. "There are no multiple kinds of gibberish."[115] Paul uses the plural form in 1 Corinthians 14 with the same connotation.[116] The apostle uses the singular in verses 2, 13, 14, and 19 where he refers to the counterfeit pagan gibberish (*unintelligible speech*) that was being used by many of the Corinthian believers instead of the true gift of languages. Fourthly, MacArthur refers to 1 Corinthians 12:10 and the "interpretation of languages." The Greek term here (*hermeneuo*) conveys the idea of *translation*. He comments: "You cannot translate ecstatic speech or babble."[117] Fifthly, 1 Corinthians 12:10 mentions different "kinds" (*genos*) of language. The term means a *family or group*. Linguists are familiar with "language families." Sixthly, 1 Corinthians 14:21, where Paul quotes Isaiah 28:11, indicates that tongues were a foreign language—the Assyrians spoke genuine Assyrian!—given as a sign to unbelieving Israel. Seventhly, MacArthur suggests that 1 Corinthians 14:27 indicates a genuine language since it was to be translated. Failure to translate the language would inevitably result in confusion (cf. verse 23).

Thus MacArthur's approach runs on similar lines to that of Hoehner. The combined testimony of their investigations support the view that *glossai* ("tongues") that are "being evidenced in churches today [are] entirely different from tongues described in the Bible."[118]

Notwithstanding this evidence, some appeal to 1 Corinthians 13:1 as supportive of *glossa* meaning *angelic speech*.[119] Here the apostle speaks of "tongues (*glossai*) of men and of angels." The claim of those advocating this understanding is that the passage refers to *ecstatic heavenly speech*. Such a view is untenable on both grammatical and contextual grounds. The Greek construction used is that of a "third class condition." The "more probable future" aspect of this "conditional sentence" category presents a condition as uncertain for the sake of argument. In this context, it is to be understood as a hypothetical Third Class Condition. Paul was using hyperbole, or exaggerated speech, as Hodges has pointed out.[120] Secondly, it may be concluded that the apostle does not mean that this description is normative for, or descriptive of, the New Testament church.

CONCLUSION

In the light of these considerations, glossa ("tongues"), in regard to its usage in the New Testament, is best understood as a language or dialect. Biblical tongues of the first century were known languages. On this definition, then, the approach espoused in this volume is justified.

Appendix C

Jesus Christ: God's Supreme Revelation

Dr. Deane J. Woods
Principal of the Adelaide College of Ministries
Adelaide, Australia

INTRODUCTION

One of the fundamental issues involved in the current charismatic debate has to do with the matter of "revelation." Is Scripture complete? Does God still speak today? Is the canon of Scripture closed? Has God's revelation ceased? What assessment can be made of alleged "words of prophecy" revealed through tongues-speakers or visionaries? How does one gauge such claims? So these and many more allied questions are raised. At the heart of the matter is what may be rightly called "the sufficiency of Scripture."

The present purpose is to address these issues with a view to arriving at a conclusion consistent with the biblical data. Consider the following statement of Deere:

> In order to fulfill God's highest purposes for our lives we must be able to *hear his voice* both in the *written word* and *the word freshly spoken from heaven*. . . . Satan understands the strategic importance of Christians hearing God's voice so he has launched various attacks against us in this area. One of his most successful attacks has been to develop a doctrine that teaches *God no longer speaks to us except through the written word*. Ultimately, this doctrine is demonic even [though] Christian theologians have been used to perfect it.[121]

Such an approach is ultimately an attack on the sufficiency of the Scriptures. As the editorial team who met with Wimber and Deere (and others) for three hours comment: "Those who believe in the sufficiency

221

of the Scriptures for Christian faith and life are caricatured as those who believed in a God who *writes* rather than a God who *speaks*."[122]

On what biblical grounds, then, is it justifiable to assert that Scripture is sufficient. Putting it another way, the question may be asked: Is Scripture complete? To this question the discussion now turns.

IS SCRIPTURE COMPLETE?

Chantry has dealt at some length on this matter.[123] He directs attention to what he describes as "An Evident Answer," in terms of several salient Scripture passages. These are set forth here with appropriate comments.

A. Hebrews 1:1-3

Actually, verse four should be included since the Prologue to this great letter embraces the first four verses of the opening chapter.

In a nutshell, the writer states that *"Jesus Christ, God's Son, is the Par-Excellence Vehicle of Divine Revelation."*[124]

In the Greek, these verses demonstrate an example of literary beauty of the highest order. It is a majestically constructed opening paragraph. Central to the presentation is the stunning phrase: "He (God) has spoken to us in his Son" (v. 2). The aorist tense of the verb "has spoken" (*elalesen*) signifies a completed act in past time. "God having spoken (*lalesas*) to the Fathers by the prophets, has, in the last of these days, spoken to us by his Son." Jesus Christ is God's last "Word" to man. God's prophetic revelation has now received its end-times climax through his Son. There cannot be, there will not be, any other "Word." The Father's revelation is complete in his Son—the Incarnate Word to whom testimony is borne in the inscripturated Word (cf. John 5:39).

Moreover, the Hebrews passage links "he sat down" (*ekathisen*) with this one who "has spoken to us." Another aorist tense is used, but this time with the nuance of personal reflection. "Having made (for himself) a cleansing of sins (*katharismon ton harmartion poiesamenos*), he sat down at the right hand of the Majesty on high." In the Cross, the work of redemption was complete. In Christ, God's revelation has found its zenith. In the Person of his majestic Son, one discovers consummate revelation.

Some have suggested that in the light of John 21:25, it is invalid to claim that Scripture is a complete revelation. Two comments are in order. Firstly, the construction in Greek is a *third class condition (more probably future)* presenting a condition as *uncertain* for argument's sake. Secondly, in context, John uses hyperbole to indicate the vastness of the materials from which he (cf. 2 Tim. 3:15-16) has made selection to fit his evangelistic purpose ((John 20:30-31). He is "sovereignly selective" in giving materials which best suited his purpose. As Leon Morris comments:

> The Gospel closes with a reminder that the author has done no more than make a selection from the mass of material available. He has not written all he knows about Jesus. If all were to be written he thinks the world itself could not contain the books to be written. With this delightful hyperbole he lets us see that there is much more about Jesus than we know. It is fitting for us to bring our study of the Gospel to a close with the reminder of the limitations of our knowledge. It is well for us to be appreciative of the knowledge we have and to show a due gratitude to God for what he has revealed. But we should not exaggerate. Our knowledge of the truth is at best partial. The reader who appreciates the significance of these final words is kept humble.[125]

Others have drawn attention to John 16:12-13 and claimed the implication of these verses is that Christ's revelatory work was not completed on earth. Again, such a view warrants comment. Firstly, the statement is to be understood in the context of God's redemptive mission. John tells us that Jesus has made God known (1:18). He has "revealed" the Father. He who has seen Jesus has seen the Father (14:9). Jesus is God's last word to man (Heb. 1:1-4; cf. Rev. 22:18-19). The Holy Spirit is the "coronation gift" of the Father to the church upon the Son's exaltation and glorification (John 15:26; Acts 2).

Secondly, consider the details of these verses as Morris comments upon them. They are pertinent to the topic being discussed.

> From the work of the Spirit in the world, Jesus here turns to his work in believers. First he speaks of leaving many things yet to say to the disciples. "Bear" is an unusual verb in this connection (*bastazo*). It may mean that their experience thus far sets a limit to their ability to perceive. There are vistas of truth set before them which they cannot yet enter, but they will enter when the Spirit comes. More probably it refers them to their inability, until the Spirit should come (*hotan elthe*), to live out the implications of the revelation

(cf. 14:17; 16:13). As the days go by the Spirit will lead them deeper and deeper into a knowledge of truth.

The Spirit's teaching is not from Himself, but he teaches "what things so ever he shall hear." It is not said whether he hears them from the Father or the Son. John is emphasizing the Spirit's ministry at this point. The expression indicates the Spirit's harmony with the Father and the Son.

"The things that are to come" is somewhat puzzling. While the Spirit has on occasion revealed the future (Ezekiel's experiences: 3:12, 24; 11:1; John 1:10; 4:1), that is not his characteristic work. Perhaps the expression means that he will supply what is needed as it is needed. Alternatively, and more likely, the phrase refers to the whole Christian system (yet future when Jesus spoke), and to be revealed to the disciples by the Spirit, not by natural insight.

There could also be an eschatological reference here (cf. Mark 13:1-11), though in context, the sense of "He will show you the whole Christian way" seems to be of primary emphasis.[126]

He is the embodiment of all truth. Indeed Chantry can say:

> . . . Our Protestant forefathers drew their dogma directly from the New Testament. Hebrews 1:3 contrasts Old Testament prophecy with New Testament revelation. The comparison is intended to display the superiority of New Testament disclosures of truth. . . .

> God's revelation of truth reached a glorious climax when Christ was on earth. In the person of Jesus Christ, revelation had been brought to completion with a dramatic suddenness.[127]

But the writer to the Hebrews, under the inspiration of the Holy Spirit (see 2 Tim. 3:15-16; 2 Pet. 1:20-21), has something further to add. He sets forth scriptural evidence to show that: *To God's kingly-Son, not to the Angels, Belongs a Triumphant Eternal Reign (1:5-14).*[128]

B. Hebrews 2:1-4

Then follows the *First Warning Passage* (2:1-4) in which our author urges his readership: *Don't neglect such great salvation.* Interestingly, he includes himself, too, when he says, "How shall we escape if we neglect so great salvation" (v. 3). He urges them all to live lives commensurate with "that ultimate deliverance from conflict which involves sharing Messiah's glorious reign."[129] Relative to the aspect of this Son being God's final revelation, this *First Warning Passage* highlights another significant fact. Again, Chantry comments:

> So complete is Christ as God's revelation, and so sufficient is his work as a prophet that the apostles and their New Testament books are viewed in Hebrews 2:1-4 as merely *confirming* what the Great Prophet had already said.[130]

These verses also imply that the confirmatory "signs and wonders" had passed[131] by the time of writing, probably just prior to destruction of Jerusalem (and its Temple) in A.D. 70.[132] Thus the apostolic writings echo (cf. John 14:26; 16:13) what was spoken by the Lord Jesus Christ—the "Word" of God.

C. John 1:1, 18
Revelation has come to an end in Jesus Christ.[133] The "Word" who became flesh is the fullest and most exhaustive expression of God. He is the complete truth of God (14:6). The apostles saw his glory full of truth (1:14). What is more, Christ is the "exegesis" of God (1:18); that is, Christ has fully "declared" (NKJV) the Father; he has "explained" (NASB) the Father. The "Word" has made him known. With such complete revelation, no more need be sought. Yet there is recorded in Scripture an incident where such a request is implied. In the light of the present discussions, the instruction given in John 14:7-10 is significant, for it impinges on the sufficiency of Scripture.

THE SUFFICIENCY OF SCRIPTURE

A. John 14:7-10
Jesus talked with his disciples about his soon departure. He noted that they knew the Father and had seen him; yet Philip sought *something more!*

Jesus gave a "withering rebuke" to Philip's request: "Have I been so long time with you . . . he who has seen me has seen the Father" (v. 9). Jesus Christ is the living glory of God. As Chantry astutely wrote:

> A similar insult is given by the modern desire for further revelation. It is an indication that seekers of "charisma" are failing to see the glory of God in the face of Jesus Christ. Though the infallible words of Jesus Christ have been so long time with them, they look for something more in order to know the living

God. They are missing the wonder of the truth that the Scripture is the all-sufficient revelation given by the Spirit of God. . . . [134]

To aspire to some subliminal heights of subjective ecstasy in search of new revelation is to do despite to God's Son and to deny the sufficiency of Scripture.[135]

The current upsurge of interest in the "Signs and Wonders" movement raises some basic questions. The emphasis on "words of knowledge" and "power evangelism," in effect, seeks to add to the Scripture. The former does so by espousing an "additional revelation" view in the ministry of the charismatic gifts.

It goes well beyond Scripture. The latter's claim to legitimacy is that such practices authenticate the gospel. Its purpose is to give validity to the spoken word through overt demonstrations of power and miracles. But the Scriptures affirm that the gospel "is the power of God unto salvation to everyone who believes . . ." (Rom. 1:16). Since God has spoken in his Son, and his revelation is complete, no "additions" are necessary.

B. John 17:4 and 15:15

The beloved apostle tells us that the task Christ came to do had been perfectly accomplished. He records that the Son of God had "given unto (the disciples) the words which (the Father) had given (him)" (John 17:8). As Chantry observes: "The indication is that there are no more unspoken words held in reserve for another era."[136] When one compares this with John 15:15, this comment comes into sharper focus: "All things that I have heard of my Father I have made known unto you." That Christ's perfect prophetic ministry concluded with his salvific death, and subsequent resurrection and ascension, is attested in his own High Priestly prayer offered to the Father just prior to Calvary.

C. Ephesians 2:20

Since Christ is the embodiment of all truth, one would be daring indeed to seek something in addition to him, or even to what the apostolic witness said of him and his revelation.

Paul affirms that the church is built upon the foundation of the apostles and prophets in Ephesians 2:20. A foundation is only laid once. To attempt to add[137] to this apostolic testimony is to again deny the validity and sufficiency of God's revelation of Christ in the inscripturated Word. God's truth has been revealed in a "fixed and finished objective revelation."[138]

IS THE CANON OF SCRIPTURE CLOSED?

Jude 3

To seek a biblical answer on this question, one must look at Jude 3. In doing so, a definition is in order. The English word "canon" comes from the Greek *kanon* meaning *rule* or *standard*. By the term *canon of Scripture* is meant "[that] closed collection of writings inspired by the Spirit of God, [having] a normative authority, and are held as the rule for our faith and life."[139]

In Jude 3, the Holy Spirit looks forward to the completion of the canon. He urges his readership to "contend earnestly (*epagnonizesthai*) for the faith which was once for all delivered to the saints." Literally, the text reads: ". . . contend earnestly for the once [for all] delivered unto the saints faith." The stress is upon the "once [for all]" nature of that which was delivered. It emphasizes that which has been done for all time. True, there will be lasting results, but there is no need for any repetition or renewed revelation. Nothing needs to be added! All this has been revealed! Why? Because this complete revelation in Scripture "has been delivered. . . ." That is, it will not require any future additions. The nuance of the aorist passive participle in the original language indicates the decisive completion of this revelation in a past time. By inference, the closure of the canon is envisaged. In this regard, MacArthur observes:

> Through the Scriptures God has given his people a body of teaching on his Son that is final and complete. Our Christian faith rests on historical objective revelation, and this rules out all prophecies, seers and new revelation until God speaks again in the end times (cf. Acts 2:16-21; Rev. 11:1-13). Because the Word of God as delivered is unchangeable and unattenable, any new doctrine or new revelation is unnecessary and false.[140]

In the light of Jude 3, then, the question "Is the Canon of Scripture Closed?" must be answered affirmatively.

CONCLUSION

This study addressed the subject *Jesus Christ: God's Supreme Revelation.* The fundamental issue of "revelation" was discussed relative to three corollary areas. The first dealt with "Is the Scripture Complete?" The second highlighted "The Sufficiency of Scripture." The final area of concern had to do with "Is the Canon of Scripture Closed?"

As the various matters were studied in the light of the scriptural evidence, the answer to the first question must certainly be a resounding "Yes!" As to the second, the Word of God is totally sufficient. It needs neither further confirmation nor continuing revelation. Finally, since Jesus Christ is God's last "Word" to man and the Scriptures bear testimony to him, the record of that testimony is complete. The canon of Scripture is closed. In short, *Jesus is God's Supreme Revelation.*

Appendix D

Faith in the Melting Pot
WCC Slides into Syncretism

Special Report on the WCC World Conference in
Sydney, Australia, in February 1991

Bob Thomas
Editor of New Life *Magazine*

"Syncretism," according to the Macquarie Dictionary, is "the attempted reconciliation or union of different or opposing principles, practices or parties, as in philosophy or religion."

"Ecumenism" was once taken to mean "the promotion of Christian unity, in particular the unification of all Christian churches." Its meaning, however, has been progressively enlarged under the auspices of the World Council of Churches (WCC).

The modern ecumenical movement is reckoned to have had its beginning with the World Missionary Conference in Edinburgh in 1910, when a great vision of winning the world for Christ through Christian unity was put as a challenge to the churches. With the passing of time, however, mission in its real sense has been submerged by the all-consuming passion for visible unity.

The ecumenical movement received its greatest boost with the inauguration of the WCC in Amsterdam in 1948. Initially composed largely of mainline Anglican and Protestant churches, it now contains a large number of Eastern Orthodox and Coptic churches, some charismatic or Pentecostal churches, and is increasingly looking Romeward.

It has eagerly assimilated Marxist principles into its broad-based philosophy, which finds its most vocal expression in so-called "Liberation Theology" in its numerous variants.

Not content, however, with building a super-church along lowest common denominator lines, the WCC is now looking towards other

229

"living faiths," as it calls Judaism, Islam, Buddhism and Hinduism, and is seeking to equate Christianity with pagan "spirituality."

Religious Plurality

WCC general secretary Emilio Castro in his report to the assembly stated:

Inter-faith co-existence is a reality of our life everywhere, but here, as elsewhere, we carry with us the burden of the past.

For churches in Africa, the relation with other religions, in particular Islam, has become concern number one. Is there perhaps in the new pluralism that we see developing everywhere in the world due to migrations, a possible way out, a way forward, a possibility to develop styles of conviviality or living alongside one another, that could take us beyond the conflicts from co-existence, to an attitude of reciprocal pro-existence? We would like to see this new pluralism as a hopeful sign, but we need to raise the question: is it only a secular world view that could affirm tolerance and collaboration among religious traditions? We have gone far in dialogue with friends of other religious convictions, but now, in the perspective of the Spirit, could we not discern signs of the Spirit's actions in other people's religious experience? This was a dividing theme in Vancouver as many of you will remember.

But it is evident that we need to develop a theological understanding of other people's convictions that could undergird a process of constructive co-participation in the building of human societies.

Clearly the WCC is moving far beyond the original dream of Christian unity to the nightmare of Christian compromise for the sake of an all-embracing syncretistic religion (boldface mine).
    Let the Spirit Speak to the Churches, a guide to the theme of the assembly, states on p.16:

Christians believe that the Holy Spirit is present wherever the name of Christ is evoked. The spirit confirms and sustains the faith of believers.

At the same time the Bible bears testimony to the activity of the Spirit in all of creation and in all of life. The Spirit is the freedom of God. Even as the wind blows where it wills, the Spirit acts in total freedom.

This conviction that the whole creation is the sphere of the Spirit's activity raises questions of discernment and of the criteria we need for discernment. As the experience of living in a pluralistic world becomes real to larger and larger groups of Christians, so does the need to discern the Spirit at work in places where the name of Christ is not explicitly invoked. For more and more Christians feel called to work for justice and peace in the world with neighbors of other faith traditions and ideologies.

This has raised in a new way the important issue of the theological significance of other religions and the spiritualities of neighbors of other faiths. Is the Spirit at work in them? Is the Spirit the source of all that is perceived as fruits of the Spirit in the lives of people and movements that are not based on the Christian understanding of God? That question is at the heart of our attempts to work with them for reconciliation and unity of the larger community.

"Inconceivable That Anyone Is Outside God"

The boldest syncretistic/universalistic statement came from the WCC's director of inter-faith dialogue, Dr. Wesley Ariarajah, a Sri Lankan Methodist, who stated:

> As a Sri Lankan Christian who has read the Hindu writings and the Scriptures of the Hindu saints, I simply cannot believe that there have not been other people (than Christians) who are familiar with God.

> It is beyond belief that other people have no access to God or that God has no access to other people.

> Who is listening to the prayers of the Hindu? Are there many Gods?

> If we are thinking about a God who is the creator and sustainer of the whole universe, as in Psalm 24, then there are not two Gods. Therefore it is inconceivable to me that a Hindu or a Buddhist or anyone is outside God.

> My understanding of God's love is too broad for me to believe that only this

narrow segment called the Christian church will be saved.

If you are a Christian you must be open and broad, not narrow and exclusive.

Dr. Ariarajah said being a good Christian did not include going around telling people of other faiths they had got it all wrong.

During conflict in Fiji between Christians and predominantly Muslim and Hindu Indians, Dr. Ariarajah said the council had expressed solidarity with the Indians and told them it was "ashamed" of Christian attitudes. He said religious faith could only be cloaked in the cultural and philosophical traditions of a people.

On the upsurge of Islam, Dr. Ariarajah said it was seen in the West as a serious challenge and there had been confrontations from the earliest times. But he rejected intolerance for Islam in the same way he was sure good Muslims condemned intolerance toward other religions.

Disturbing Korean Performance

Of all the disturbing events witnessed at the assembly, the most disturbing was a presentation by Ms. Chung Hyun-Kyung, a minister of the Presbyterian Church in the Republic of Korea and professor at Ewha Women's University, Seoul.

At a press conference prior to her lecture, she dismissed the imagery given by the Lord Jesus of the gospel as a seed planted in the soil, claiming that it presents a static picture of theology as something once given and now fixed. She replaced the seed/soil imagery given by our Lord with an image drawn from human fertility; when a sperm makes contact with an ovum, a new genetic make-up results. The press was told that when the Christian gospel takes root in a given culture, it so mingles with the ancient spirituality as to produce a new form of religion.

Prior to delivering her lecture, she took part in a ceremonial dance with two Aboriginal men and several Korean men. She invited all present to "get on holy ground with me by taking off your shoes while we are dancing to prepare the way of the spirit." Several did. She then invoked the presence of the dead, with a candle burning on each side of her.

Come. The spirit of Hagar, Egyptian, black slave woman exploited and abandoned by Abraham and Sarah, the ancestors of our faith (Genesis. 16-21).

Come. The spirit of Uriah, loyal soldier sent and killed in the battlefield by the great King David out of the king's greed for his wife, Bathsheba (2 Samuel 11:1-27).

Come. The spirit of Jephthah's daughter, the victim of her father's faith, burnt to death for her father's promise to God if he were to win the war (Judges 11:29-40).

Come. The spirit of male babies killed by the soldiers of King Herod upon Jesus' birth.

Come. The spirit of Joan of Arc, and of the many other women burnt at the "witch trials" throughout the medieval era.

Come. The spirit of other people who died during the Crusades.

Come. The spirit of indigenous people of the earth, victims of genocide during the time of colonialism and the period of great Christian mission to the pagan world.

Come. The spirit of Jewish people killed in the gas chambers during the Holocaust.

Come. The spirit of people killed in Hiroshima and Nagasaki by atomic bombs.

Come. The spirit of Korean women in the Japanese "prostitution army" during World War II, used and torn by violence-hungry soldiers.

Come. The spirit of Vietnamese people killed by napalm, agent orange or hunger on the drifting boats.

Come. The spirit of Mahatma Gandhi, Steve Biko, Martin Luther King Jr., Malcolm X, Victor Jara, Oscar Romero and many unnamed women freedom fighters who died in the struggle for liberation of their people.

Come. The spirit of people killed in Bophal and Chernobyl, and the spirit of jelly babies from the Pacific nuclear test zone.

Come. The spirit of people smashed by tanks in Kwangju, Tiananmen Square, and Lithuania.

Come. The spirit of the Amazon rain forest now being murdered every day.

Come. The spirit of earth, air, and water, raped, tortured and exploited by human greed for money.

Come. The spirit of soldiers, civilians and sea creatures now dying in the bloody war in the Gulf.

Come. The spirit of the Liberator, our brother Jesus, tortured and killed on the cross.

At this point she burned the list, then continued:

I came from *Han*. Han is anger. Han is resentment. Han is bitterness. Han is grief. Han is broken-heartedness and the raw energy for struggle for liberation. In my tradition people who were killed or died unjustly became wandering spirits, the Han-ridden spirits. They are all over the place seeking the chance to make the wrong right. Therefore the living people's responsibility is to listen to the voices of the Han-ridden spirits and to participate in the spirits' work of making the wrong right. These Han-ridden spirits in our people's history have been agents through whom the Holy Spirit has spoken her compassion and wisdom for life.

Without hearing the cries of these spirits we cannot hear the voice of the Holy Spirit. I hope the presence of all our ancestors' spirits here with us shall not make you uncomfortable. For us they are the icons of the Holy Spirit who became tangible and visible to us. Because of them we can feel, touch and taste the concrete bodily historical presence of the Holy Spirit in our midst. From my people's land of Han-filled spirits I came to join with you in another land of spirits full of Han, full of the spirits of the indigenous people, victims of genocide.

After expounding various elements of Korean spiritism and equating them with elements of the Christian message, she concluded:

For me the image of the Holy Spirit comes from the image of Kwan In. She is venerated as goddess of compassion and wisdom by East Asian women's popular religiosity. She is a bodhisattva, enlightened being. She can go into Nirvana any time she wants to, but refuses to go into Nirvana by herself. Her compassion for all suffering living beings makes her stay in this world enabling other living beings to achieve enlightenment. Her compassionate wisdom heals all forms of life and empowers them to swim to the shore of Nirvana. She waits and waits until the whole universe, people, trees, birds, mountains, air, water, become enlightened. They can then go to Nirvana together where they can live collectively in eternal wisdom and compassion. Perhaps this might also be a feminine image of the Christ who is the first born among us, one who goes before and brings others with her?

Dear sisters and brothers, with the energy of the Holy Spirit let us tear apart all walls of division and the "culture of death" which separate us. And let us participate in the Holy Spirit's political-economy of life, fighting for our life on this earth in solidarity with all living beings, and building communities for justice, peace, and the integrity of creation. Wild wind of the Holy Spirit, blow to us. Let us welcome her, letting ourselves go in her wild rhythm of life. Come Holy Spirit, renew the whole creation. Amen!

Finally, she teamed with one of the Aboriginal dancers and performed a dance which we could not defile the pages of *New Life* with by describing.

Where Will It End?

Last week (see *New Life*, February 14, 1991) we reported that the WCC assembly began with a pagan ceremony, and asked the question: Where will it end? With three days to go (at the time of writing this report) we wait with apprehension.

May the Holy Spirit smite these people with a deep sense of sin for their blasphemy. May he open their eyes to the truth of the Word of God, the truth as it is in Jesus. May he give them the grace of penitence. May he give them cleansing with the blood of Christ, shed on the cross of Calvary, as the only means by which we may be made right with God. In short, may the Holy Spirit come and renew the whole creation— beginning with the World Council of Churches![141]

Endnotes

Preface

[i]Stanley M. Burgess and Gary B.McGee (eds.) *Dictionary of Pentecostal and Charismatic Movements* (Grand Rapids, Michigan: Zondervan Publishing House, 1988), pp. 186ff.
[ii]Ibid., p.186.

Introduction

[1]The early centuries of Christianity witnessed the rise of many movements which did not stand the scrutiny of Scripture: Arianism (denying the deity of Christ); Gnosticism (which fostered a false duality between matter and spirit); Marcionites (who tried to corrupt the canon of Scripture); and Sabellianism (a form of moralism that taught it was God the Father Who became incarnate, suffered, died, and raised Himself). Probably the most interesting, from its relation to the present study, was the heresy fostered by Montanus. Note the comments of Paul Enns which summarize the basic issues raised by Montanus: "At his baptism Montanus spoke in tongues, declaring that the age of the Holy Spirit had come and that the end of the world was near. The New Jerusalem was soon to come down out of heaven and inaugurate the millennial age. He and his disciples were the last prophets, bringing the revelation of God to the world. Two women, as his disciples, also were known as prophets giving new revelation. Montanus found refuge in the writings of John and taught that he (Montanus) was the mouthpiece through whom the Paraclete, the Holy Spirit, was revealing Himself to the world. While being generally orthodox in his doctrine, Montanus taught 'that the Holy Spirit continued to speak through prophets, and among these it included women.' Because it was the end of the age, the gifts of the Spirit were

237

being manifested. . . . Although the Council of Constantinople condemned Montanism in A.D. 381, the teaching enjoyed considerable popularity, even converting Tertullian to its teaching." Paul Enns, *The Moody Handbook of Theology* (Chicago: Moody Press, 1989), pp. 416-17.

[2]Although these writers are well respected, even the arguments which they put forth are based on logic or experiential comparisons, rather than on a thorough analysis of the scriptural issues. See J. I. Packer, *Keep in Step with the Spirit* (Old Tappan, New Jersey: Fleming H. Revell Company, 1984), pp. 171-199; D. Martyn Lloyd-Jones, *Prove All Things* (Eastborne, England: Kingsway Publications Ltd., 1985); C. Peter Wagner, *On the Crest of the Wave* (Ventura, California: Regal Books, 1983), pp. 127-136; John White, *When the Spirit Comes in Power* (Downers Grove, Illinois: InterVarsity Press, 1988). For further discussion see B. B. Warfield, *Counterfeit Miracles* (Edinburgh: The Banner of Truth Trust, 1972).

[3]The *Dallas Times Herald* recorded this event in a special feature article that appeared in the *Dallas Life Magazine* on April 17, 1988. In the article, the issues surrounding the resignation and dismissal of Jack Deere, Walter Bodine, and Donald Sunukjian are addressed. While Jack Deere's personal pilgrimage into Wimber's Vineyard Movement is the primary focus of the article, all three men voice the opinion that Scripture cannot prove the cessation of the sign gifts. One key observation is made that may explain the decision of these men. Drowning in intellectualism and academic pursuits, the Deeres confessed to being spiritually cold and having a spiritual void—like a parched desert. He also confessed that his basic thrust was to "be right" rather than to "love God." This thirst for more of God led him and the other men into the realm of the experiential. In response, a Christian's faith should never be devoid of experiential contact with God. There should be the vibrant side that transcends mere intellectual assent. There should be the passionate concern for souls and for the welfare of people. And there should be a relationship with the Lord that brings a consuming love to the heart. Yet, these can be found in everyday walk with the Lord through Scripture and communion with the Spirit. If one does not avail himself to these God-ordained avenues, there will always be experiential alternatives to beckon. Glenna Whitley, "True Believer," *Dallas Life Magazine* (April 17, 1988), pp. 11-14. For a more detailed testimony of Deere's pilgrimage, see Kevin Springer (ed), *Riding the Third Wave* (Scoresby, Victoria: The Canterbury Press, 1988), pp. 86-101.

[4]Jack Deere, *Surprised by the Power of the Spirit* (Grand Rapids: Zondervan Publishing Company, 1993).

Question One

[5]Packer, *Keep in Step*, p. 177.
[6]Ibid., pp. 177-78.
[7]It is significant that the Book of Acts only records three instances of tongues: chapters 2, 10, 19. Why? In promising the coming of the Holy Spirit, Jesus had outlined to the apostles the advance of the gospel through their witness: "*But you shall receive power when the Holy Spirit has come upon you; and you shall be witnesses to Me in Jerusalem, and in all Judea and Samaria, and to the end of the earth*" (Acts 1:8). The gospel was to advance from Jerusalem and Judea, through Samaria, and into the uttermost parts of the world. And that is exactly the pattern that unfolds in the Book of Acts.

The first recorded instance of tongues occurred in a Jewish setting in Jerusalem. The witness of the gospel was thus confirmed there through the coming of the Holy Spirit to indwell the church. Jews were inducted into the Body of Christ. The second recorded instance of tongues took place in Samaria, at the home of Cornelius. Now Gentiles were inducted into the Body of Christ. An apostle was present so that the movement of the Spirit in Samaria would come under the stewardship of the apostles. A separate church movement in Samaria, independent from apostolic oversight, would have threatened the unity of the early Christian witness. The presence of an apostle was crucial in view of the long-standing enmity between the Jews and the Samaritans.

As one comes to the last recorded instance of tongues in Acts (ch. 19), one sees Paul's witness to the disciples of John the Baptist. The setting is Ephesus and fulfills Jesus' command that His followers would be witnesses to the "end of the earth." The gospel had now gone beyond Judea and Samaria. In this third recorded instance of tongues, Paul testified to those disciples of John the Baptist who were "caught" between the old order and the new. As they heard the message of Jesus and of the coming of the Spirit, they too believed and became part of the Body of Christ. The tongues stood as a confirming sign that the gospel had advanced and embraced these new believers (19:1-6).

The three instances of tongues in the Book of Acts thus instruct the reader as to their purpose. They were an evangelistic gift. They confirmed the promise of Jesus that the witness of the Spirit would proceed from Judea, to Samaria, and to the uttermost parts of the earth. Tongues also served as an outward testimony of the inclusion of Jews, Gentiles, and the former followers of John the Baptist into the Body of Christ. Moreover, such served to confirm apostolic authority in the administration and stewardship over the early churches. All in all, tongues served as a testimony that the gospel was going beyond the bounds of Judaism; all peoples and all languages would hear the word of Life!

[8]Some expositors strongly suggest that tongues were solely signs to unbelieving Jews. Thus, whenever tongues were used, they were used in the company of unbelieving Jews.

[9]For a full discussion of the biblical nature of tongues, see the article by Harold W. Hoehner entitled "The Purpose of Tongues in 1 Corinthians 14:20-25" in *Walvoord: A Tribute*, Donald K. Campbell (ed.), (Chicago: Moody Press, 1982), pp. 53-66.

[10]John F. MacArthur, Jr. *The Charismatics: A Doctrinal Perspective* (Grand Rapids, Michigan: Zondervan Publishing House, 1978), p. 163. MacArthur goes on to note that two predominate mystery religions of that day (Cybele and Dionysius) used tongues (i.e., ecstatic speech) in their worship services. Moreover these were accompanied by clanging cymbals, smashing gongs, and blaring trumpets. Ibid.

[11]Packer, p. 211.

[12]Kenneth L. Woodward, "The Giggles Are for God," *Newsweek* (February 20, 1995), 54.

[13]Ibid. While the Bible urges believers to be "filled with the Spirit" and to sing and make "melody in your heart to the Lord" (Eph. 5:18, 19), the confusion and questionable phenomena accompanying the laughing revival reveal a source other than God.

[14]The writer is well aware that even many evangelical scholars reject the authenticity of the last twelve verses in Mark's Gospel. Indeed, in the field of textual criticism, this subject occupies a major focus. However, the longer reading has gained increased support since 1974 when Cambridge University Press published William Farmer's work, *The Last Twelve Verses of Mark*. While Farmer does not firmly attribute the last twelve verses to Mark, he proves that the position is a viable one. This writer would accept the authenticity of these verses and point the reader to the following: William R. Farmer, *The Last Twelve Verses of Mark* (Cambridge: Cambridge University Press, 1974); John William Burgeon, *The Last Twelve Verses of The Gospel According to Mark* (Oxford: 1871); Jacob Van Bruggen, *The Ancient Text of the New Testament* (Winnepeg: Premier Press, 1976); Wilbur N. Pickering, *The Identity of the New Testament Text* (Nashville: Thomas Nelson Publishers, 1977).

[15]A parallel to this use of sign gifts can be found in the ministry of Jesus. Even Peter's message at Pentecost stressed that signs and miracles done by

Jesus were for the purpose of confirming His own ministry to unbelieving Israel (cf. Acts 2:22).

[16]MacArthur, *Charismatics*, pp. 74, 75.

[17]Robert Doyle (ed.), *Signs and Wonders and Evangelicals* (Homebush West, NSW: Lancer Books, 1987).

[18]Ibid., p. 43.

[19]Warren W. Wiersbe, *The Bible Exposition Commentary*, Vol. 1 (Wheaton, Illinois: Victor Books; 1989), pp. 293-294. See also R. Kent Hughes, *Are Evangelicals Born Again?* (Wheaton: Crossway Books, 1995).

[20]One should also note the incident recorded in Acts 8:9-25 where Simon was strongly rebuked for seeking to buy the power of the Holy Spirit. He was more interested in the signs and wonders than in the condition of his own heart. Such is the danger of making signs and wonders an end in themselves.

[21]Walter J. Chantry, *Signs of the Apostles* (rev. ed.; Edinburgh: The Banner of Truth Trust, 1976), pp. 35-37.

[22]The reader is referred to an excellent article by Harold W. Hoehner, "The Purpose of Tongues in 1 Corinthians 14:20-25." This article is part of a compendium of articles written in honor of Dr. John F. Walvoord, former president of Dallas Theological Seminary. Donald K. Campbell (ed.), *Walvoord: A Tribute* (Chicago: Moody Press, 1982), pp. 53-66.

[23]See Cyril H. Maskrey's *The Pentecostal Error*. In this small booklet the author stresses that the Triune God gave Israel three major opportunities to turn to Him in faith. Sadly, Israel rejected each overture from the Lord. These opportunities involved special intervention by each Member of the Godhead: the Father, through special revelation and miracles from the Exodus to the prophets who ministered during the divided kingdom era; the Son, through the Incarnation and His ministry accompanied by miracles; the Holy Spirit, through Pentecost and the ministry of the apostles. Each period was significant because new revelation and miracles were the order of the day. Maskrey argues that with Israel's continued refusal of the Lord during the Apostolic Era, the day of signs and wonders ceased. The Godhead had completed all overtures to the nation. Only the judgment of the tribulation would turn the nation's heart to welcome the Lord Jesus Christ. Cyril H. Maskrey, *The Pentecostal Error* (White's Printing Company: E. Cannington, Western Australia, 1953).

[24]The majority of commentators would regard Mark's Gospel as being written prior to that of Matthew's. Others would also place the Galatians letter after 1 Corinthians. Nevertheless, most would agree that only four to five books of the New Testament had been written prior to

the writing of 1 Corinthians. See D. Edmond Hiebert, *An Introduction to the New Testament*, 3 vols. (Chicago: Moody Press, 1977). Merrill C. Tenney, *New Testament Survey* (Grand Rapids, Michigan: WM. B. Eerdmans Publishing Company, 1961); H. C. Thiessen, *Introduction to the New Testament* (Grand Rapids, Michigan: Wm. B. Eerdmans Publishing Company, 1943).

[25]MacArthur, *Charismatics*, p. 166.

[26]Joseph Dillow gives an excellent discussion on the reasons why the "perfect" of 1 Corinthians 13:10 cannot refer to the second coming of Christ. Though some of the arguments are of a technical nature, Dillow offers at least seven lines of evidence for his position. Joseph Dillow, *Speaking in Tongues: Seven Crucial Questions* (Grand Rapids, Michigan: Zondervan Publishing House, 1975).

[27]The reader is referred to the sources cited previously which deal with New Testament background and introductory considerations. The majority of conservative expositors all agree on this point. The Jewish nature of the epistle; the opening greeting *"to the twelve tribes which are scattered abroad"* (1:1); the reference to believers still assembling in the synagogues (2:2); the great body of Old Testament Scriptures which are quoted; all point to an early date—A.D. 40-50.

[28]While the phrase "face to face" throughout the Old Testament and New Testament refers to seeing or speaking to *another person,* the introduction of the "mirror" concept overrides this consideration (see Appendix, Question #15). Some would question, however, the use of the "mirror" in the 2 Corinthians 3:18 passage. The verse seems to say that **we see the Lord's glory when we look into the "mirror"** and that **one day we will bear that image.** *"But we all, with unveiled face, beholding as in a mirror the glory of the Lord, are being transformed into the same image from glory to glory, just as by the Spirit of the Lord."* Thus we do see another's "face" in the mirror of 2 Corinthians 3:18. We see the "glory of the Lord." However, when one compares this verse to the context of verses 7-17, one sees that the "glory of the Lord" which is seen in the mirror is that shining through **believers.** As we look into the mirror (i.e. the Word), we are able to see the measure of the Lord's glory shining through in us. Moreover, the verse affirms that through the ministry of the Holy Spirit believers are being changed into the image of Christ (cf. Rom 8:29). Indeed, one day His image shall be our image; His reflection in the Word shall be our reflection.

There is also another way in which 2 Corinthians 3:18 may be taken. The force of the verse could be the following: in the Word of God (i.e., the mirror) we behold the *reflected* glory of the Lord. Through God's

Word and through the Spirit of God we are being changed into His likeness so that we too may reflect that glory.

We must await the full transformation process which will only be complete when we are with Jesus. Either way, the phrase "as beholding in a mirror" must be viewed as one looking into the Word of God. This rendering is consistent with James 1:22-25 passage and the "mirror" of 1 Corinthians 13:12.

[29]Joseph Dillow, *Speaking in Tongues*, pp. 127-136

[30]Ibid., pp. 108-133.

[31]Ibid., pp. 114-116. Other Scriptures such as Ephesians 4:8-11, 11-16, and 1 Corinthians 12:28 also link prophecy with the ministry of the apostles. Both were gifts to the early church to nurture believers and to bring them to a position of maturity.

[32]Masters builds a strong argument that the sign gifts were given primarily to the apostles to confirm their apostolic office and to confirm their witness to the resurrection. The following passages form the basis of Masters' thesis: John 15:7; Luke 24:46-48; Acts 1:8; Acts 1:1-13; Acts 2:32; Acts 3:15; Acts 5:31-32; Acts 10:39-42; 1 John 1:1-3; Acts 22:14-15; 1 Cor. 9:1; 1 Cor. 15:8; Acts 4:33; Acts 2:43; Acts 5:12; Heb. 2:2-4; 2 Cor. 12:12. Masters also places great emphasis on the apostles and prophets being the foundation of the church. As such, one should not expect to find them in the superstructure. Peter Masters, *The Healing Epidemic* (London: The Wakeman Trust, 1988), pp. 112-135. See also Acts 4:29-30, Acts 15:12, and Romans 15:19.

[33]Peter Wagner, *On the Crest of the Wave* (Ventura, California: Regal Books, 1983), pp. 131-141.

[34]Sandra Hart (ed.), *God Still Steps In* (Lawson, NSW: Mission Publications of Australia, n.d.).

[35]*The Willowbank Report* quoted from *Perspectives on the World Christian Movement: A Reader*, ed. by Ralph D. Winter and Steven C. Hawthorne (Pasadena, California: William Carey Library, 1981), p. 525.

[36]For further reading on tongues and spiritual gifts, see the following: Kenneth O. Gangle, *Unwrap Your Spiritual Gifts* (Wheaton, Illinois: Victor Books, 1983); Robert G. Gromacki, *The Modern Tongues Movement* (Phillipsburg, New Jersey: Presbyterian and Reformed Publishing Company, 1967); William McRae, *Dynamics of Spiritual Gifts* (Grand Rapids, Michigan: Zondervan Publishing House, 1976). For an overview of related issues from proponents of the charismatic movement, see: John L. Sherrill, *They Speak With Other Tongues* (Old Tappan, New Jersey: Fleming H. Revell Company, 1964); Samuel Chadwick, *The Way to Pentecost* (Old Tappan, New Jersey: Fleming H. Revell Company).

Question Two

[37]John Warwick Montgomery, *Damned through the Church* (Minneapolis, Minnesota: Bethany Fellowship, Inc., 1970).

[38]One need only consult Paul's instruction in 1 Corinthians 14:16 to see that it was the common experience of the first-century churches to confirm blessing in word or song through the expression "amen!" The writer urges readers to take a concordance and look at the various ways in which "amen" is used in Scripture.

[39]See R. Alan Streett, *The Effective Invitation* (Old Tappan, New Jersey: Fleming H. Revell Company, 1984). Peter's preaching at Pentecost alone would give biblical grounds for concluding a public preaching service with an appeal for people to make a commitment to Christ (Acts 2:40, 41).

[40]Neil Babcox, *A Search for Charismatic Reality* (Portland, Oregon: Multnomah Press, 1985), pp. 53-55.

[41]"The 'New Age'—Is It Serious?" (Advertising Feature), *The Advertiser* (Saturday, September 30, 1989), p. 17.

[42]Ibid. The article goes on to record "The Great Invocation" of the New Age Movement. Note the refrain: *From the point of Light within the Mind of God, Let light stream forth into the minds of men, Let Light descend on Earth; From the point of Love within the heart of God, Let love stream forth into the hearts of men, May Christ return to Earth; From the centre where the Will of God is known, Let purpose guide the little wills of men—The purpose which the Masters know and serve; From the centre which we call the race of men, Let the Plan of Love and Light work out, And may it seal the door where evil dwells; Let Light and Love and Power restore the Plan on Earth.*

[43]Dave Hunt and T. A. McMahon, *The Seduction of Christianity* (Eugene, Oregon: Harvest House Publishers, 1985); Dave Hunt, *Beyond Seduction* (Eugene, Oregon: Harvest House Publishers, 1987).

[44]Hunt, *The Seduction of Christianity*, especially pages 58, 144-188; *Beyond Seduction*, pp 205-264.

[45]Hunt, *Beyond Seduction*, pp. 242-43.

[46]Tal Brooke, *When the Word Will Be as One* (Eugene, Oregon: Harvest House Publishers, 1989).

[47]Ibid., p. 95.

[48]Robert Muller's address cited in Dean Halverson, "Transformation Celebration," *SCP Magazine* (January, 1984), p. 4, and quoted by Rooke, *When the World Will Be As One*, p. 207.

[49]John Naisbitt, *Global Paradox* (New York: Avon Books, 1994), pp. 191-232.

[50]Peter Masters, *The Healing Epidemic*, pp. 181-182.

[51]"Spiritual Warfare: The Critical Moment" by Andrew Shead in *The Briefing* (April 24, 1991), 45/46, p. 9.

[52]"Spiritual Warfare: What Happens When I Contradict Myself" by Mark Thompson in *The Briefing*, p, 11.

[53]Ibid., p. 12.

[54]Michael Horton (ed.), *The Agony of Deceit* (Chicago: Moody Press, 1990).

[55]D. R. McConnell, *A Different Gospel,* Updated Edition (Peabody, Massachusetts: Hendrickson Publishers, 1995); Hank Hanegraaff, *Christianity in Crisis* (Eugene, Oregon: Harvest House Publishers; 1993); John F. MacArthur, Jr., *Charismatic Chaos* (Grand Rapids, Michigan: Zondervan Publishing House; 1991). Note that McConnell writes his critique as a charismatic who is concerned about the excesses and heresies within the movement.

[56]Horton, *Agony of Deceit*, pp. 89-120.

[57]Kenneth Copeland, tape of "Victory Campaign," Dallas, Texas cited in Horton, *The Agony of Deceit,* p. 116.

[58]Norman Geisler, *Signs and Wonders* (Wheaton, Illinois: Tyndale House Publishers, 1988), pp. 157-168. In Horton's *The Agony of Deceit,* an excellent discussion is offered on "Seven Rules for Testing Prophets," pp. 259-261. These seven rules, with some amplification by this writer, may be summarized in the following manner:

1. *The Degree of Authoritarianism*—false prophets rule by their own authority (Jer. 5:31) and insist that their pronouncements are above question or scrutiny; true prophets of old invited comparison and accountability to the Word of God (cf. 1 Cor. 14:29; Acts 17:11).

2. *The Degree of Credibility and Track Record in Faithfulness*—false prophets sometimes make mistakes in the accuracy of their prophecies or pronouncements; true prophets of old displayed one hundred percent accuracy in their prophecies (cf. Deut. 19:22; Jer. 23:25, 25; Deut. 18:15-22).

3. *The Degree of Judgment Declarations*—false prophets appeal primarily to human nature (cf. Isa. 30:10-11; 2 Tim. 4:3, 4); true prophets of old proclaimed both blessings and judgment.

4. *The Degree to Which the Message is Man-Centered*—false prophets elevate man and temporal considerations (cf. Isa.

29:16; Jer. 5:24); true prophets of old elevated the Lord and related temporal considerations to eternal accountability.

5. *The Degree of Isolation from Scripture or Historical Doctrines*—false prophets claim direct insight or revelation which is superior to the wisdom and the teachings of historic Christianity and the faith once delivered to the saints in Scripture (Jude 3), and they also mock "the ancient paths" (Jer. 6:16); true prophets of old held in high regard the Scriptures and the doctrines which flowed from the Word of God (cf. Rom. 16:17; 2 Pet. 2:1-3; Acts 20:26; Gal. 1:6-9).

6. *The Degree of Greed or Emphasis on Money*—false prophets focus personal gain and try to defend such (Jer. 6:13; 2 Pet. 2:1; Acts 8:20); true prophets of old did not make merchandise of God's blessings (cf. 2 Kings 5:16).

7. *The Degree of Personal Power, Special Access to God, and Influence Claimed*—false prophets elevate themselves to a special mediatorial role; true prophets understood the temporary nature of their office in view of completed revelation and the unique ministry of the glorified Lord Jesus Christ (cf. 1 Cor. 13:8-12; 1 Tim. 2:1-6).

[59]White, *When the Spirit Comes With Power*, p. 24.

[60]Packer, p. 198.

[61]Doyle, *Signs and Wonders*, pp. 40-41.

[62]While the word "apostle" in the New Testament was not restricted to the Twelve, Scripture affirms that the Apostolic Office was restricted. It was not perpetual, for those who occupied the office must have lived during the ministry of Christ and been witnesses of the resurrection (cf. Acts 1:21-26; 1 Cor. 9:1; Rev. 21:14). Even though the apostolic office and prophecy ceased with the completion of Scripture, the role of evangelists, pastors, and teachers has continued to function until this day.

[63]Packer, *Keep in Step*, p. 210.

[64]"Tabor Charismatic Conference" (Advertising Feature), *The Advertiser* (Friday, January 5, 1990), p. 9.

[65]Ibid.

[66]For an excellent and detailed report of the growth of the charismatic movement, and especially the Catholic Charismatic Renewal, see the following articles in *Dictionary of Pentecostal and Charismatic Movements*, ed. by Stanley M. Burgess and Gary B. McGee (Grand Rapids, Michigan: Zondervan Publishing House, 1988; "Catholic

Charismatic Renewal," by Francis A. Sullivan, 110-126; "Charismatic Movement," by Peter D. Hocken, 130-160.

[67]Jackie Pullinger, *Life and Death in Kowloon Walled City* (London: Hodder and Stoughton, 1989), pp. 28, 37-41.

[68]"Catholic Charismatic Renewal" by F. A. Sullivan in *Dictionary of Pentecostal and Charismatic Movements,* ed. by Stanley M. Burgess and Gary B. McGee (Grand Rapids, Michigan: Zondervan Publishing House, 1988), p. 116.

[69]Packer, *Keep in Step,* p. 171.

[70]Tom Smail, Andrew Walker, and Nigel Wright, *Charismatic Renewal: A Search for a Theology* (SPCK: London; 1993), pp. 20, 50.

[71]For an excellent discussion of the biblical teachings regarding separation of the believer from others who deny the essentials of the faith, see: Gary G. Cohen, *Biblical Separation Defended—A Biblical Critique of Ten New Evangelical Arguments* (Phillipsburg, New Jersey: Presbyterian and Reformed Publishing Company, 1966).

Question Three

[72]Dillow, *Speaking in Tongues*, pp. 9, 10.

[73]This writer hastens to add that not all effects are positive. In many instances tongues have served to split marriages and entire churches. It is interesting to note that when tongues appear amidst strong evangelical and fundamental circles, strife and division are the by-products; yet, when tongues occur among liberal and neo-evangelical circles, there is unity.

[74]For further study on the significance of the word barach and its relation to he overall theme of the Book of Job, see: William Henry Green, *The Argument of the Book of Job Unfolded* (reprint ed.; Minneapolis, Minnesota: James and Klock Christian Publishers, 1977), pp. 23-25; Edgar C. S. Gibson, *The Book of Job* (reprint ed.; Minneapolis, Minnesota: Klock and Klock Christian Publishers, 1978), pp. 3, 4.

[75]The reader is referred to McDowell and Stewart's handbook on cults and religions: Josh McDowell and Don Stewart, *Handbook of Today's Religions* (Here's Life Publishers: San Bernadino, California; 1983). Note also that places and names in this section have been altered to protect anonymity; however, the rest of the account is true as given.

[76]I am indebted to Pastor Larry May who first introduced me to these overall concepts. Pastor May shepherds a thriving Baptist church in the Dallas, Texas, area.

[77]See George Orwell, *Animal Farm* (New York: Signet Classics. 1957).

Question Four

[78]Stanley M. Burgess and Gary B. McGee (eds.), *Dictionary of Pentecostal and Charismatic Movements* (Grand Rapids, Michigan: Zondervan Publishing House, 1988). See also Elmer L. Towns, John N. Vaughan, and David J. Seifert, *The Complete Book of Church Growth* (Wheaton, Illinois: Tyndale House Publishers, 1981), pp. 148-155.

[79]Stanley M. Burgess (ed.) and Edward M. Van Der Mass (assoc. ed.), *The New International Dictionary of Pentecostal Charismatic Movements—Revised and Expanded Edition* (Grand Rapids, Michigan: Zondervan Publishing Company, 2002), p. 284.

[80]Ibid., p. 285.

[81]Some commentators have said that Paul was wrong in paying for offerings that included a blood sacrifice. Was this compromise? If the offering had been for a sin offering alone, it would have been an affront to the Cross. However, the sin offering in this instance was one of many sacrifices; it was part of a whole and the total testimony of the ceremony was one of praise, not the enactment of spiritual forgiveness.

[82]Charles Caldwell Ryrie, *The Ryrie Study Bible* (Moody Press: Chicago, 1985), p. 1828.

[83]Francis A. Schaeffer, *The Great Evangelical Disaster* (Crossway Books: Westchester, Illinois, 1984).

[84]Ibid., pp. 37, 38

[85]Ibid., p. 67.

[86]Ibid., p. 151.

[87]Ibid., pp. 50, 51

[88]Throughout this study, the writer has emphasized time and again that forces working within the charismatic movement seek to woo the believer away from the Scriptures. These forces do not emerge from merely the minds of men. Many arise from Satanic and demonic sources. Remember, the Christian's warfare is against spiritual entities (2 Cor. 10:4, 5; Eph. 6:10-12). Donald Barnhouse, in his classic work *The Invisible War*, gives the following instruction: "To the Corinthians Paul wrote that we are not ignorant of Satan's devices (2 Cor. 2:11). The word is a very interesting one. The dictionary definition is 'something devised or contrived for bringing about some end or result; an arrangement, plan, scheme, project, contrivance; an ingenious or clever expedient; often one of underhand, or evil character; a plot, stratagem, trick.' In the days of the King James translation, Shakespeare was writing

in *Twelfth Night*, 'Excellent, I smell a device.' The original word in the New Testament was one used from the time of Homer for the source of thought, intelligence, and thus for intentions, projects and plans, generally in an evil sense. It is the word used for the minds that are blinded or corrupted by Satan (2 Cor. 3:14; 4:4; 11:3), and the mind which shall be kept by the peace of God (Phil. 4:7). It is the thought that is to be brought into captivity unto the obedience of Christ (2 Cor. 10:5)." Donald Grey Barnhouse, *The Invisible War* (Grand Rapids, Michigan: Zondervan Publishing House, 1965), p. 155. This entire study is a call to Christians to increase their sensitivity to devices which are presently being unleashed upon believers on a worldwide scale. The impact of these satanic stratagems extend beyond global significance. They are reflections of a cosmic struggle which began with the first rebellion in the kingdom of God (Isa. 14:12ff.). Though our Lord will ultimately triumph (1 Cor. 15:20-28), we must be vigilant as soldiers in the kingdom to never lay down the Sword of the Spirit even for a moment.

Appendix A

[89]*Evangelicals and Catholics Together: The Christian Mission in the Third Millennium* (New York: The Institute on Religion and Public Life, 1994).

[90]John F. MacArthur, *Reckless Faith* (Wheaton: Crossway Books, 1994).

[91]*Evangelicals and Catholics Together*, Reprinted by the Ankerberg Theological Research Institute by permission of The Institute on Religion and Public Life, p. 8.

[92]See David Jeremiah's *Invasion of Other Gods: The Seduction of New Age Spirituality* (Dallas: Word Publishing, 1995).

[93]For further understanding of Roman Catholic beliefs, see *Protestants & Catholics: Do They Now Agree?* by John Ankerberg and John Weldon (Eugene, Oregon: Harvest House Publishers, 1995).

[94]Charles Hodge, *An Exposition of the Second Epistle to the Corinthians* (reprint ed.; Grand Rapids, Michigan: Wm. B. Eerdmans Publishing Company, 1973), pp. 76, 77.

Appendix B

[95]Homer, *Odyssea* 3.332; Aristophanes, *Vespae,* 547.

[96]Aristotle, *Historia Animalium* 6.10 (565a. 24).

[97]Herodotus 1.57; 1.142; 4.183.

[98]See *de Usu Partium.*

[99]Cf. 2.406f.

[100]*Punic Wars* 8, 18 (Libuke 121).

[101]Oxyrhynchus Papyri 1.138. See also Griechische Papyri zu Giessen, 1.99 cited in James Hope Moulton and George Milligan, *The Vocabulary of the Greek Testament Illustrated from the Papyri and Other Non-Literary Sources* (London: Hodder and Stoughton, 1930), p. 128.

[102]Romans 3:13, 14:11; 1 Corinthians 12:10 (twice), 28, 30; 13:1, 8; 14:2, 4, 5 (twice), 6, 9, 13, 14, 18, 19, 22, 23, 26, 27, 39; Philippians 2:11.

[103]Romans 3:13; 14:11; and Philippians 2:11. All references use the term in the sense of *physical organ.*

[104]Johannes Behm, *TDNT,* ed. G. Kittel, 1:722; cf. the discussion in Walter Bauer, W. F. Arndt, F. W. Gingrich and F. W. Danker, *A Greek-English Lexicon of the New Testament and Other Early Christian Literature* (University of Chicago Press, 1979), p. 162.

[105]Harold W. Hoehner, "The Purpose Of Tongues In 1 Corinthians 14:20-25" in *Walvoord: A Tribute,* Donald K Campbell, ed. (Chicago: Moody Press, 1982), pp. 53-66, esp. p. 55.

[106]The reader is referred to John F. MacArthur, *The Charismatics: A Doctrinal Perspective* (Grand Rapids: Zondervan Publishing House, 1978), pp. 156-163, esp. pp. 159-161; Merrill F. Unger, *New Testament Teaching on Tongues* (Grand Rapids: Kregel Publications, 1978), pp. 1-168, esp. pp. 79-1 69.

[107]Hoehner, op. cit., p. 55

[108]Jean Hering, *The First Epistle of Saint Paul to the Corinthians* (London: Epworth, 1962), p. 128.

[109]J. G. Davies, "Pentecost and Glossalalia," *Journal of Theological Studies* 3 (October 1952): 229-30.

[110]James D. G. Dunn, *Jesus and the Spirit* (Philadelphia: Westminster, 1975), p. 224.

[111]For further study, see Robert H. Gundry, "Ecstatic Utterance" *Journal of Theological Studies* (17 October 1966): 299-307.

[112]MacArthur, *The Charismatics,* pp. 159-61.

[113]This term occurs in Acts 1:19; 2:8; 21:40; 22:2; 26:14. The term *glossa* in Acts occurs in 2:3, 4, 11, 26; 10:46; and 19:6.

[114]MacArthur, *The Charismatics*, p. 159.

[115]Ibid.

[116]The only exception is 14:27 where the apostle apparently referred to the real gift but while mentioning a single man speaking a single language thus demanding a single form.

[117]MacArthur, *The Charismatics,* p. 160.

[118]See "The Biblical Nature of Tongues" in Question One of the main text of this present study.

[119]See p. 7 of this present work for a discussion on this passage.

[120]Zane C. Hodges, "The Purpose of Tongues," *Bibliotheca Sacra* 120 (1963); 231, n.4. See also John F. MacArthur, *The Charismatics*, p. 163.

Appendix C

121Cited in "*The Briefing*" Issue #45/46, April 24, 1990, p. 11; italics mine. Jack Deere (former Professor of Old Testament, Dallas Theological Seminary) served as John Wimber's (Vineyard Ministries) theological adviser. At a "Spiritual Warfare" conference in Sydney's Hordern Pavillion in March, 1990, over five thousand registrants met. In teaching workshop two, headed "A Demonic Doctrine Illustrated," the quotation cited above is found.

122Ibid; italics mine

123Walter Chantry, *Signs of the Apostles* (rev. ed.; Edinburgh: The Banner of Truth Trust, 1976), pp. 22-37.

124Zane C. Hodges, "Hebrews" in *Bible Knowledge Commentary,* John F. Walvoord and Roy B. Zuck, eds. (Wheaton: Victor Books, 1983), p. 780.

125Leon Morris, *The Gospel According to John* (Grand Rapids: Wm. B. Eerdmans, 1971), p. 881.

126Ibid., pp. 699-700.

127Chantry, *Signs of the Apostles*, pp. 29-30.

128Hodges, *Bible Knowledge Commentary*, p. 781.

129Zane C. Hodges, Class Notes, "Hebrews," Dallas Theological Seminary, 1985. Attention is drawn to the future nuances each time "salvation" (*soteria*) occurs in Hebrews (1:14; 2:3, 10; 5:9; 6:gf; 9:28).

130Chantry, *Signs of the Apostles*, p. 31; emphasis mine. It has been alleged by some that, in light of Hebrews 2:3, *rhema* (uttered word) should confirm Scripture today. Is this a valid claim? Not from the view espoused consistently in this present study. Firstly, the term *rhema* does not occur in Hebrews 2:3, but it does in 6:5. The word *logos* (word) is used. Secondly, Scripture does not need "confirmation." It is complete in and of itself. It is God's final revelation. It bears witness to the Word of God Incarnate, Jesus Christ. He is God's last word to man (Heb. 1:1-4). God's word is truth (John 17:17), and truth is absolute. It needs no confirmation to prove validity.

131Notice: ". . . which at the first (*archen*) began to be spoken by the Lord . . ." (v. 3).

132F. F. Bruce, *Commentary on the Epistle to the Hebrews* (Grand Rapids: Wm. B. Eerdmans Publishing Co., 1972), pp. xliii-xliv.

133Bruce's heading for the Prologue of Hebrews (1:1-4) reflects this avowal. He speaks of "God's Final Revelation in His Son." Ibid., pp. 1-9.

[134]Chantry, *Signs of the Apostles*, p. 33.

[135]Cf. the comments relating to Deere and Wimber, who in their own admission do not believe in the sufficiency of Scripture. *The Briefing*, op. cit., p. 5.

[136]Chantry, *Signs of the Apostles*, p. 34.

[137]The reader's attention is again drawn to the detailed treatment concerning Revelation 22:1-19 in the main text of this present work.

[138]Chantry, *Signs of the Apostles*, p. 34.

[139]Adapted from an article by N. H. Ridderbos, *The New Bible Dictionary* (Leicester: Inter-Varsity Press, 1962), "Canon of the Old Testament," pp. 186 94, esp. p. 186.

[140]MacArthur, *The Charismatics*, p. 18.

Appendix D

[141]Bob Thomas, "Faith in the Melting Pot," *New Life* (February 21, 1991), pp. 1, 13. Used by permission.